ESSAYS:

HISTORICAL,

LITERARY,

EDUCATIONAL

BY

WILLIAM CHAUNCEY FOWLER, LL.D.

Printed by
THE CASE, LOCKWOOD & BRAINARD CO.
HARTFORD;
1876.

CONTENTS.

INTRODUCTORY NOTE.

A considerable number of the following essays have been published in "The Christian Spectator," or "North American Review," or "The Theological and Literary Journal," or "The Knickerbocker," or "The American Journal of Education," and are collected now for the first time.

ORIGIN OF THE

Theological School

OF YALE COLLEGE.

BY PROF. WILLIAM C. FOWLER, LL.D.

In the vacation following the Commencement of 1817, I went to New Haven to make some arrangements for entering the Theological Seminary at Andover. This was the same year that was darkened by the death of Prest. Timothy Dwight. Accidentally meeting Samuel B. Ingersoll, who had just taken his degree, I was urged by him to give up my purpose of going to Andover and to study theology under Professor Fitch, if he would receive us. I entertained his proposals so far as to consent to an interview with Professor Fitch on the subject. Accordingly we immediately went to see him. He appeared to be very much pleased, and told us he would take the subject into consideration. On our second visit he expressed great readiness to receive us as students, saying that he thought it would be a great advantage to himself, inasmuch as it would necessitate a review of his studies, which would help to qualify him to prepare a course of sermons on doctrinal subjects, as Professor of Divinity in Yale College. While the matter was pending, I was urged to accept the office of rector of the Hopkins Grammar School, a position which I had occupied for a portion of the summer term of my senior year. I concluded to accept the appointment and also study theology with Professor Fitch, who had impressed me very favorably.

Accordingly Mr. Ingersoll and myself commenced our course in theology with Professor Fitch, at the commencement of the next college term, visiting his house, the same which is now occupied by Professor Thacher, two evenings a week, and confining our attention for the first term to Biblical criticism. In the course of the term we were joined by Wm. Graham, a graduate of Jefferson College, Pa., of the year 1816; during the same term I received letters from Edward Bull, my class-mate, writing for himself and David N. Lord, inquiring about the advantages they would enjoy, in studying theology in New Haven. I wrote in reply, urging them to join us at the commencement of the next term. This they concluded to do.

Thus at the commencement of the second term our class consisted of five in number. Soon after Horace Hooker and Joseph D. Wickham joined us, who were then tutors in Yale College. After this our class was increased by Epaphras Goodman, a graduate of Dartmouth College, of the class of 1816. The next year Edward Hitchcock joined us, who received the degree of A. M. from Yale College in 1818; and also Lyman Coleman, a tutor in the college, and Levi Smith, who graduated at Yale College in 1818. At a later period, Stephen D. Ward, a graduate of Princeton College, of the class of 1819, also joined us. The whole number of the class was twelve.

After the commencement of the second term, the class requested one of the tutors, either Mr. Hooker or Mr. Wickham, to invite Professor Kingsley to instruct us in the Hebrew language, which he consented to do. Some months later, I was requested by the class to invite Professor Goodrich to instruct us in elocution, and the composition of sermons.

At the commencement of the second term, January, 1818, I invited the class to hold their recitations in the Hopkins Grammar School-house, on the corner of Temple and Crown streets. Accordingly the recitations were afterwards held there. In our exercises we pursued much the same course as the one pursued at Andover.

Professor Fitch, " with the vision and faculty divine," Professor Kingsley with his thorough scholarship and keen sagacity, Professor Goodrich, with his earnest and discursive mind, kindling as it ran, united their efforts for our improvement. With these efforts the class were not only entirely satisfied, but were grateful for them, and the professors appeared to be highly pleased with our progress.

In our exercises with Professor Fitch, we were especially interested in the science of Biblical criticism, or Exegesis, a term that was beginning to be current. The opinion that the language of the Bible must be interpreted in the same way as the language of any other book, was readily welcomed. This opinion seemed to dispel the cloud of mysticism or mystery, that in some of our minds, had enveloped that sacred book. Several of us imported and read German books, one of which, Ernesti, three of us united to translate into the English language; certain portions being assigned to each. We carried our design into execution so far, that each of the three read portions of the book to the tutors' club, which met weekly. While thus engaged, Professor Stuart's translation of the book was announced, and this relieved us from our labors.

In our investigations in theology proper, we pushed our discussions on some points to the utmost limits of orthodoxy. Professor Fitch himself was a seeker after truth, and thus was in the same attitude of mind that we were. He was not polemic; he was not dogmatic; and if he was didactic, he was so rather in regard to the means of arriving at the truth, than in regard to the ultimate conclusions. It was pleasant in the class-room, to hear him state an abstract doctrine to us, as if he was a pure intelligence addressing pure intelligences; and then to hear him in the chapel on the Sabbath, exhibiting the same doctrine in the relations of logic, rhetoric, and poetry, sometimes in thrilling tones, as if he was a human being addressing human beings. It was no wonder that, on one occasion when he had preached in the chapel, before his ordination, Governor John Cotton Smith, who heard him without knowing his name, exclaimed, as he came out, " Who is this angel from heaven, who has preached to us this morning?" We enjoyed other advantages. The class, though organized by a voluntary association, enjoyed the advantage of being considered a part and parcel of Yale College—that school of the prophets.

On the death of President Timothy Dwight, January 11, 1817, great anxiety was felt for the college. Men who still retained distinct impressions of the energetic intellect and fervid eloquence of President Stiles, " the most learned scholar in America," and fresher impressions of President Dwight, imperial in mind, manner, and person, in their opinion the beau ideal of what a president of Yale College should be, in their regret and despondency were ready to say, " These suns have set, O rise some other such!" In the expected political change from the charter of Charles II., to a constitution adopted by the people, they feared that in some way the interests of Yale College would be compromised.

After the appointment of President Day, it became known generally among the friends of the college, that in him the elements were so mixed that there was no redundancy and no deficiency; that "good without pretence," his "mind of large discourse was able to look before and after," and was thus not liable to be jostled from its place by the surging impulses of the present; that he was to be the Palinurus, the pilot who could weather the storm and with a wary eye and steady hand could take the ship into port. The public were reassured. At a festival attended by the citizens of New Haven, a toast was drank:—" We want no brighter light than that of Day." Strangers were strongly impressed in his favor. When two from abroad were speaking of him with admiration, one said, " Why, he has the head of Leo."

Five of the class were tutors in the college. At one period when there were only three tutors, who were members of the class, the other three tutors were William T. Dwight, Professor Alexander M. Fisher, and Rufus Woodward. Mr. Dwight was by inheritance a theologian, being a son of President Timothy Dwight; and though then studying law, afterwards became an eminent divine in Portland, Maine. Professor Alexander Metcalf Fisher, the eminent mathematician, who was lost in the "Albion," in the year 1822, had studied, after his graduation, a year under his pastor, Dr. Emmons, that Corypheus in theology, and another year at Andover. Dr. Emmons had discussed with him the many knotty questions connected with this science. He put into his hands the objections of leading skeptics, as nuts for him to crack. He put into his hands a small tract by Hume, not published in his works, in which the author, then a young man, treats the common arguments in favor of existence of the Deity as fallacious. Professor Fisher's mode of treating subjects may be seen in the *Christian Spectator*, Vol. I., monthly series, p. 414.

Mr. Woodward fully equaled these two in breadth of mind and depth of research even in theological subjects, especially the Evidences of Christianity. Mr. Woodward also contributed a number of able articles to the *Christian Spectator*. (See Memoir, *Christian Spectator*, Vol. VII., p. 113.)

The class, too, had the advantage of witnessing and aiding a great revival in New Haven. For an account of this revival see *Christian Spectator*, Vol. III., p. 49, signed by Samuel Merwin, and Nathaniel W. Taylor, in which mention is made of the theological students. It was during this revival that the lay preachers of New Haven became distinguished and called forth the letter of Professor Stuart, to correct or prevent any evils attendant upon their course. These men believed in the great power of prayer, united with personal appeals to the unconverted. They visited other towns and made their reports Saturday evenings at Mr. Timothy Dwight's. Several evenings I was present when the reports were given in. The persons that I remember among them were Timothy Dwight, Dwight Williams, Levi Stillman, Seth Bliss, S. P. Davis, Sherman Converse, and S. S. Jocelyn. In many cases their public addresses and their private appeals and prayers appeared to be attended with a divine blessing. This was more strikingly the case at first than it was after the novelty had passed by. They may some of them have been over-confident at first, but afterwards were more inclined to sustain a divinity school than to exercise any clerical functions themselves.

Apprehensions were entertained by clergymen and others, that evils would grow out of this system injurious to the clergy, and the order of the churches. At one time there seemed to be some ground for that apprehension. Embracing the opinion that prayer and correspondent exertion could at any time produce a revival of religion, they were inclined to blame those ministers and those churches where there was no revival. Said one, in his report: "We visited such a minister and such a church, we found the sentinel (the minister) sleeping at his post." A good woman present, in the warmth of her feelings, exclaimed, "He ought to be shot." But, this feeling gradually died out and none were more efficient or generous patrons of the future theological school than were the so-called lay-preachers. Mr. Timothy Dwight gave five thousand dollars for founding a professorship in it.

At the period we are considering, distinguished preachers addressed audiences in New Haven. Dr. Asahel Nettleton, with his strong scriptural doctrines, pungent appeals to the conscience, and his sepulchral voice coming up from the depths of his soul, would hold a great audience breathless, as if eternity and heaven were everything, and time and earth nothing.

Then, too, there was Dr. Lyman Beecher, with so much of the old and familiar as to furnish a basis of argument in the minds of his hearers, and so much of the new as to keep their attention; with so much of the abstract as to require the exercise of their reason, and so much of the concrete as to make his thoughts intelligible; with so much of graphic power as to awaken the imagination, and so much of his own will as to make his subject a personal matter between him and them.

Then there was Dr. Nathaniel Hewitt, from whose lips, when his soul was charged, would "leap the live thunder" to the heads and hearts of his congregation. There was also Dr. Thomas H. Skinner, whose soul was so full of life that he vitalized all the truths which he uttered.

Then there was Dr. John Rice, whose large mind and large heart were so "touched to fine issues," that his hearers readily gave themselves up to his guidance. It was of him that President Jefferson said: "If that measure is adopted, John Rice will set all Virginia in a blaze." Other distinguished preachers might be mentioned. I should not omit to mention Rev. Samuel Merwin, who was pastor of the North church in New Haven, saintly in character, in aspect and manner,—a model pastor. Dr. Taylor was pastor of the Center church, and was at the height of his popularity as a preacher and a man.

Rev. Dr. Emmons, having been called to preach an ordination sermon in North Guilford, was invited to visit New Haven, and to preach in the North Church. There was a general attendance of the intelligent Christians of New Haven to hear this far-famed theologian. He preached a sermon on the relation between the fore-knowledge of God and His decrees, to an appreciating and admiring audience, which was a fine specimen of his terse and compact style of writing, and of his inferential theology.

The religious controversies formerly existing in New Haven had at that time died out, but had left the leading men there well acquainted with the doctrines at issue in those controversies, and ready to converse intelligently about them. Some of these men had sat under the pastoral ministration of the venerable Chauncey Whittlesey, of that profound metaphysician, the younger Jonathan Edwards of the White Haven church, of James Dana, that man of high culture, and of his successor Moses Stuart.

Among them were James Hillhouse, the statesman, the strong prop of Yale College during the years of its weakness; Judge Charles Chauncey, often consulted by President Dwight on theological subjects; Noah Webster; Judge David Daggett, an amateur hearer of sermons and a prophetic judge of young preachers, generous and appreciative; Judge Simeon Baldwin, ever candid and gracious; Elizur Goodrich, Samuel Darling, Joseph Darling, Judge Dyer White, Stephen Twining, Timothy Dwight, William Leffingwell, and others. These men seemed to take great interest in the class, and showed a readiness to converse with them. Indeed, the religious people of New Haven seemed to view the class with favor, were disposed to hear them preach, and were ready to subscribe to the endowment of the Dwight Professorship by which the school could become permanent.

There had been in Connecticut, from the first, a union, or quasi union between Church and State, sanctioned as was supposed, by the God of Israel; "Thou leddest forth thy people as a flock by the hands of Moses and Aaron." But by the State constitution of 1818 Aaron was deposed from his joint leadership with Moses. The aureola which encircled his head faded off. The clergy, most of them, had laid aside their wigs. Some of them had come down from their pristine elevation "to become all things to all men." Had they kept on their wigs, had they not come down from their elevation, they might, perhaps, according to the remark of Roger Minot Sherman, have kept back the revolution for a time. After 1818 they could no longer be recognized by the General Assembly as a power in the State. They could no longer take their annual public dinner at Hartford, furnished at the expense of the State. The people, by their vote declared in favor of "toleration," and the clergy had nothing to do but gracefully submit to the loss of their prestige.

With some feeling of bereavement and degradation they naturally turned their thoughts to Yale College, which had always been their pride and their love. It was at first the child of the clergy, and afterwards the Alma Mater of most of them. The ministers of the "standing order" of Connecticut had their attention especially turned to our class of theological students. Indeed, they seemed to have been taken almost by surprise. They had expected nothing of the kind after the death of President Dwight, who had given occasional instructions to students in theology; but here was a school composed of twelve promising young students, regularly taught at stated times by three accomplished professors, who were devoted to their work. Nothing equal to it had ever been seen at Yale before.

There was a good deal of curiosity expressed by the clergy in regard to this school, both as to the instructions given and as to the proficiency of the students. At an early period we were given to understand by some of the associations that they were ready to receive our application for licenses. Somewhere about the year 1860, President Day informed me that he walked all the way to Woodbridge in order to be present at the examination of one of the class, before the New Haven West Association.

After we were licensed to preach, we were received with favor by the ministers and the churches. Invitations came in upon us from different quarters to preach as candidates, even before we were ready to accept them. In one or more cases the invitation came in advance of the license. After we were licensed, all the pulpits were opened to us. One of the class preached his first sermon to the students in the college chapel at the earnest request of Professor Fitch, and another preached to the students during a summer term in the absence of Professor Fitch.

Sometime in the year 1822 a Memorial, signed by a portion or all of the class, was addressed to the corporation of the college, requesting them to establish a Theological Department. The corporation listened to the "memorial," and appointed Nathaniel W. Taylor to the chair of Didactic Theology. There were also certain literary advantages outside of the school and the college which contributed to the improvement of some or all of the class. Dr. Benjamin Trumbull, in that period, was engaged in publishing his "History of Connecticut," at New Haven; Dr. Noah Webster was there preparing his great American Dictionary for the press; Professor Silliman commenced the publication of the *American Journal of Science and Art* in the year 1818; the same year the Rev. Thomas Davies commenced the publication of the *Christian Spectator;* in 1820 Cornelius Tuthill began the publication of the *Microscope;* James A. Hillhouse spent a portion of the time there; so did James G. Percival, the "walking encyclopedia;" and Carlos Wilcox, who was sometimes called the "beloved disciple," published there his "Age of Benevolence;" then there was Nathaniel Chauncey, Henry Dwight, and Mr. Torrey, for a short period afterwards professor at Burlington. Then there was Eli Whitney, whose invention introduced a new era for the cotton fabrics of the civilized world; and, for a small portion of the time, Rev. Jedediah Morse and his excellent sons, Samuel Finley Breese, Sidney Edwards, and Richard.

The medical department of the College was in operation. Its faculty were Prof. Æneas Munson, a man of various acquisitions, and as good a joker as Abraham Lincoln; Prof. Nathan Smith, one of nature's gifted sons; Prof. Eli Ives, learned and high principled; Prof. Knight, whose merit was equaled only by his modesty.

At the bar there was David Dagget, whose clear and adroit statements of a case in court sometimes won it before he commenced the argument; Nathan Smith, who successfully addressed the common sense and the common heart of the jury; Seth P. Staples, learned in the law with his fierce and fiery logic; Ralph I. Ingersoll, whose "soul of honor was seated in a heart of courtesy;" Roger S. Baldwin, endowed with hereditary talents for the law, *a patre et avo*, and Dennis Kimberly, who, by his high intellectual and moral qualities, won all hearts that he approached.

The literary atmosphere of New Haven was genial and invigorating. The educational influence of the community in which a college is placed, upon the officers and students of the college, has long been well understood. Thus, in ancient Oxford, England, there were laws prohibiting any of the students of the university from entering into any house in the town. It was feared they would be contaminated by contact with the community. They were expected by their segregation from it, to ascend into a higher plane of learning, religion, morals, manners, and refinement. It was expected that the scholars, after they had enjoyed the advantages of a university education, would endeavor to elevate the community. After a long period, when the people of Oxford had become elevated by the influence of graduates of the colleges, these prohibitory laws were abolished, and the undergraduates derived great advantage from an intercourse with families of cultivation and refinement.

About one hundred years had elapsed since the establishment of the college at New Haven, and one hundred and eighty years since the time that John Davenport, himself an Oxford student, had led a "London Company" to settle at New Haven. Intelligence, courtesy, and refinement of manners, transmitted from the "London Company," had been increased through the influence of the college, so that the people of New Haven generally were intelligent, pious, and refined. There were, moreover, generally in the community, habits of industry, order, and frugality.

The social atmosphere of New Haven, on the high grounds, was pure and exhilarating, tempered and made fragrant by airs from what Bunyan calls "the delectable mountains." Breathing this atmosphere, with "looks commencing with the skies," the young theological aspirant could easily send his thoughts to the region where there is a *largior ether*, where there is a higher communion, where there is the city of the living God, the home of his own soul, and of the souls of all whom he may in his ministry lead to Jesus.

—

Edward Bull was born in Saybrook, Conn., November 26th, 1791, and died in Cheshire, Conn., April 25th, 1869. He was fitted for college by his pastor, Rev. Aaron Hovey; graduated at Yale College in 1816; was teacher in the Grammar School in New London, Conn., for nearly two years; was tutor in Yale College five years; was ordained September 29th, 1825, paster of the Congregational Church in Lebanon, Conn., and was dismissed in 1837. The rest of his life was spent in Cheshire, where he received a few pupils for instructions, chiefly the children of his friends, who repaid his care by their proficiency and their friendship. He was an excellent classical and English scholar; was independent in the expression and formation of his opinions; was constant in his friendships, and much beloved by those who knew him intimately. Mr. Bull was married about the time of his ordination to Miss Eliza Ann Hallam, of New London, Conn. She died October, 1872, and left, by her will, $2,000 to found a scholarship for the Yale Divinity School, to be called the Edward Bull Scholarship.

Lyman Coleman was born in Middlefield, Mass., June 14th, 1796, graduated at Yale College in 1817; was rector of the

Grammar School in Hartford, Conn., three years; was tutor in Yale College four years and a half; was seven years pastor of the church in Belchertown, Mass.; was Principal of the Burr Seminary, Vt., five years; subsequently was five years Principal of the English Department of Phillips Academy in Andover; studied and traveled a year in Germany; was connected with Amherst College three years; was Professor of German in the New Jersey College two years; visited Europe a second time and traveled extensively in Egypt, the Desert of Sahara, and Palestine; was a Professor of Latin and Greek in LaFayette College; is still connected with that college. He is the author of a number of valuable works: "Antiquities of the Christian Church," "The Apostolic and Primitive Church," "Historical Geography of the Bible," "Ancient Christianity," "Historical Text-Book and Atlas of Biblical Geography," "Genealogy of the Lyman family." He has received the degree of D. D.

WILLIAM C. FOWLER was born in Killingworth (now Clinton), Conn., September 1st, 1793; was fitted for College by Rev. John Elliot, D. D., of East Guilford (now Madison); was rector of the Hopkins Grammar School a portion of the summer term of 1816, also nearly a year in 1817–18; was tutor in Yale College five years, wanting one term; was ordained pastor of a Congregational Church August 31st, 1825, in Greenfield, Mass.; was eleven years Professor of Chemistry and Natural History in Middlebury College; was five years Professor of Rhetoric in Amherst College; was a member of the Massachusetts House of Representatives in 1851, and of the Senate of Connecticut in 1864; delivered lectures before the Smithsonian Institute in 1851; traveled in Europe in 1852; was accredited Representative of the United States at the meeting of the British Scientific Association in Belfast in 1852; is the author of "The English Language in its Elements and Forms," and of two abridgements of the same; "Memorials of the Chaunceys," "The Sectional Controversy," "The History of Durham," "Local Law in Massachusetts and Connnecticut," Historically considered; Editor "University Edition of Webster's Dictionary," and author of a considerable number of pamphlets, and various articles in periodicals, and Sermons. He received the degree of LL. D. Resides in Durham, Conn.

William Graham was born in Fayette county, Penn., in 1793; was graduated at Jefferson College in 1816; studied at Yale College two years, and afterwards at Andover three years; was settled in the ministry, first at Chillicothe, Ohio, in 1828; in 1834 or '35 was installed at Oxford, Ohio; in 1847 he was settled over the Presbyterian Church in Woodbury, New Jersey, where he died in 1856; in 1824 he married Miss Jane Ridgely, daughter of Dr. Frederic Ridgely, of Lexington, Ky., and left a son, Frederic Ridgely Graham, who graduated at Amherst College in 1847, and who is now a physician in Chester, Penn. The following is a copy of the inscription on his monument, which was erected by his church:

Rev. William Graham,
who fell asleep in Jesus,
December 18, 1856,
in the 58th year of his age,
the 34th of his ministry,
and the 9th of his pastorate
in the
Presbyterian Church
in Woodbury.

As a preacher
he was earnest and solid:
As a pastor, active and laborious;
judicious in counsel:
of affable manners and warm affections;
faithful to admonish, skilful to console;
an example to his flock.

By their affection,
this stone
is erected to his memory.

" The morning cometh."

Epaphras Goodman was born in West Hartford, January 22d, 1790; was graduated at Dartmouth College in 1816; was ordained pastor in Torringford March 6th, 1822, and was dismissed January 12th, 1836; was installed over the first church in Dracut, Mass., June 15th, 1836, and was dismissed June 7th, 1838; from 1840 to 1850 was editor of the *Watchman of the Valley* at Cincinnati; in 1851 was editor of the

Christian Era for one year, at Chicago; was secretary of the American Missionary Association. He died at Chicago, June 12th, 1862; aged 72. He appears to have been a very useful and successful minister.

HORACE HOOKER was born in Berlin, Connecticut, March, 1793; was graduated at Yale College in 1815; was teacher of the Hartford Grammar School two years; was tutor at Yale College five years; was ordained pastor of the Congregational Church, Watertown, Connecticut in 1822; in 1824 he returned to Hartford and became editor of the *Connecticut Observer*, a religious newspaper, which he conducted with ability for many years; was secretary of the Connecticut Missionary, and Home Missionary Societies; was Chaplain of the Retreat for the Insane; was author of several valuable books; was appointed by the General Association in Connecticut, together with Dr. O. E. Daggett, to prepare a psalm book for the churches of Connecticut, which is still in use. Mr. Hooker was a clear thinker, and expressed his thoughts in a style remarkable for its neatness and perspicuity. He died in Hartford, December 17th, 1864, aged 71.

SAMUEL B. INGERSOLL was born at Salem, Mass., October 13th, 1785. He became a mariner and commander of a ship that traded at Archangel, Russia, on the White Sea; was graduated at Yale College in 1817; was licensed to preach by the New Haven West Association, May 25th, 1819; was married to Susan Whittlesey of New Haven, December, 1819; was ordained at Shrewsbury Mass., as colleague with the Rev. Dr. Sumner, June 14th, 1820; and died at Beverly, Mass., November 14th, 1820, having preached only one sermon after his ordination, to the people of his charge. During his last illness he composed a hymn, breathing a Christian spirit, of which this is the first stanza:

> " And does affliction press thee down,
> And dost thou see thy Father's frown?
> Turn not away, but kiss the rod,
> Be still and know that I am God."

This hymn can be found in the *Christian Spectator*, vol. 3, page 59. He was universally respected as a gentleman and a christian. See Memoir.

Edward Hitchcock was born in Deerfield, Mass., May 24th, 1793; died at Amherst, Mass., Feb. 27th, 1864; received the degree of A. M. at Yale College in 1818; was Principal of the Deerfield Academy from 1815–1818; was ordained pastor of the Congregational Church in Conway, Mass., in 1821; was professor of Chemistry and Natural History in Amherst College from 1825–45; was President of Amherst College and professor of Natural Theology and Geology from 1845–54; was appointed State Geologist of Mass., in 1830, of the first district of New York in 1836, and of Vermont in 1857; in 1850 was commissioned by the State government to examine the agricultural schools in Europe. His publications are numerous and well known throughout the country. He received the degree of D. D. and LL. D.

David N. Lord was born in Franklin, Conn.; was graduated at Yale College in 1817; supplied the pulpit in the chapel at Yale College one summer during the absence of Professor Fitch; his health failing, he devoted himself to business pursuits in New York city, where he did for several years a large and successful business; was author of "Views in Theology"; for thirteen years conducted a quarterly, entitled *The Theological and Literary Journal*, New York, a great many of the articles being written by himself; was author of an able exposition of the "Revelation of John," and a poetical work entitled "Visions of Paradise." He has in his productions shown himself a learned, vigorous, and logical writer, earnestly devoted to the defence of Scripture truths. He is now engaged in the management of a very large estate left him by his brother, Rufus Lord, the well-known millionaire, of whose will he is one of the executors.

Levi Smith was born in Litchfield County, Conn., in 1790; was graduated at Yale College in 1818: was ordained as an evangelist, and labored very successfully as such several years; he was sometimes called the second Nettleton; was first settled at Wayland, Mass., in the winter of 1828–29, where he remained four years. Dr. Lyman Beecher having preached his ordination sermon, was afterwards settled at Kennebunkport, Me., where he remained seven years ; subsequently was settled at South Windsor, Conn., where he remained ten years. He died at South Windsor, Conn., January 15th, 1854. Dr. Bennett Tyler preached his funeral sermon.

STEPHEN D. WARD was born in New Jersey; was nephew of the Rev. William Dodd, of East Haven; was graduated at New Jersey College in 1819; was rector of the Hopkins Grammar School two years 1821–23; completed his theological studies at Andover; his first place of settlement was Machias, Me., where he was ordained in 1834, and remained ten years; he then preached in various places in New Jersey and Virginia; he was installed over the Congregational Church at Agawam, Mass., October 18th, 1853, and died June 11th, 1858, after a pastorate of four years. "He was a good scholar, a sound theologian, and an able preacher." "He left a sweet savor among his people, and must have been an eminently godly man."

JOSEPH D. WICKHAM was born at Thompson, Conn., April 4th, 1797; in 1800 his parents removed to the city of New York, where he was brought up; was prepared for college at a boarding school in Stamford, Conn.; was graduated at Yale College in 1815; the first year after leaving college he was amanuensis for Dr. Dwight; the year following, was rector of the Hopkins Grammar School; then tutor at Yale College for about three years; was licensed to preach by the New Haven West Association, January 2d, 1821; his first ministerial labors were as a missionary on Long Island; then he traveled in Western New York in an agency for the Presbyterian branch of the American Education Society; was ordained at Oxford, Chenango county, N. Y., July 31st, 1823, where he remained two years; then he removed to Westchester county, N. Y., where he remained somewhat longer, preaching at New Rochelle and West Farms; in 1828 became a partner in the Washington Institute, and ultimately its sole proprietor and manager; was installed pastor of the Presbyterian Church at Matteawan in the town of Fishkill, N. Y., November, 1834; was principal of the Burr Seminary, at Manchester, Vt., twenty-five years; he also acted as professor in Middlebury College (of which he is a trustee) one year during that period; has received the degree of D. D. His present residence is Manchester, Vt.

A STATEMENT SUBMITTED TO THE PRUDENTIAL COMMITTEE, BY THE PROFESSOR OF DIVINITY IN YALE COLLEGE.

Gentlemen:

Several members of the present Senior Class, desirous of pursuing their theological studies at this college, have applied to the professor of divinity to engage in the business of their instruction, and he begs leave on this occasion, deeply interesting to his feelings, to avail himself of that provision in the laws of the college, which declares that he may "receive" from the Prudential Committee "their advice and direction in all matters relating to the business of his office."

By the laws, it is made his duty to attend to the instruction which has been requested of him in this application. Such is the construction he has ever given to the clause, which enacts that "it shall be his duty to give from time to time, such lectures and private instruction, to the resident graduates and students, as he shall judge may best preserve and promote the religious interests of the college, and tend most effectually to form for future usefulness in the work of the evangelical ministry, such of the students as shall appear desirous of being prepared for it." The clause is indeed worded in accordance with the spirit of the times, in which theological studies were commenced before the expiration of the collegiate course, but it contemplates one important design entertained in calling a professor of divinity to the college—that of "supplying the churches with a learned, pious, and orthodox ministry."*

In accordance with this duty of his office, he has given private lectures, once or twice weekly, ever since his induction into office, to such theological students as have chosen to remain here. In doing it, however, he has had to struggle

* Pres. Clapp's Hist. Y. C., p. 61.

with embarrassments which the present application,* if complied with, must greatly enhance, which he will now state to the committee, and out of which there arises an interesting practical question on which he solicits their advice.

His chief embarrassment in the discharge of this duty, has arisen from the present advanced state of theological instruction. He looks back to the state of theological education at the period in which his office was instituted, when the instructions of a single divine, in systematic theology, formed the highest standard of such education, and he looks abroad on its advanced state at the present period when the labors of two or more instructors are wholly devoted to it, and Scriptural interpretation and sacred eloquence as well as systematic divinity are comprised in its standard, and he feels embarrassed with the duty of continuing an old establishment that exhibits to students, under the present raised standard of education, such comparative disadvantages. The professor of languages is willing to afford assistance and all that is necessary in the department of Hebrew criticism. The professor of rhetoric and oratory is willing to do something in the department of sacred eloquence; yet the state of his health, and the pressure of his duties in the classical department, require him to leave the main burden unsustained. The whole burden therefore of Greek criticism and Scriptural theology, and of didactic and polemic theology, and the main burden of sacred eloquence rest upon the professor of divinity, if any attempt be made, under present circumstances, to give to theological students the advantages required by the present standard of education. He need not say that the burden is more than he can assume. Accordingly, he is thrown back still on the embarassments of being obligated to continue an old establishment under its disadvantages.

Another embarrassment arises from the state of his own health. The labors of the Sabbath and of preparations for it are so exhausting to him, that altogether unaided in these, he could hardly contribute to this branch of instruction the labors of a single man.

---

* A class more numerous than had applied to him for previous years.

In these circumstances of embarassment, he has ever felt himself placed, while he has held the office; and he has felt at a loss what reply to make to young gentlemen who have desired to pursue their theological studies here. To advise them to remain, under disadvantages to themselves, was repugnant to his feelings: to refuse them instruction, seemed abandoning an important design of his office: and he has hitherto avoided the decision himself by stating the superior advantages to be enjoyed elsewhere, and engaging in the instruction of those who, after all, chose to remain.*

These difficulties are presented afresh to his mind by the application now brought to him by the seniors; and from these difficulties he can be freed by nothing short of having assistance, on the one hand, adequate to place this department of education on a suitable foundation, or else, on the other hand, of having this important duty disconnected from his office.

The question which arises on this statement, and which he respectfully submits to the Committee, is the following: *Shall exertions be made to add a new professor to the College who shall take a part in the education of theological students, and the duties of the Chapel; or, shall the education of students in theology be wholly discarded from the college?*

The preceding statement, he conceives unavoidably leads to the great practical alternative presented in this question, whether the object of educating theological students shall be *pursued* or *abandoned* in the college; and in this attitude he chooses to present the subject, without specifying particularly here, the branches of instruction a new professor, were he introduced, should assume other than such a share in chapel duties as would afford a necessary relief to the professor of divinity, were he to engage earnestly in this instruction. The specification of his duties can be made afterwards. The question *what* shall be done may be raised, when the main points is decided whether *any thing* shall be done.

---

*During this interval, the following persons pursued their Theological studies here: J. D. Wickham, Edward Bull, William C. Fowler, Edward Hitchcock, Lyman Coleman, Samuel B. Ingersoll, David N. Lord, H. Hooker, Levi Smith, C. Whittelsey.

The question, it will be perceived, is one of momentous interest to the college, (to mention no other relation which it bears,) on which its constituted guardians will not act without serious deliberation, and in submitting it to the Prudential Committee, he begs leave to append, with modesty, the following considerations which, in his opinion, ought to have an influence on the result to which they come.

I. *The primitive design of the college demands consideration.*

More than a century has rolled by since the clergy and pious laymen in the colony of Connecticut contemplated the establishment of this college. By adverting to the circumstances of the age, the acts that were passed respecting the college and its past history, it is apparent that the chief design of establishing it was, that it should be a school to prepare men for the ministry of the Gospel.

At that age our ancestors had no idea of the severance of theological schools from the schools of philosophy. They derived their views from the higher schools of Europe in which the four branches of philosophy, law, medicine, and theology, were united, and maintained the sentiments of that age—that the primary design of the superior schools of learning was to educate young men for the ministry.* The fathers of New England have left their sentiments on this subject in sundry expressions in their early synodical acts.† The circumstances of the colonies did not permit of their establishing schools at the first, comprising all the advantages of the higher schools of Europe; and out of these exigencies arose the practice of pursuing theological studies with individual clergymen of eminence, as well as in the schools supported by the colonies of Massachusetts and Connecticut. But most remote was it from their intentions to erect mere schools of philosophy. "*Christo et ecclesiae*" was the dedicatory motto of Harvard, and the ministers who first concerted the plan of this college proposed to call it "The School of the Church."‡

* Cent. Magdeb., Lib. i., Cap. vii.; Lib. xi., Cap. vii.; Lightfoot's Works, Vol. 2d, p. 80; Stillingfleet's Works, Vol. 3, p. 878; Alsted, Chron. Scholarum.

† President Clap's History of Yale College, page 1.

‡ Clap's History of Yale College, page 2.

The acts which have been passed from the first respecting this college exhibit this as its primitive design. When the charter was granted and the college was organized in 1701, the trustees gave special directions to the rector "to instruct and ground the students well in theoretical divinity," in order "to promote the power and purity of religion, and the best edification of *these New England churches*.* The General Assembly of the colony, in 1753, "recommended a general contribution to be made in all the religious societies in the colony, for the purpose of settling a professor of divinity in the college," considering "that one principal end proposed in erecting the college was to supply the churches in this colony with a learned, pious, and orthodox ministry."† In 1756 a professor of divinity was attached to the college, whose duty it was made in the statutes, not only to be a pastor of the church and a religious teacher of the pupils, but also, as has already been explained, to furnish such students in theology as might be reared in the college or chose to resort to it, with assistance in their studies preparatory to the university.

The history of what has been done in theological education in the college is in conformity with this design of its founders and benefactors. Theological instruction has always been given to the pupils of the college and to students in divinity, and there has been maintained in the college a strictly theological school. The Rev. Professors Daggett and Wales, and the Rev. President Dwight, in his capacity of professor of divinity, have each successively given instruction to students in theology, and prepared many for the ministerial office, who have been highly distinguished for their usefulness in the churches. In 1765 President Clap, speaking of the progress of the college, says: "The principal design of the institution of this college was to educate persons for the work of the ministry; which design has been so far succeeded as that above four hundred worthy ministers have received their education here." From that date to the present period several times that number have been added to the catalogue, and out of this

---

* Clap's History of Yale College, page 11.

† Clap's History of Yale College, page 60.

large number of students who have entered into the ministry, a great portion have been qualified for their labors by pursuing their theological studies at this college.

The committee then will take into consideration this primitive design of the college while deliberating on the question which the professor of divinity now proposes to them; and may he be permitted respectfully to ask of them whether, when acting as guardians over the trusts of our pious ancestors, they can consistently convert a school, held sacred by them to the purposes of the ministry, into a mere school of science? Whether, when they have already augmented the scientific department, and have already annexed a medical department completely organized, and may yet be called upon to add the department of law, they shall wholly discard a theological department, so clearly intended by the founders to be the chief pillar and ornament of the college.

II. *The support of a theological department in the college interferes not with existing theological institutions.*

The friends of religion take a deep interest, as well they may do, in those theological seminaries which have been recently instituted in our country, and have extended such aid to the work of preparing men for the ministry. Any measure undertaken with the design of interfering with the welfare of these seminaries must meet with the decided disapprobation of their many and devoted friends. The committee then will consider whether the support of a theological department in this college, according to the primitive design of its founders, and on a foundation adequate to the present standard of theological education, would be justly considered, either in design or in effect, as an interference in the welfare of existing theological seminaries.

Not in design surely; for the design in them, who hold as trustees the sacred bequests of past generations, would be no other than that of consulting with fidelity the high interests committed to their guardianship—a design which they are bound equally to entertain in their consultations and decisions, whether any, or however so many, new institutions spring up around them into existence.

Nor in its effect could such a support of a theological department here as is necessary, be justly deemed an interference with existing theological seminaries. Not an interference in regard to any claim of precedence in such seminaries, in regard to their students, or in regard to their funds.

Not in regard to any claim of precedence they may have upon the public patronage, for the department of theology had long been known here, as the most precious branch of instruction, in the estimation of the founders, before any of these institutions ever had an existence, and it has languished for want of suitable encouragement while these more recent institutions have been attracting, in an unprecedented degree, the patronage of the wealthy; and if so ancient a school of theology, so long languishing for want of necessary support, should now lift its supplicating voice for aid, no claims of precedence from any quarter could arise to resist its claims.

Not, in regard to the number of students in existing seminaries, would the support of this department be an interference. For, it is obvious that a maximum number of students may be assumed, beyond which it is not desirable, either in regard to study, piety, charity funds, or the interests of the church, that an individual theological seminary should go, and one of these seminaries has nearly attained, it will be acknowledged, it is believed, by the professors themselves, to this maximum. But it will be perceived, on a statistical view of the number of pious students in the colleges of New England, that more than a maximum are coming forward for existing institutions; and on reverting to the efforts making by the education societies, it will be perceived that this overplus must be expected still to increase; so that without any infringement on the number of students in existing seminaries, this department may speedily expect, if supported, a suitable number of pupils.

Nor, finally, will the support of this department interfere at all with the funds of such institutions. For as to students, an increase of their number in charity students is but a consumption of their funds, and in other students is but a bare re-payment of simple expenses; and as to the community, they look to a different portion of it from that on which this department must chiefly rely.

While the committee then consider the obligations of pursuing the primitive design of the college, the professor of divinity would beg leave to ask whether they are not encouraged to pursue it by the ability they possess of doing it without interfering at all with those existing seminaries that are held deservedly in high estimation by the friends of religion?

He would suggest also as another encouraging consideration—

III. *The facilities of supporting a theological department in the college.*

For much that is needed for the proper organization of such a department is already in their possession. They have a library that is more ample on this department than on any other, and which might, at little expense, be made adequate for all the purposes of both the instructors and the pupils. They have one professor who, by his very office, is devoted to this department, and have the promise of partial assistance in it from two others. The whole department seems already organized to their hands, with the exception of merely an additional instructor; and will they abandon these advantages?

What they have not in possession they may easily obtain—the additional instructor. For so far as the subject has been broached among the clergy or among laymen, it meets with that warm reception which promises that solicitations, becomingly urgent, made on private individuals of wealth, or, if need be, on the community, will be productive of the necessary funds. With adequate funds it can hardly be supposed but that a man can be found who is suited to fill the station.

IV. *The positive advantages of upholding such a department of instruction in the college are also to be taken into consideration.*

The professor of divinity might suggest the advantages which the school would afford to its own students arising from its location, and the benefits it would impart to the church of Christ, but he omits these topics most deeply interesting, to hint merely at some of the advantages likely to arise from it to the college, in which they must be supposed to take a lively interest as the constituted guardians of its welfare.

The complete organization and successful operation of such a department of education, it is confidently believed, would exert a most auspicious influence on the college in regard to the character of its students, its reputation in the community, and the augmentation of its funds.

The influence must reach the students of the classical department, and be highly auspicious in favor of their order, morals, and religion. For it would bring the weight of the character and instructions of a new professor and religious teacher, and the conversations and examples of a more advanced grade of students, to bear on the minds of the classical students.

The influence of the department too, if successful, (as the professor of divinity flatters himself it would be,) would be felt on the reputation of the college in the community. For much might be done by the students of six or seven years standing, like those in this department, and their instructors in connection with them, to exalt the standard of literature in the college; and the approaches it would make by the full organization of this department towards the character of a university, would exalt its reputation in the view both of the religious and literary part of the community.

The influence of it would, it is presumed, reach also the funds of the college. The religious and the literary both would feel stronger motives to send their sons to a college of increased sanctity and celebrity, and the wealthy of whatever character would more willingly have their names and donations identified with its reputation, and the poor more readily connect the silent rivulet of their gifts with the broad tide of its prosperity.

The guardians of the college then, while taking into deliberation the question now submitted to them by the professor of divinity, will doubtless look with an impartial eye on the considerations which he has suggested—the primitive design of the college, the ability of pursuing it without interfering with

4

existing institutions, the facilities that are in their possession, and the advantages likely to accrue to the college—and to their decision he now cheerfully submits the deeply interesting question arising out of his statement.

ELEAZAR T. FITCH.

NEW HAVEN, YALE COLLEGE, April 23d, 1822.

A true copy. GEORGE E. DAY.

THEOLOGICAL DEPARTMENT OF YALE COLLEGE,
December 4th, 1869.

The following gentlemen were the Prudential Committee to whom the statement of Prof. Fitch was addressed: viz., President Jeremiah Day, Rev. John Elliott, D. D., Rev. Calvin Chapin, D. D., Hon. David Tomlinson.

WILLIAM C. FOWLER.

THE APPOINTMENT OF NATHANIEL WILLIAM TAYLOR TO THE CHAIR OF THE DWIGHT PROFESSORSHIP OF DIDACTIC THEOLOGY IN YALE COLLEGE.

The clergy were always prominent in Connecticut from 1636 down to 1822, the era that I am considering.

After the authorities of Yale College had decided to establish a department for the instruction of a permanent school in theology, the question came up—who shall fill the place? In order to answer that question correctly it was necessary to take into view the "form and pressure of the time," and also those antecedents which had given shape to that form, and force to that pressure.

The origin of the vital forces that were then at work in the living present could be found only in the dead past, by looking at those antecedents through the period of one hundred and eighty-four years. In order to learn what were the peculiarities of that great stream of human population in Connecticut, which in 1822 was hurrying along into the vast future, it is necessary to follow that stream up to its spring head in 1636. The mental and moral characteristics of a community are transmitted through the successive generations, with some modifications, as are the attributes of blood in a family, cropping out here and there in various strains.

The founders of Connecticut wished to build up a "peculiar" structure of society for themselves and their posterity. In order to do this successfully they needed the united wisdom of all. They needed the wisdom of Hooker—"the light of the western churches"—and of Stone, both of Hartford, and of Wareham, of Windsor, and of Davenport, of New Haven—"the ornament of New England"—and of Prudden, of Milford, and of Whitfield, of Guilford. These men were the most learned, the most able, and the best men in the two colonies. They had led their followers across the ocean, and into the wilderness, and they were now needed for the higher work of laying the foundations of civil and religious society. Accordingly they were brought to the front.

In the minds of these Puritan leaders the religious interests, the civil interests, and the educational interests, were so intertwined with each other that they felt it impossible to legislate successfully for one class of these interests without legislating for the other two. They did not complain of the union of church and state simply in itself considered, but they did complain of that union so far as the church in England inspired the state to pass and execute bad laws against themselves. If they looked to the Hebrew commonwealth they found a union of church and state, in which the priests had their share in the government; if they looked to England they found there a union of church and state, in which the sovereign was the head of the church, and the bishops had their seats in Parliament.

Accordingly when they laid the foundation of the government for the colony on the Connecticut River, and for the colony on Long Island Sound, they established a union of church and state, in which it was expected that the church would inspire the state to pass good laws; and they were not disappointed. The ruling idea in their minds was, that what the state could not do for the benefit of itself the church should do; and what the church could not do for itself the state should do. Thus the church and the state were complements of each other, and when united formed a complete whole.

As all derived great advantages from religious institutions, so all were taxed for the support of those institutions, on substantially the same ground that all are now taxed to support common schools. After the union of the two colonies in 1665, the legislature gave permission to form new towns and establish new churches; and as a condition it seems to have required that certain allotments of land should be set apart to the first *settled* minister of the town, to be held by him in fee simple, and certain other allotments for the support of the ministry in all future time.

The towns appear to have been co-ordinate with the churches in the call of the minister, and in the invitation to the council which was to ordain him. Sometimes, indeed, the towns seem to have called the minister and invited the council for his ordination before the church was formed. When the churches of Connecticut framed the Saybrook Platform in 1708, the General Assembly, at Hartford, passed an act approving of that platform as a constitution for the churches, and recommended it for their adoption. When the churches found themselves in difficulty they applied to the General Assembly to assist them in the settlement of it.

The clergy generally visited Hartford at the annual election in May. Here, in their clerical dress, they marched in a long procession to the church, where a sermon was preached by one of their number to the Governor, Lieutenant-Governor, Assistants, and General Assembly. In this sermon the duties of the Legislature were carefully and often earnestly set forth. On these occasions they felt the strong tie of sympathy binding them together as ministers of Christ. And after enjoying the stalled ox and the luscious shad, at the public dinner provided for them at the expense of the Commonwealth, and assisting in preparing the nomination of candidates for future election, they went to their several homes, strengthened in their desire to do everything for their beloved commonwealth; and there musing on what they had seen and enjoyed, some of them might be ready to exclaim:

> "Roll on loved Connecticut, long hast thou ran,
> Giving blossoms to nature, and morals to man."

Or christianizing the words of Virgil, to say

> "Deus nobis haec otia fecit."

In many of the towns of Connecticut the clergyman was in a highly respectable and desirable position. After enjoying the advantages of a liberal education, and after his baptism by the Holy Ghost, and after taking his ordination vows as a pastor, his influence among his people was almost unlimited, if his mind belonged to a superior order. Settled for life and devoted to the best interests of his people, they, in return, paid him respect, admiration, love. Besides his annual salary, if he was not the first minister of the town who received an allotment of land, he received from the town what was called a " settlement," namely, a sum of money which would assist him to purchase a house and land. This settlement implied that the contract between him and the town was to continue during his life, just as a marriage covenant is for life. He was the most learned man in town, the first gentleman, and regarded as the best christian;

> " The glass of fashion, and the mould of form,
> The observ'd of all observers !"

If his was a long ministry he could look back upon more than one generation which he had moulded into form, and after he had gone to his rest he would be long remembered as he was in the pulpit, as he was by the baptismal font, as he was by the bedside of the sick, as he was by the open grave, as he was administering consolation in the house of mourning. The sermon preached at his funeral would be printed, would be often read by weeping eyes, carefully preserved, and transmitted as an heir-loom in the family. His influence extended to all his people in all their spiritual and in all their earthly concerns. If he was not the "Father Confessor," he was the "Father Adviser" of all.

The clergy carefully remembered the words of the New Testament, " Given to hospitality: and be not forgetful to entertain strangers." They considered hospitality as a christian duty.

President Timothy Dwight, before he was settled in Greenfield Hill, Conn., told the committee who were appointed to agree upon the terms of his settlement, that he must have enough to support his family and educate his children, and provide for *hospitality*, and lay up something for old age.

In a pleasant country town Dr. P., at the annual meeting of the society, told the people that one reason why he must have a large salary was the expense of entertaining company;

that he kept as many as five horses a week through the night, upon an average, during the year. One of his parishioners rather doubting this statement offered to keep the horses for a stipulated sum. The minister agreed to it, but upon trial the parishioner found he had made a bad bargain.

If a minister, or any other gentleman, instead of stopping at the sign of the tavern should stop at the minister's for hospitality, he was said to "put up at the sign of the steeple."

Macauley, in his History of England, speaks of the Nonconformists as follows:

"The ablest and most eloquent preachers among them had, since the Declaration of Indulgence had appeared, been very agreeably settled in the capital, and in other large towns, and were now about to enjoy under the sure guarantee of an act of Parliament, that toleration which, under the Declaration of Indulgence, had been illicit and precarious. The situation of these men was such as the great majority of the divines of the Established Church might well envy. Few, indeed, of the parochial clergy were so abundantly supplied with comforts as the favorite orator of a great assembly of non-conformists in the city. The voluntary contributions of his wealthy hearers, aldermen and deputies, West India merchants and Turkey merchants, wardens of the company of fish-mongers, and wardens of the company of goldsmiths, enabled him to become a land-owner, or a mortgagee. The best broadcloth from Blackwell hall, and the best poultry from Leadenhall market, were frequently left at his door. His influence over his flock was immense. Scarcely any member of a congregation of separatists entered into a partnership, married a daughter, put a son out as an apprentice, or gave his vote at an election, without consulting his spiritual guide. On all political and literary questions the minister was the oracle of his own circle. It was popularly remarked, during many years, that an eminent dissenting minister had only to make his son an attorney, or a physician, that the attorney was sure to have clients, and the physician to have patients. While a waiting-woman was generally considered as a helpmeet for a chaplain in holy orders of the established Church, the widows and daughters of opulent citizens were supposed to belong in a peculiar manner to non-conformist pastors. One of the great Presbyterian rabbis, therefore, might well doubt whether, in a worldly view, he should be benefited by a comprehension. He might, indeed, hold a rectory or a vicarage, when he could get one; but, in the mean time, he would be destitute; his meeting-house would be closed; his congregation would be dispersed among the parish churches; if a benefice were bestowed on him, it would probably be a slender compensation for the income which he had lost; nor could he hope to have, as a minister of the Anglican Church, the authority and dignity which he had hitherto enjoyed. He would always, by a large portion of the members of that church, be regarded as a deserter. He might, therefore, on the whole, very naturally wish to be left where he was."—Vol. III., *page* 88.

NOTE. See also, Addison's Spectator, 317. See also, Sir John Hawkin's Life of Johnson, page 210, as follows:

"The interest which the dissenting teachers had with the members of their several congregations, though now but little known, was formerly very great, and in my memory was such, that scarcely any member of a separate congregation would dispose of a daughter, or make a purchase, or advance a sum of money on a mortgage, without first consulting his pastor."

The condition of the clergymen of Connecticut at the first settlement of both the primitive and derivative towns, was as much inferior to that of their non-conformist brethren just described, as the general condition of New England at that time, was inferior to that of England. Instead of the "gorgeous palaces and solemn temples," they lived in humble habitations and worshiped God in meeting-houses of the humblest pretensions. Instead of the "finest broad-cloth of Blackwell," they were often dressed in home-spun manufactured in their own families by their wives and daughters. Instead of a bottle of "Brooks and Hellier," with which the retired citizen regaled his minister, Mr. Nisby (John Nesbit), see Spectator as above, the Connecticut clergyman had to content himself with small beer until cider became the favorite beverage in the Commonwealth.

It is no wonder that some of them looked to England with earnest longing:

"In the primitive towns, at their first settlement, there were those who looked back, with yearning hearts, across the waters to their first home. Some actually returned thither. Others wished to do so. And numbers who left England under the monitions of conscience, in the spirit of adventure, in the hot blood of controversy, or in the bad blood of resentment for injuries, real or threatened, would, in the sun-set and twilight of age, look back with softened hearts and tearful eyes to the home of their childhood; to the church-yard, where their parents were sleeping; to the churches and cathedrals in which they had offered their youthful devotion. Methinks some of those aged pilgrims, in moments of fond recollection, exclaim,"

> "Oh thou Queen,
> Thou delegated Deity of earth,
> Oh dear, dear England!"

From History of Durham.

But in time things changed for the better. The general condition of society became improved, and the minister frequently had the best house, and sometimes the best farm in town. His family, often a large one, a minister's blessing, was educated better than the families around him. His sons he could sometimes educate at the college, which was his own Alma Mater. His daughters were sometimes the belles at the College Commencements, and the same might be said of them as was said of the daughters of Job: "And in all the land no women were found so fair as the daughters of Job."

In one important respect their condition was better than that of their English brethren. The latter, belonging to the subject party, had to think and to act under the over-bearing domination of Church and State. A sense of this inferiority probably had some influence in lessening freedom of thought and the highest manhood.

The clergy of Connecticut, on the other hand, belonged to the dominant party, both in religion and politics. They could think freely, and speak freely, and act freely, without feeling the superincumbent pressure of King, Parliament, or Bishops. The Commonwealth could pass laws which went into operation without requiring the signature of a Governor appointed by the Crown. This consciousness of freedom continuing through several generations, contributed to form that individualism in the character of the people of Connecticut, for which they have been distinguished in comparison even with the people of some of the States in our own country, who did not enjoy, as Connecticut did, the full measure of the power of local self government.

The clergy, also, virtually had the control of the public schools, and thus educated the children in the rudiments of learning in good manners and in the principles of religion.

This union of Church and State had its influence in bringing together the leading men of the clergy, ("God sends us bishops whether we will or no,") and the leading men of the Commonwealth and their families. Thus there was a higher aristocracy in the Commonwealth at large, while in each town there was a lower aristocracy composed of the minister and the town authorities, and others. And as the ministers were settled for life, and the leading rulers enjoyed long terms of office, this aristocracy was, in a certain sense, permanent.

In a letter, dated July 24th, 1874, my life-long friend and teacher, Rev. Dr. Leonard Withington, of Newbury, Mass., wrote to me as follows:

"I often think of East Guilford, (now Madison,) as a perfect specimen of old Connecticut manners before the Revolution, which Democrats and Episcopalians joined to make. The aristocracy of the centre; the population on the outside; the central influence of the minister, Mr. Elliot; the deacon, the Squire, the Colonel, who used to meet at his house on Sabbath evenings, when the Sabbath was over according to their reckoning, and they felt at liberty to discuss politics. Ah! those scenes are departed never to return. It seemed to me a beautiful form of society, when voluntary strength was checked by sober principle, and man was almost as happy as freedom could make him."

For a considerable period after the settlement of Connecticut the minister's house was the centre of intelligence for the whole town. He was the best educated man, had the best library, and was the most hospitable in the entertainment of strangers. After newspapers were established in Boston, he was often the only man in town who took any of them. As there were no post-offices in those days, private conveyance furnished the only means for obtaining those papers. As a considerable trade was carried on between Boston and the towns on the Connecticut River and the Sound, the papers were sent by the vessels engaged in this trade. In this way people could obtain the news which, in these days, we should esteem stale, it not being received until weeks after publication. Some of the first newspapers published were the "Boston News Letter;" the "New England Courant," edited by James and Benjamin Franklin; and the "Boston Weekly Post Boy."

The minister and town authorities were mutually helpers. When the State received an injury from the violation of the laws, the minister hastened to the aid of the civil ruler, as Aaron and Hur upheld the hands of Moses. When the Church was in danger from the intrusion of ungodly men, the civil ruler hastened to the relief of the minister, as Moses sustained Aaron and the Priesthood against the pretentions of Korah.

For a long period this union of Church and State, in Connecticut, was productive of the best results. It would be difficult in any Christian country to find a population more religious, more church-going, more moral, more happy, than could be found in the towns of Connecticut; or where the ministers were more pains-taking, more respected, or more useful. For a long period the people of the Commonwealth were all or nearly all of one denomination.

But the minor denominations became deeply dissatisfied with the existing state of things. They raised the cry of Toleration so long and loud, that in union with the Democrats in 1817, they elected Oliver Wolcott Governor, in opposition to the candidate of the hitherto dominant party.

The downfall of the "Standing Order" sent sorrow into many habitations in the several towns in the State. "I remember that time. John P. Brace came up to our house on the day of the election, and mother asked him how it had gone. 'Oh,' said he, 'the Democrats have beaten us all to pieces!' and a perfect wail arose."—H. B. S.

"I remember seeing father, the day after the election, sitting on one of the old-fashioned rush-bottomed kitchen chairs, his head drooping on his breast, and his arms hanging down. 'Father,' said I, 'what are you thinking of?' He answered solemnly, 'The Church of God.'"—C. E. B.—*Autobiography of Lyman Beecher*, Vol. I. p. 344.

The adoption of the State Constitution in 1818, in place of the Charter of Charles II., completed the downfall of the "Standing Order," and the "Federalists." The Democrats and the minor religious denominations, exulted in this downfall. After the Convention which framed the Constitution had finished its work, a leading member of the Convention, Mr. E——— said to Mr. L———, who had thought himself badly used by a certain Congregational Church, "Now you go right home and mount your horse and ride right over the top of the meeting-house."

Thus fell a party representing the union of Church and State for one hundred and eighty-four years. It struggled hard for life, but it fell as gracefully as Cæsar under the wounds of his assassins, muffling his face and falling at the base of Pompey's statue. They had claimed to be the party of law and order while they were dominant in the Commonwealth, and now, becoming subjected, they proved the truth of their profession. There had been some relentings in the

Convention, and the victorious party did not abuse their newly acquired power as it was prophesied they would. For a number of years after 1818 the clergy continued to be free from taxation, and retained their former honorable position in society. The revolution was in 1818 an accomplished fact, but the old ideas and the old habits of thought continued to prevail for some years afterwards.

The inquiry is sometimes made, how it happened that for a number of years the Congregational clergy of Connecticut, and the Democrats, were not upon very good terms.

Before the Revolutionary War, the Charter of King Charles II., which conferred great privileges on the people of the Colony, was highly valued by the whole population. But after the adoption of the Federal Constitution in 1788, this charter some of the people wished to change for a State Constitution. The clergy, who enjoyed certain privileges under this charter, were unwilling that this change should be made. After the Democratic party was formed in Connecticut, they were in favor of the change. The Federalists, on the other hand, uniting with the clergy, were with them opposed to the change. There was a good deal that was unreasonable, said and thought on both sides.

Not long after 1800, the Rev. Mr. C———, stopped to water his horse at a small brook not far from Durham. A farmer, Mr. A———, drove his ox team into the brook and said: "Good morning, Mr. Minister." He replied, "Good morning, Mr. Democrat." Mr. C——— then said, "How did you know I was a minister?" The other replied, "By your dress. And how did you know I was a Democrat?" "By your address," was the reply.

A very devout Congregational old lady, in Hartford, went to a neighbor's to ask a favor. She understood that when the Democrats came into power, under the new constitution, all the Bibles were to be taken away, and she wanted her neighbor, one of the Democrats, to keep her Bible for her. "Certainly, my good woman," said he, "if it will do any good; but if *all* the Bibles are to be taken away, your book will be no safer in my hands than in your own." "Oh, yes, it will, sir," she exclaimed, "for nobody will suspect a Democrat of having a Bible!"

The Democrats and Episcopalians, however, used the power acquired in 1817–18, with so much wisdom and forbearance that the Federalists and the clergy could not complain greatly. The State Constitution which they formed proved to be a very good one, and the Bibles were safe in every household.

Another great work of the clergy of Connecticut, was to form an ecclesiastical constitution for the churches. From the first settlement, after ecclesiastical questions arose, the churches were exposed to great difficulties from packed councils, and successive councils, and *ex parte* councils, and no councils. The evils of independency and isolation were tried. Accordingly there were those who were not inclined to remain in the "wilderness of Congregationalism," when they might enter into enclosures which by cultivation they thought they could make like the Garden of God.

The venerable Thomas Hooker, of Hartford, had said: "We must agree upon constant meeting of ministers, and settle the consociation of churches, or else we are undone." The great Synod of 1662, which met at Boston, had recommended consociation of churches.

Accordingly, under the direction of the Colonial Legislature, a Synod, composed of representatives of the churches of the several counties of Connecticut, met in Saybrook, Sept. 9th, 1708.

From the council of Hartford county: The Rev. Timothy Woodbridge, Noadiah Russell, and Stephen Mix; Messenger, John Haynes, Esq.

From the council of Fairfield county: The Rev. Charles Chauncey and John Davenport; Messenger,—Dea. Samuel Hoyt.

From the council of New London county: The Rev. James Noyes, Thomas Buckingham, Moses Noyes, and John Woodward; Messengers,—Robert Chapman, Dea. William Parker.

From the council of New Haven county: The Rev. Samuel Andrew, James Pierpont, and Samuel Russell.

The Rev. James Noyes and Thomas Buckingham being chosen Moderators. The Rev. Stephen Mix and John Woodward being chosen Scribes.

The Synod thus composed formed an ecclesiastical constitution for the Colony, called the SAYBROOK PLATFORM. This they did so wisely and so well that the Legislature, at its next session, approved of this platform and recommended it to the churches of the State for their adoption.

For an account of the Saybrook Platform, see President Clapp's Defense of the Doctrines of the New England Churches.

When the Puritans first came to Connecticut they agreed in doctrine with the thirty-nine Articles of the Church of England. Thus, in the first of the Seven Articles of the Church of Leyden, presented to the King by John Robinson and William Bruster, there is the following:

I. "To ye confession of fayth published in ye name of ye Church of England, and to every artikell thereof wee do wth ye reformed churches where we live and also elswher assent wholly."

The children of the schools were taught the Westminister Divines' Catechism, which they recited every Saturday in the school-room; before the minister, as school visitor; and also Saturday evening and Sunday afternoon, in the family. Such being the practice throughout the State, to a greater or less extent, it would seem that there would be no great danger that the people would become heterodox. There seems to have been no very great difficulty in respect to doctrinal points, especially after the Saybrook Platform was adopted.

But after a time there sprang up what was called "New Divinity," in distinction from the old forms of belief or "Old Divinity." The originators and advocates of "New Divinity," sometimes called, whether in compliment or disparagement, "New England Theology," were Jonathan Edwards, the elder; his pupils, Samuel Hopkins and Joseph Bellamy; Jonathan Edwards, the younger; Levi Hart, and John Smalley, pupils of Bellamy; Charles Backus, pupil of Levi Hart; and Nath'l Emmons, pupil of John Smalley. All of these excepting one, Jonathan Edwards, the younger, were natives of Connecticut, and graduates of Yale College; and he resided in Connecticut during twenty-nine years of his life. Of this theological constellation, Jonathan Edwards, the elder, was the leading star. He was not only the "cynosure of neighboring eyes," but also of eyes of men in another hemisphere, who admired his powers of reasoning, even when they rejected his doctrine. These very able men, and their pupils, whom they introduced into the ministry, inculcated the new doctrines with much earnestness and success, notwithstanding great opposition in different places.

On the one side, men who preached "Old Divinity" were represented as being Arminians, and as inviting their hearers to feed on the empty husks of morality.

On the other side, men who preached "New Divinity," were charged with representing God under the guise of an oriental demon who invited men to "sup on horrors." Besides these differences in their own denomination, the Congregationalists were, after a time, attacked by other denominations, Methodists, Episcopalians, and Unitarians.

The following extract will show what were the feelings of the first mentioned denomination: "To Asbury, afterwards Bishop, who often traversed New England till his death in 1816, the religious life of New England presented an example of the rigid Hebrew legalism, strangely combined with the speculative dogmatism of the early Greek Church, but unrelieved by the spiritual mysticism of the latter, and nearly destitute of the vital charity and joyousness of the primitive faith. Its distinctive theology he literally detested; it seemed to him to bind, as in iron bands, the souls of the people; depressing by its tenets of election and reprobation, with uncomplaining but profound distress, scrupulous, timid, and therefore often the best consciences; inflating the confidence and pharisaism of the self-reliant or self-conceited, who assumed their predestination to heaven; enforcing the morality without the gracious consolation of religion; and giving to the recklessly immoral an apology for their lives in their very demoralization, their lack of 'effectual grace,' of an 'effectual call.'"—See *Stevens' History of Methodism*, Vol. III.

Similar charges were brought by the Episcopalians against the "distinctive theology," or the doctrines taught by some of the leading Congregational divines in the Connecticut churches.

It is remarkable that, during the twenty years previous to 1818, there were two factors in the controversies, the political and the religious. After 1818, one of the factors, the political, was dropped out of the controversies, which thus became purely religious, into which the minor denominations on the one side, encouraged by their success, were ready to enter; and the Congregational denomination, on the other side, was equally ready for the encounter. Indeed, in many parts of the State there seemed to be a kind of guerrilla warfare in a hand to hand contest. As exponents of this warfare, there were certain controversial sermons published; there was also published a series of doctrinal tracts. There was also a tract entitled, "A Serious Call to those who are without the Pale of the Episcopal Church;" and a reply to this, entitled, "A Sober Appeal to the Christian Public;" and a reply to the last, entitled, "A Candid Appeal." There was an attack, about the same time, on the character of Dr. Dwight, in the North American, by the editor, Edward Everett, and a defence by Mr. Rufus Woodward and Professor Kingsley. There was a pamphlet issued by Prof. Andrews Norton, of Harvard College, on "True and False Religion," which was reviewed in the Christian Spectator, in June, 1822, by Rev. Matthew Rice Dutton. An able answer to this review was written by Prof. Norton.

Thus the Congregationalists, beset before and behind, on the right hand and on the left, felt deeply the need of a Theological School, in which their young men could be educated to defend and enforce the truth.

But the Congregationalists were divided, not only in regard

to doctrines, but likewise in regard to measures for promoting religion. They had originally adopted their own measures and their own means to this end. They relied—first, on the public preaching of the Word in the Sanctuary; secondly, on the example and influence of the members of the Church; thirdly, on family religion, the daily reading of the Bible in the family, and family prayers night and morning; fourthly, on catechetical instruction in the schools, and by the minister.

When about 1740, the eloquent and erratic Whitefield from England, and the morbid and enthusiastic Davenport, from Long Island, came preaching in Connecticut, many of the ministers and the people naturally viewed their coming as an intrusion; and when the full effects of their visits appeared, and the measures adopted by their followers became known, they were still more disgusted. They felt that the territory which they inhabited belonged to the people of the Commonwealth by Charter, and by the right acquired by their labors in reclaiming it from the wilderness. They were not willing to have their ecclesiastical domain invaded by religious gypsies and squatters, whether from the Old World or the New. Those who were in favor of the measures employed were called "New Lights," and those who were opposed to those measures were called "Old Lights." For a full account of the condition of things at that time, see "Seasonable Thoughts on the State of Religion in New England," by Charles Chauncey, D. D., and also, "A Plain Narrative," by Rev. Philemon Robbins; and a "Defense of the Doings of the Consociation and Association of New Haven county, in the case of Philemon Robbins."

This division of opinion, in regard to the Great Awakening of that period, continued to prevail in Connecticut in regard to revivals of religion generally, to the means and agents employed and the joint results, whether good or bad.

In the revival in Yale College in 1815, in which I took a great interest, there was something of the spirit of the "New Lights." When President Dwight refused to encourage the students to be absent from their regular recitations to attend religious meetings, and also refused to multiply those meetings, he was accused of being opposed to the revival, and of being an Arminian. These charges were repeated after he had delivered an excellent address to the students from the following text: "For the Kingdom of God is not meat and drink, but righteousness and peace and joy in the Holy Ghost." These charges seem to have come from lips that had been touched by a live coal from the altar lighted with the strange fires of the "New Lights."

Even in the great revival in New Haven in 1820, objections were made by clergymen to the course pursued by the lay preachers, so called. In one of the Associations of Litchfield county, these objections were strongly expressed by some of the clergymen, among whom was the excellent John Langdon, of Bethlehem, the worthy successor of Backus and Bellamy. After a speech, made by him, of great earnestness and power, setting forth the present and prospective evils of lay-preaching, Dr. Beecher said to him; "Will you take a walk with me, Brother Langdon?"

Accordingly he joined arms with him, but instead of going out the door, he led him in a half circle in the room, and said: "Brother Langdon, we commenced our walk in one direction and closed it in another direction; instead of opposing the lay-preachers, lead them."

They were willing to be led. The following is a letter written by Prof. Moses Stuart to Timothy Dwight, one of their number.

ANDOVER, April 27th, 1821.

My Dear Sir:—Yours, written some time since, was duly received, and has been read until it is literally worn out. Soon after receiving it, I communicated the substance of it to our meeting, on the evening of the general Monthly Concert of Prayer. This occasioned it to be inquired after and read by all those persons among us who take peculiar interest in doing good. This very day, I have lent it, to be read to-morrow evening in the Conference, at Salem, conducted by laymen; and where, at present, a revival is begun.

I thank God that I have lived to see the day, in which laymen are beginning to feel as if they had something to do, as well as ministers, in propagating the truths of the gospel. Thus did they in primitive ages. (See Acts VIII., 1–4.) It is a most preposterous thing for any man to suppose, that he is not under obligation to use his powers in the service of the Church. I bid you God speed with all my heart; and hope in God, that the spirit which is kindled at New Haven, will speedily pervade the Christian world.

I have only two cautions to suggest,—and these, I think, important to the object in question:

1st. Let no one undertake to teach any more than he has learned. Let him not usurp the place, or claim the prerogatives of a regularly ordained minister. This caution is necessary to preserve good order.

2d. Guard well against all approaches to mere excitement of the passions, and appeals to simple natural feelings; in other words, against any enthusiasm or extravagance. Guard well against a censorious spirit in respect to Christians who do not at once fall in with our views, and who are afraid of enthusiasm. While the object is not at all abandoned, they may be treated with tenderness; and when they see the good effects of the practice, they will fall in with it. Guard well against being proud of success; or being disposed to feel elevated, so as to look with disdain on a humble minister whose labors have not been blessed. The greatest danger of those whose labors are blessed, is spiritual pride. If this once enter the sacred enclosure of the church, it will mar the fairest portion of God's inheritance.

" These things, if ye observe, ye shall do well." And observing them—go on, labor, prosper, esteem the reproaches of men as nothing; look at the glory of God and the salvation of never-dying souls; and then rouse up to renewed and still more vigorous action. That the Almighty God may bless the labors of you and your coadjutors in this glorious work is, the sincere and fervent prayer of

Yours, sincerely and affectionately,

M. STUART.

This letter, wisely written by one in whom they all had great confidence, was well received by them, and had its appropriate influence.

Considerable opposition was made to the introduction of conference meetings by the "New Light" or "New Divinity" pastors. As a specimen of the opposition take the following:

A Mr. Nelson, a Baptist clergyman, went to Hartford somewhere about the commencement of the present century, where there were two or three Baptist families residing. He was made welcome in those families and commenced holding evening meetings, sometimes in one family and sometimes in the other, to which their neighbors and acquaintances were invited. Evening meetings were, in Hartford, a new thing, and there was a good deal of curiosity manifested in regard to them. The weekly attendance grew to be so large that an invitation was given to them by Mr. Nelson for a meeting on the Sabbath, whether at a private house or at some schoolhouse, I do not remember. The attendance grew larger and larger each Sabbath, until one Sunday, when Dr. Nathan Strong, the minister of the First Congregational Church, made an exchange with the minister in East Hartford. Some of his people, taking advantage of his absence, attended the meeting of the young Baptist minister. Dr. Strong, finding how matters stood, called upon Mr. Nelson and invited him to preach in his church. This invitation Mr. Nelson declined. "I did not feel," said he, "qualified to stand up before Dr. Strong's intelligent congregation. I felt, indeed, that such an act would ruin my hopes of building up a Baptist congregation in Hartford." These facts I had from the lips of Mr. Nelson himself, who spent his last years in Amherst.

Not a great while afterwards Dr. Strong appointed evening meetings for his own church and congregation. One Monday morning, several of the leading men of Hartford happened to meet at one end of the bridge over the small river, and held an animated conversation, in which they all agreed in disapproving of these evening meetings on the ground that they were injurious to family order and family piety. While thus engaged Dr. Strong, came near them, at first unobserved; immediately the conversation was hushed, and the salutations of the morning offered. One of them said, "Dr. Strong, we have just been talking about you." "And what did you say?" Then each in order expressed his disapprobation of these evening meetings, giving his reasons. After they had concluded, he replied: "Gentlemen, you don't understand this matter. If I was to refuse to have evening meetings, in three weeks one third of my congregation would be in Connecticut river.—Good morning, gentlemen." There was then silence for a moment, when one of them remarked:—"Well, I believe the old fellow understands his own business better than we do."

One reason which operated extensively to produce opposition to conference meetings, was that an impression prevailed that some of the ministers insisted that the young people should give up balls and parties and attend these meetings, thus officiously interfering with the common amusements of the young people.

It may be added, that many of the leading men in Connecticut and Massachusetts, who still remained Congregationalists, were opposed to the distinctive theology of New England. After the State election in Massachusetts, in 1824, when William Eustis, a reputed deist, sustained by the Democrats and the Orthodox people, was elected Governor, he was met one day by Harrison Gray Otis, who was the defeated candidate of the Federalists and the Unitarians, who said to him, "Mr. Eustis, it seems you have become a believer in the doctrines of Calvinism." He replied, "I am a believer in the doctrine of *Election*."

New Haven has always been one of the great centers of the religious and social system of Connecticut, which communicates an influence to other towns and receives an influence from them. The history of New Haven is therefore to some extent the history of other towns, so far as it is an exponent of them. Here there has been more intelligence to perceive differences in doctrines and in measures and in forms, more fullness in expressing them, and more care in recording them.

The ministers of the First Congregational church in New Haven, namely John Davenport, who came to New Haven April 18th, 1638, Nicholas Street, James Pierpont, Joseph Noyes, Chauncey Whittlesey, and James Dana, the latter of whom was dismissed in the fall of 1805; all of them preached "Old Divinity" to their congregations.

Rev. Moses Stuart was settled March 5th, 1806, the period of his ministry being a little less than four years. He was graduated at Yale College in 1799, was admitted to the Bar in Danbury in 1802, and served in the office of tutor from 1802 to 1804.

He was an eloquent, out-spoken man. His statements were so distinct that he was easily understood by his hearers; his descriptions so vivid that he fixed their attention; his arguments were so condensed that he gained the conviction of his hearers; and the force of his will was such that he carried them along to his own conclusions and to the course of action prescribed by him. During the short period of his ministry, the church was greatly increased from the fruits of a great revival.

Still there were those of his church and congregation who were not satisfied with his doctrines or his spirit. In the main, his doctrines were those of "New Divinity"; though he sometimes enunciated peculiar doctrines of his own, as for instance, on Baptism. In the fervors of his youthful feelings, he was sometimes thought to be hasty in his judgments and severe in his censures. He once, after he had been a tutor in the college, said to Dr. Dana, "There is very little piety in the college. Of the tutors, one is a Deist, one is an Arian, one is a Universalist, one is an Orthodox man, and one is a Christian." In early life his mind was like new wine, effervescing, somewhat turbid and austere. Later in life that same mind became clear, strong, and mellow, "like wine on the lees well refined."

Nathaniel William Taylor was settled over the same Congregational Church, April 8th, 1812, and was dismissed November, 1822.

The Second Congregational church of New Haven was composed of "New Light" members who seceded from Mr. Noyes' church. They settled a pastor, the Rev. Mr. Bird, in 1751. This church was called the White Haven Church, and their place of worship was on the corner of Church and Elm streets. Mr. Bird was dismissed January 19th, 1768. Jonathan Edwards was settled in 1769, and dismissed May 19th, 1795.

From this seceding church and society which worshiped in the White Haven church, a secession took place according to a vote of sixty-eight members, September 4th, 1769. Mr. Edwards, in common with other "New Divinity" ministers, was opposed to the "Half-way Covenant;" these seceding members of the church were in favor of it; hence the secession. They were constituted a church in June, 1771, with the name of the Fair Haven church. Their place of worship was on the site of the present North Congregational church. The first settled minister of this church was Mr. Allyn Mather, who was ordained February 3d, 1773. He died on the 12th of November, 1784.

November 9th, 1786, Mr. Samuel Austin was ordained as their minister, and was dismissed January 19th, 1790.

On the 27th of November, 1796, these two churches were united under the denomination of "the Church of Christ in the United Societies of White Haven and Fair Haven." In November, 1798, the Rev. John Gemmil was installed pastor of the church and society, and was dismissed November, 1801. Mr. Samuel Merwin was ordained their pastor on the 13th of February, 1805, and dismissed on the 29th of December, 1831.

The secession from the Rev. Mr. Noyes' church was mainly a secession of "New Lights." It is instructive inasmuch as it shows the repellency between "New Lights" and "Old Lights" in many other places as well as in New Haven. It was from this repellency that a considerable number of congregations of separatists, or strict congregationalists, as they called themselves, were formed, especially in the eastern portion of the Commonwealth. In a printed statement I find that as late as 1791, there were as many as ten congregations of separatists. The "New Lights" gradually faded off into the common light of day.

The secession from the White Haven church, then under the care of Rev. Jonathan Edwards, in order to form the Fair Haven Church, was a secession of men who adhered to the practice of baptism of children under what was called the "Half-way Covenant." For a considerable period the general and perhaps universal practice of the Congregational churches of Connecticut was to baptize the children of parents who themselves had been baptized, and who "owned the covenant," as it was called; that is the baptismal covenant made by their parents, though they were not admitted to full communion and did not partake of the Lord's Supper.

In most of the congregations there were persons of orderly lives and good conversation who were very anxious to have their children baptized, though they themselves were not members of the church in full communion.

This was the condition of things until the "New Divinity" ministers brought in a disturbing force which produced great dissatisfaction. They insisted that only those children should be baptized whose parents, or one of them, were in full communion with the church. I have heard worthy persons complain very bitterly of this change of practice; but in most cases their numbers were so few that they could not, as in New Haven, form a new church, and therefore had to submit to the grievance. Some of them did go over to the Episcopalians and the Methodists, where the practice in regard to the baptism of children was supposed to be more liberal.

The experience of these two churches, the Centre and the North Church, was very different in regard to secessions and reunion; but the results in each case in 1822, were very much the same. They were sisters in doctrine, in forms, and in spirit, and they were sisters in the tenderest meaning of the term.

The Association of New Haven County was divided by vote May, 1787, into the two associations of New Haven East and New Haven West. It was then voted to call a meeting of the consociation to effect a like division in that body.

There was a tradition that one reason why the division of the Association took place at that time was doctrinal, and that the movement for a division came from those who favored "New Divinity," of which Edwards the younger, then a pastor in New Haven, was the champion, who, with him, would fall into the Western District or Association. Some color of truth is given to this tradition by the circumstance that Dr. Trumbull of North Haven, a "New Divinity" man, whose geographical position was in New Haven East, followed Dr. Edwards into New Haven West; and Rev. Mr. Foote of Cheshire, the father of Gov. Foote, an "Old Divinity" man, whose geographical position was in New Haven West, joined New Haven East. The Quinnipiac river was the geographical boundary of the New Haven East and the New Haven West. See "Contributions to the Ecclesiastical History of Connecticut," p. 323.

"Old Divinity" and "New Divinity;" "Old Lights" and "New Lights;" "Calvinism" and "Arminianism;" "Stoddardean" and "Edwardean;" "Hopkinsianism" and "Emmonsism;" the "Taste" scheme and the "Exercise" scheme; "Owning the Covenant" and the "Half-way Covenant;" were terms in current use in certain religious circles in 1822.

During my ten years residence in New Haven, I never supposed that the extreme views of "New Divinity," were adopted by any considerable number of religious people there.

We have already seen that the Episcopalians, Methodists, and other denominations gained a great victory over the Congregationalists in 1817–18. The fruits of that victory were seen in the rapid growth of these denominations in New Haven and elsewhere. The diocese of Connecticut had been in charge of Bishop Hobart for a number of years, until October

27th, 1819, when Dr. Brownell was appointed Bishop. He afterwards took up his residence in New Haven for the purpose of giving instruction to the pupils of the General Theological Seminary of the Episcopal Church, which was established there, September 13th, 1820. The learned Professor Turner delivered the inaugural address on that occasion. The Episcopalians were evidently increasing.

The Methodists, too, somewhere about this time, who had hitherto worshiped in a small church at the south end of Temple street, commenced the erection of a new edifice on the northwest corner of the upper green. That society, and their leaders, were accused of ambition in thus placing their church in this conspicuous position. In reference to this charge, Mr. Thatcher, then the Methodist minister, in New Haven, was in the habit of praying in the family where he boarded: "If the building of this church proceeds from unworthy motives, come four-winds from the four-corners of the earth and demolish it."

Strange to say, in the September gale, after the rafters were placed and the roof laid, wholly or in part, the winds swept it off and demolished a considerable portion of the wall. This house was afterwards completed and occupied by distinguished preachers of that denomination; among others, by Summerfield, who was followed by crowds.

The growth of these denominations, made at the expense of the Congregational, seemed to demand some effort to strengthen the latter.

Yale College seemed to be an organic part of New Haven, connected as it was with it in business, history, and social life. When a quarter before five, in the morning, in summer,

> The clear toned bell
> Danced merrily to tell

it was the students' hour of prayer, many families were soon astir. In their movements in business they seemed to keep time with the music of the Chapel bell. This was before the steam fiend shrieked the hours of labor to the operatives. Many had received their education in the College, and the community generally felt a great interest in the College as a religious and literary institution. Accordingly when the subject of establishing a department of theology in the College was brought before the leading inhabitants, they readily subscribed three-quarters of the sum necessary, as a foundation for a new professorship,—Timothy Dwight, the eldest son of President Dwight, subscribing five thousand dollars.

Before the appointment of Dr. Taylor it was understood that the subscribers to this fund, as well as other leading citizens, would be well satisfied with the appointment of Dr. Taylor to fill the chair. As a student in College, as a student in Theology with Dr. Dwight, as a licentiate, and as a settled minister, he had been a resident of the city for something like eighteen years, so that they had had the best opportunities to judge of his qualifications for the place.

New Haven Subscribers to the Dwight Professorship :

Jeremiah Day, New Haven,		$700.00
B. Silliman,	"	150.00
J. L. Kingsley,	"	500.00
E. T. Fitch,	"	1,666.66
C. A. Goodrich,	"	500.00
Timothy Dwight,	"	5,000.00
Wm. Leffingwell,	"	2,000.00
Anna Townsend,	"	500.00
Stephen Twining,	"	250.00
Hull & Townsend,	"	500.00
Dyer White,	"	300.00
Sherman Converse,	"	500.00
Wm. H. Elliot,	"	300.00
John H. Coley,	"	100.00
Jehiel Forbes,	"	50.00
Elihu Sanford,	"	50.00
Titus Street,	"	1,000.00
David Daggett,	"	600.00
Harriet Webster Cobb, New Haven,		50.00
Abraham Bradley, Jr., and James Bradley,	Real Estate,	1,000.00
Sum total,		$15,716.66

Other Subscribers:

Nehemiah Hubbard, Middletown, - -	$1,000.00
H. L. Ellsworth, Hartford, - -	1,000.00
W. W. Ellsworth, " - - -	800.00
Thos. S. Williams, " - -	500.00
Stephen Van Rensselaer, Albany, - -	500.00
A Lady, - - - -	90.00
	$3,890.00
Smaller sums (a portion of which was from New Haven,) say - - -	$400.00

The noblest work ever done by the Congregational clergymen of Connecticut, was the establishment of Yale College. For this they should be held in everlasting remembrance. The first act was dramatic. Ten ministers had a meeting in Branford, at the house of Mr. Russell, in the year 1700; each of them in turn deposited on a table a bundle of books and said: "I give these books for the founding of a College in this Colony." President Abraham Pierson was elected November 11th, 1701.

In that microcosm, a college, there are influences at work which preserve its identity. This is true, at least of Yale College, from 1701 to 1822, the era I am considering. The several Presidents, namely: Abraham Pierson, Samuel Andrew, Timothy Cutler, Elisha Williams, Thomas Clap, Naphtali Daggett, and Ezra Stiles, who died in 1795, were all "Old Divinity men." Timothy Dwight, his successor, was appointed President by an "Old Divinity corporation." Sometime about 1820, I was informed by a gentleman connected with the corporation, and who was as well qualified to express an opinion as any other, that the majority of the corporation of Yale College had always been "Old Divinity" men, or as they were sometimes called by their opposers, Arminians.

The views of Dr. Dwight can be found in his published works. He satisfied "Old Divinity" men. He was supposed to be opposed to the extreme views of "New Divinity" men.

The primary object for the establishment of a College in Connecticut, was to raise up a learned and pious ministry for the service of the church without the inconvenience and expense of sending young men for their education to another Colony. Accordingly we find, in the history of the College, that this object was accomplished. In the first twenty-five years there were one hundred and seventy-one graduates, of whom ninety-five, more than one half, were ministers. In the next twenty-five years, namely, from 1726 to 1751, there were four hundred and seventy-seven graduates, of whom two hundred and eleven were ministers. From 1752 to 1822, the comparative number of ministers was much less.

The ministers educated in the College naturally retained a very strong love for their Alma Mater. Many of them fitted their sons and other young men for the College. Many of them every year, at the commencement, would go to New Haven, as on a pilgrimage, thus keeping alive their affectionate feelings and tender recollections. Many of them in their rural homes would labor in their studies, and on their farms, wearing homespun provided for them by their wives and their daughters. One of their number educated five sons at College, who were all clothed from the wool and the flax manufactured in the family.

But, on the Sabbath day, and in their visits to the College, they wore a professional dress suitable to the occasion.—The beaver-hat, whether cocked or not, the wig or the cue, the black dress, whether of broadcloth or silk, the bands, the knee-buckles, the shoe-buckles, and sometimes the gold-headed cane. They joined in the long procession, "calm and beautiful," they listened to the commencement exercises; they partook of the festivities of the dinner, and even the wine which, in their simplicity, they believed made glad the heart of man, with happy and exultant feelings. They went to their several homes reinforced for the performance of the duties of another year by the feeling that they were still a part and parcel of a noble institution.

One ground of complaint on the part of other denominations against the Congregational order was, that the latter had entire possession of Yale College; that though the State had aided it, its interests were in the hands of a Corporation, all of whom were Congregationalists; that the Faculty were required to subscribe to the following test law of the corporation:

"I ——— ———, being chosen ——— of Yale College, do hereby declare my free assent to the confession of faith and rules of Ecclesiastical discipline, agreed upon by the churches in the State of Connecticut, A. D., 1708."

The students, it was said, were placed under congregational preaching, the professor of divinity who preached to the students every Sabbath was a Congregationalist. The students were obliged to obtain permission to attend upon preachers of their own church.

Wise counsels prevailed. The fundamental law of the State adopted in 1818, introduced into the Corporation six Senators, the Governor and Lieut. Governor, as an equivalent for the six assistants, and the Governor and Lieut. Governor. Students were allowed, upon the application of their parents, to attend other churches, and a monitor was appointed for the Episcopal church in New Haven, to secure their attendance. These changes, removing the ground of complaint against the College as sectarian, were generally so satisfactory that it was hoped that there would be no more talk about establishing another college.

When the subject was agitated, of establishing a distinct department in Yale College for the instruction of a permanent school in Theology, the jealousies which had been allayed by the conciliatory course of the College, were revived so that in six weeks after the establishing of that department and the appointment of a Professor of Didactic Theology, there was a preliminary meeting of gentlemen for consultation on the subject of establishing a new College in the State. In December, 1822, there was another meeting held at the house of Bishop Brownell, in New Haven, consisting of eighteen clergymen, to take the preliminary steps to obtain a charter. A memorial was presented to the Legislature at their next session and a Charter was granted on the 16th of May, 1823, to Washington, now Trinity College.

The Test-law of the Corporation of Yale College, cited above, was repealed May 7th, 1823.

At the organization of the Andover Theological Seminary in 1808, the Corporation appointed Rev. Eliphalet Pearson, D. D., an "Old Divinity" man, one Professor, and Rev. Leonard Woods, a "New Divinity" man, who had studied Theology with Rev. Charles Backus, of Somers, Conn., another Professor. President Dwight preached the sermon, when the Rev. Eliphalet Pearson was inaugurated.

Thus they endeavored to satisfy the "Old Divinity" men of Massachusetts, and elsewhere, and the "New Divinity" men. In 1822, fourteen years later, the Corporation of Yale College appointed Nathaniel W. Taylor, D. D., professor of Didactic Theology, and in so doing they satisfied the "Old Divinity" men of Connecticut, and the "New Divinity" men.

Nathaniel William Taylor, the son of Nathaniel Taylor, was born in New Milford June 23d, 1786, and died in New Haven March 10th, 1858.

His grandfather, Rev. Nathaniel Taylor, a distinguished "Old Divinity" clergyman, was born at Danbury, Conn., Aug. 27th, 1722, was graduated at Yale College in 1745, was settled in New Milford in 1748, was a chaplain at Ticonderoga in the war of the Revolution, was an efficient member of the corporation of Yale College for twenty-six years, and died at New Milford December 9th, 1800, after a successful ministry of fifty-three years. The celebrated Stanley Griswold, afterwards Judge of the United States Court, was settled as his colleague in 1790, and continued pastor of the church until 1802.

Nathaniel William Taylor was graduated at Yale College in 1807, not long after he became amanuensis to Dr. Dwight and a pupil in theology under his instruction. He was licensed to preach in 1810 by the New Haven West Association, and was ordained pastor of the first Congregational church in New Haven April 8th, 1812. His Ordination Sermon on

The Dignity and Excellence of the Gospel, was preached by Dr. Dwight. He was appointed to the Dwight Professorship of Didactic Theology in Yale College at the Commencement 1822; was dismissed from his church and congregation November, 1822.

As amanuensis and pupil of President Dwight, his mind was brought in close contact with the mind of that distinguished man, for whom he entertained reverence, admiration, and strong personal attachment. President Dwight on his part felt for his pupil a strong attachment, and entertained high hopes for his success in the profession which he had chosen. It is understood that President Dwight recommended him in the highest terms as a suitable candidate for settlement in the Center Church.

Those of his church and congregation who favored "Old Divinity" and those who favored "New Divinity," those who favored "Old Lightism," and those who favored "New Lightism," all united in giving him their confidence and support during the whole of his ministry. He was popular among all classes, and especially with the young. *Gratior et pulchro veniens in corpore virtus.*

> Each youth cried, charming!
> Each nymph, divine!

While the North church and the Center church were in progress of erection, two boys were, at a certain time, discussing the comparative beauty of the two houses. One said, "We have got a mahogany pulpit in our house (the North church)," and the other boy replied: "We have a mahogany preacher in our house."

It was a very significant fact that Dr. Dana, who, after the settlement of Mr. Stuart, had withdrawn from the pulpit and house of God, where he used to preach, and worshiped in the College Chapel, under the preaching of President Dwight, when Mr Taylor was settled, reappeared in the Center church and took his seat, at the invitation of the Society, in the pulpit with the young minister, and was always well satisfied with his ministrations.

During his ministry, the attendance on Sunday at his house of worship, was large, and the number belonging to the church was greatly increased. In 1820, his church and the North church enjoyed a powerful revival of religion. A very interesting account of it is given in the Christian Spectator, Vol. iii, page 49,—by himself and Mr. Merwin.

Dr. Taylor was settled over the Center church the same year that I entered College, and he was elected Professor one year before I left the tutorship. He was in the flower and flush of his professional life during the ten years that I was in New Haven. In stature he was taller than the middle height, with a frame rather squarely built but well knit, a full muscular development, but without any tendency to leanness on the one hand or obesity on the other. He had a clear complexion, a bright beaming black eye, black or dark brown hair, and clear cut features.

He had a strong intellect to grasp truth, a strong heart to feel it, a strong conscience to apply it to his own soul, and a strong will to carry it out in practical results. He had both personal and moral courage. About the year 1816, a tall, active, strong man, said to him, " Were it not for your coat I would give you a whipping." Mr. Taylor calmly replied, "I can take it off." What he thought true he was not afraid to speak, what he thought right he was not afraid to do, limited only by the proprieties of time, place, and persons.

He was laborious in preparing his sermons. An aged gentleman, greatly respected by Dr. Taylor, told me that he " saw him one morning writing in his shirt-sleeves, and said to him, 'you are stripped to your work. Sermons, now-a-days, are not written with the coat off.' " It was pleasant in my morning walks to see him thus employed, and Mrs. Taylor, with her broom in hand, and Mrs. Professor Goodrich, and Mrs. Professor Ives, and Miss Betsy Whittlesey, all of them sweeping the door-steps and exchanging the morning salutations directly across the streets and diagonally, while the young children were playing or toddling on the side-walk. It was a beautiful picture of good housewifery, of good neighborhood, and of domestic felicity.

In the first part of 1815, there was a revival of religion in Yale College, in which William C. Woodbridge, Ward Safford, and Elias Cornelius, were very active and useful. Near the close of the revival Mr. Taylor was invited to address the hopeful converts. Accordingly we met him in one of the College rooms, and he delivered an excellent address to us on the Nature of the Christian Life, entirely in harmony with the teachings of President Dwight on the same subject. We were all much interested in what he said to us.

One Sabbath morning, at nine o'clock, in 1821, Edward Beecher, a student, came to my room bringing a request from Dr. Taylor that I should preach for him that morning as he was unwell. I felt myself obliged to decline until he told me the nature of his complaint, when I consented, with some reluctance. Dr. Taylor met me afterwards and thanked me for my services, and said some kind and encouraging words to me. At some period after this I invited him to visit our Theological school, and went with him to the recitation, where he made some remarks appropriate to the subject under discussion.

After his appointment to the Chair of Didactic Theology, I had many long conversations with him, always upon elevated topics, generally on Theological subjects. On one occasion we were conversing upon the influence of intense application of the mind in study on the bodily system; when he remarked that he believed when his mind was engaged in intense thought, there was a third more blood in his head than at other times, laughing as he spoke. He dwelt upon this with a good deal of earnestness, citing many facts. Years afterwards I went, in company with the celebrated Richard Owen, the great Naturalist of Great Britain, to visit the Giant's Causeway. In connection with a case of sea-sickness he mentioned that there was a much greater quantity of blood in the head sometimes than at others, and in order to show it, pursued the same line of argument which Dr. Taylor had followed twenty or thirty years before.

After I left the tutorship, I used, for several years, to see Dr. Taylor always in my frequent visits to New Haven. His smile of welcome was delightful.

In the pulpit his face was bright with intelligence and instinct with emotion. His manner was dignified and self-possessed, as if he was master of the situation. His voice was deep-toned and impressive. And often his word, like the Word of God, was a hammer which, by successive blows, broke the sinner's heart, and the waters of contrition flowed forth.

In his intercourse with men he showed, that in him there was a great deal that was human in the best meaning of the word. The native quality of his soul, the *indoles*, was of a high character.

There are men whose eyes are as keen as those of the fabled Epidaurian Serpent to discover the faults and foibles of other men. He was not of this class. There are men who use the weaknesses of others for their own advantage. He was not of *this* class. He had no taste nor talent for intrigue; he left this to others. The native fine qualities of his soul led him to notice the same qualities in others. The following is one of the letters that I received from him:

New Haven, November 4th, 1825.

Dear Sir:—Mr. George Carrington, one of our students, who has been here two years, I have learned this fall, is willing to go to Coleraine and see the ground, provided they will employ him a few Sabbaths, with the usual compensation. I suppose you may know something of him. As a writer of theological dissertations he is highly respectable; he has read one or two of his first sermons to me, which are not wanting in sensible and useful remark. How he will succeed as a speaker I cannot tell, though I doubt not he will speak with propriety, in many respects, if not with force. His extempore powers in debate are also respectable; he has, I think, a good spirit, and would engage in the kind of labor you speak of, with diligence and success.

The exhilarating paragraph of your good wife, was peculiarly acceptable; less so, however, than would be the *Webster scream*, should it be my good fortune to enter your habitation with such a salutatory. For this I thought I owed her an entire letter, but I dare not pay the debt in this manner, lest I should contract another which I should never pay. Let her however write paragraphs or whole letters, I will never refuse to acknowledge my obligation.

Mrs. Taylor was gratified to hear of her happiness; nor was it less gratifying to me in this respect; but there was also the stir of emotion, and the hearty good laugh—of such inconceivable value to the abstract, sober-looking didactic, I hope at least for future morsels of the like kind.

I have no doubt that you are right in the opinion that Unitarianism is on the increase in that part of the country of which you speak. I have my fears that it is, generally, in your State, at least so far as it has obtained what may be called a footing. I do not believe it is sufficiently counteracted by able discussion. It needs to be kept in sight and followed up, and when taken hold of, never abandoned, while the people will read,—unfortunately they will have the last word, and will keep it going, and in this way they accomplish much. I greatly wish to keep on, as I have begun, (a word about original sin of course,) but the courage of those who should stand by me fails, and my own purse still more. I have written partly an answer to Lords' Pamphlet, as I call it, but probably it will never be published, even if finished.

I like what you say about Theology in relation to the *present times* and *habits of thinking* among our intelligent countrymen. These times are widely different from those that have preceded them, and whether my thoughts and yours would run in the same specific channel or not on this subject, I can easily see what appears to be a highly important, not to say indispensable, field of inquiry. The man, however, who thinks of a subject is the man to write on it. So, I hope you will go to work without delay. I would give you some of my thought, if I had time. I can only say that one thing has struck me often, viz: that thinking people, of the latitudinarian cast, are really standing on ground where, in most of our theological discussions, we do not reach them. President Adams traveled from New York to Boston lately in company with

Rev. Mr. Cox, of the former place. He gave me a detailed account of the conversation in which, by the way, they were occupied during the journey. The President ultimately said, that it was impossible for God to make a creature who should be accountable under a law whose penalty should be eternal death. Now this is way off yonder, where few of our folks are wont to go. You, I trust, are not reluctant to undertake a journey of discovery even into this region. We must have a sound, deep philosophy, and yet it must be common-sense-philosophy, such as all the world can understand if we would defend orthodox theology. This can be done in my humble but very considerate opinion. But I am going beyond my intentions. I would conclude with the assurance that I shall be as truly happy to hear from you on paper as I have been *viva voce* on these topics,—you know I like *your* cue. It is the way to do good at this day in one most essential respect.

I am sincerely yours,

N. W. TAYLOR.

An Address delivered at the funeral of Dr. Noah Webster, May 31st, 1843, by Nathaniel W. Taylor, D.D.

This is not the time for attempting a full delineation of the character of the distinguished man, whose death we mourn, and whose funeral has assembled us. His life and character, however, are not of ordinary but of peculiar interest, and as furnishing many useful lessons to the living, are, with propriety, made the theme of a few brief remarks on the present occasion.

Generally, it may be said, that Dr. Webster has long been before the public as a man distinguished for great worth and excellence of character, and for high literary attainments and valuable literary productions, for true patriotism, and for Christian benevolence. With this comprehensive view of his character before us, as one well known to most of us, and without attempting to fill up the outline with the detail of those virtues which constitute it, I shall only advert to some few things which naturally occur as topics of interesting and useful contemplation.

Dr. Webster has lived long, and the character of such a man derives from this consideration a peculiar interest. He was born Oct. 16th, 1758, and died at the advanced age of 84. He had lived to see successive generations of men pass away. He had marked the vicissitudes of all human affairs, the changes in all the departments of life. He lived to see a new country become, at least in some respects, an old one. He witnessed the revolution which first gave this country its independence and freedom, the formation of its present government, its subsequent administration, its practical operations, and its glorious results. He witnessed the conflicts, the successes, the defeats, the violence and the crimes of political parties. He lived to note the revolutions of other nations, their causes, progress and consequences, to see kings and princes fall, and others take their thrones, to see peace and war and war and peace again; he lived to witness the progress of art and of science, of truth and error, to see the principles of wisdom and the dreams of visionaries tested, in politics, in religion, in science, and other things,—in a word, during his long life, he saw our world, as it were, in all its forms and phases pass away, and a new world rise around him. Amid all these changes, himself and character unchanged, he lived and died the friend of his country, the friend of man, the friend of God. Such a character has the aspect of perpetuity, and derives additional dignity and lustre, the bright impress of truth and rectitude from a life of four score years. It is the excellence, the beauty of virtue, unchanged by every cause of change, made permanent by habit, and venerable by age. "The hoary head is a crown of glory, being found in the way of righteousness."

The character of Dr. Webster is one of unusual interest as one of unusual prominence. Of the distinguished individuals of our country, no one, with the exception of the father of his country, has been more extensively known to its population. He has been extensively known in various departments of society, but pre-eminently as the instructor in the rudiments of learning of almost our entire population. In 1783, he commenced the publication of the first, second, and third parts of a Grammatical Institute of the English language. These books, especially the first, have been in constant use in most of the primary schools of the country, from that time to the present. And who, born since that time,—what man, woman, child, through our broad land, has not been taught to read our language from these books? The proof of the extent to which the name of Dr. Webster has been known, is in the fact, that, fourteen millions of his spelling book have been published and sold since its first publication. In being known as the author of these books, he has been known also in his general character. The vast numbers who have thus known him, have known him also as the friend of good morals, of virtue, of religion,—the devoted cultivator of the intellect of his country,—the man who has done more than any other, not to say than all others, in what may be called fundamental, for the elevation, the culture, the refinement of the mind of this great people, and with this, contributed incalculably to their moral improvement. While our children have admired and revered him as the great man,—we have all been children and know how children feel,—his character, his example, invited none to vice, but combined with his lessons, to allure only to virtue. "A voluntary descent from the dignity of science," said Dr. Johnson, in his life of Dr. Watts, "is perhaps the hardest lesson that humility can teach." Who does not revere the man who comes down from these heights to write books and systems of instruction for children adapted to their wants and capacities, from the very dawn of reason through its gradations of progress to maturer years, and while he teaches all to read, teaches none to sin,—who points to virtue and leads the way. As such a man, solitary and alone as it were, has Dr. Webster stood for half a century before this great nation.

The life of Dr. Webster is one of peculiar interest, as one of great industry. As a student in College, as a volunteer in the American army, as the instructor of children, as a student of law, politics, general literature, as an author, Dr. Webster found something to do. During the comparatively short period in which he was employed as the editor of a daily paper in New York, devoted to the defence of Washington's administration, it is supposed that his writings, including translations from foreign languages, would amount to some twenty octavo volumes. Without referring to his many other publications which, by their number and their contents, are decisive of singular industry and untiring application of mind, we need only reflect on the great work of his life, the American Dictionary. That we may form some just estimate of the labor employed on this work, we must reflect that since the publication of Johnson's Dictionary—a period of more than seventy years, scarcely any improvement had been attempted, and to make even a defining dictionary, adapted to the present state of the language, was to produce an entirely *new work.* It contains 20,000 words, and between 30 to 40,000 definitions, not to be found in any preceding work. For this purpose, he had thoroughly to investigate the origin of our language and its connections with other languages, and actually examined the vocabularies of twenty of the principal languages of the world, and made a synopsis of the most important words of each, arranging them under the same radical letters, translating their significations, with references from one to another, and thus tracing the affinities real or probable, between these different languages—the high character of this work, and the manner in which this character is given it, in the view of those best qualified to judge, are proofs of the labor bestowed on it. It is not too much to say, that as an instance of literary toil, and of unfaltering, persevering industry, it is at least without a parallel in this country.

It is this part of Dr. Webster's life which says, to the young men of this country, especially those who engage in literary pursuits, *always have something to do*, some object to employ the mind, to call forth its incipient action. If there is any defect in this class of our young men, which needs to be supplied, it is in literary pursuits, that want of energy of soul which is requisite to every successful exertion, that habit of activity which applies itself to everything. Even mental recreation consists not in mental inaction, but in diversity of mental employment. Man is not like the soil on which he lives, which exhausts its powers by production. Activity is an essential attribute of mind. Its powers exist only, so to speak, when they are exercised. It gains new accessions of strength from every exertion, and the greater the acquisitions it makes, the greater it is enabled to make. Such a mind is not the turbid brook formed by a shower, but a living fountain, ever flowing and ever full. Mental sloth enfeebles the whole intellectual system. It unmans the whole man. A habit of activity by ever pursuing some great object, something that rouses the mind, and keeps it always roused to action, qualifies for everything. Nothing is in vain that rouses the soul—nothing that keeps this ethereal fire ever alive and glowing. If there is any void which nature and which God abhors, it is a mental void, while the pleasure of accomplishing something—the pleasure, the joy, the mind takes in its own successful action—is its own rich reward. Of the truth of these remarks, I have known few men whose life and character furnish a more striking confirmation than those of Dr. Webster. He began, continued, and ended his life, a life which, in the end, he pronounced to be in full, perpetual, useful occupation.

The life of Dr. Webster is one of peculiar interest as devoted to intellectual acquisition. I need advert to no proofs of this fact. Few there are, who do not know enough concerning him to know that he was one of those men who sought for knowledge on all subjects speculative and practical, great things and small things, God, His works, great and marvellous, his ways just and true, and yet past finding out,—man in his nature and relations, his condition, his destiny, in this and other worlds, society, politics, government, law, divinity,—language, its meanings, its words, its letters,—diseases, their causes, their remedies,—agriculture, gardening, the weather, and of course, that the only approximation toward knowing all things perfectly, was knowing something about everything.

though all cannot devote their life as exclusively even as he did, to intellectual acquisitions, all may aim at acquisitions and still further acquisitions in knowledge. I will not here dwell on the advantages, the ability, the pleasure of knowledge, nor attempt to show how it expands the mind, exalts this higher part of our nature in all its faculties, opens innumerable sources of high enjoyment, and qualifies man to fill happily to himself and to others all the relations of life. The pleasures of knowledge are without satiety, they enable us to despise the pleasures of sense as they ought to be despised, and to feel the superiority of the spiritual and divine part of our nature, to the material and animal part. They are self-created satisfactions, and are heightened by the labor they cost, the difficulties and obstacles surmounted in successful pursuit. He who by intellectual toil overcomes formidable obstacles, in lighting on some happy discovery, either this of truth, or by some other high intellectual achievement, which will bless the world while it lasts, has more than the pleasures of a thousand brilliant victories. In this respect,—for let us estimate things as they are,—our departed friend and fellow citizen was a greater and happier man than any Alexander or Bonaparte, that once tortured the world. I only add, on this topic, that it is pre-eminently the moral good which results from knowledge that commends its acquisition. Who does not know that by this means the degraded are to be raised, the immoral to be reformed,—vice, with its infamy and miseries to be prevented; again, who does not know that in this way the good are to be made better, that even the character of the Christian is to give forth its light, its lustre, and its charms. Man, in his intellect, is made in the image of his God, and why should this feature of the resemblance be marred. This lesson, this great lesson, this lesson which is so familiar, should be learned anew, and impressed anew, by the example of our departed friend. We who knew him, know what resources he had, and we know what cheerfulness, what equanimity, serenity, what rich and independent pleasures it afforded him through his long and happy life.

The life of Dr. Webster is one of peculiar interest, as devoted to objects of utility to others. On leaving College he engaged in the instruction of a school, an employment—as it should be a profession—which, in my opinion, and we may all enjoy our own, is not inferior in usefulness, and ought not to be in dignity, to any other except that which is of divine institution. With this exception no other has the same benign influence in the promotion of the character of individuals and of the community. Dr. Webster was distinguished as a politician. He was a Judge of one of our courts, and frequently a member of the Legislatures of Connecticut and Massachusetts, in which stations his labors were always devoted to the public good. He was extensively employed as a political writer. Though, of necessity, more or less a party man, he acted not, and wrote not for party purposes, a distinction not so rare in former days, as for his country's good, in defence of the great principle of Washington, of the revolution, of the rights and remuneration of its army, which achieved our independence. It is believed he made the first distinct proposal through the press for a new constitution of the United States. He wrote, by solicitation, an examination of the leading principles of that constitution, with Gen. Hamilton, Chancellor Kent, and others, he vindicated the treaty with Great Britain, made in 1795, and called Jay's Treaty, opposition to which was so violent as for a time to stagger the firmness of Washington, and to threaten us with commotions. These papers were said to have contributed more to allay the discontent and opposition to that treaty than any others. He wrote sketches of "national policy;" he warned his country against the corruptions of the French Revolutions; he defended General Washington's Proclamation of Neutrality, contributed thus to allaying the effervescence in favor of embarking in the wars of revolutionary France. Of the design and object of his elementary books, and of his greater work, we need not speak. What has been accomplished by the former we all know concerning. What has been, and will be, accomplished by the latter, both at home and abroad, there can be but one opinion on the part of those who are qualified to judge. In his family, and in his intercourse with others, his life was marked with singular benignity. He lived pre-eminently to do good, to promote the true and best interests of his country and the world.

To you also, my young friends, the world is all before you, when to act, and what to do. It still spreads out before you, as a theater of benevolence, the field for virtue, for self-denying active beneficence to expatiate in, with its sure, delightful activity in imparting its results to others. None are so destitute of the gifts of grace, of nature, or of fortune, as to have no mite to contribute to the well-being of others. As in the example now before us, aim to do good. Let your goodness extend to all around you, to society—let it spread over the land, and over the world, like the light of the morning. Can any employment to cheer and bless existence, to brighten the face of sadness and sorrow, to wipe away the tears of grief, to turn the voice of mourning into notes of praise, and to cause the widow's heart to sing for joy, to open the eyes which prejudice has shut, to instruct the ignorant, to improve the mind from infancy to age, and thus to cultivate the soil on which the fruits of immortality shall grow,—to chain down the spirit of party, and to unite all in one great family of love, to reform a selfish world, to bring it under a spiritual dominion, and impart to it a principle of eternal life, thus to cause misery and war to vanish from the world like darkness before the rising sun,—to refresh with showers of blessing this dry and barren region, where no water is, and to accomplish the beneficent design of the Author of all, by watching, living, acting, and, if need be, dying for the happiness of the world. Is not the employment *God-like*—are not its joys *divine*.

The life of Dr. Webster is one of interest, as answering the end in some good degree, for which life is given. I have thus spoken of the great object of his life, not of the principle by which he was governed. He knew, we all know, that here a fundamental vital distinction must be made. He had learned, that though we give all our goods to feed the poor, without love it is nothing—nothing in an high relation as subjects of God's dominion, and going to the retributions of eternity. He fully believed what may be called the Gospel, not merely as a preceptive, but as a moral and religious system, with its peculiar, its sublime, its awful, its glorious truths. He believed in the depravity of the heart, and just desert of sin, the necessity of a change of heart by the Spirit of God and of pardon by the atoning blood of Christ. Nearly forty years since he publicly professed to embrace this gospel with spiritual sincerity, to become in heart the disciple of the law of God. On this greatest event of his life we have no time to eulogize. We can say all that need to be said in a few words. He lived, he died, like a Christian.

His was the religion, not of forms, not of mere external morality, and yet of this he had more than most men, not an impulse, not merely excited emotion, but an habitual internal principle, which is the only principle the sum and substance of all religion,—the only preparation of the immortal spirit for the purity and joys of heaven. In short, it was, as we believe, that true piety of heart, which loves man, but which loves God more, and befits one who is to live and act under His government forever,—for that higher theater, where he will live and act amid the grandeurs of eternity, in fellowship with God, as one with Him. His hope, as was to be expected, was as an "anchor to the soul, sure and steadfast." His dying testimony to the excellence of religion and to the power and grace of his Redeemer, was given in that peaceful serenity which discrowns death of its terrors, and falls asleep in Jesus. He met the last enemy, saying, "I know in whom I have believed," "I have no doubts—no fears."

If ever Christianity appears in its power, it is when it erects its trophies on the grave—when it takes its disciples from the grasp of death, the last enemy—and in the dying hour, gives to them and their surviving friends, its own immortal hopes. Imperfect as is human character, still by the eye of faith, and in the light of their own Christian example, we trace our departed friends to another world. They leave us, their days of trial are over. They have entered into rest. Sheltered now from the storms of life, the dangers of sin and temptations, they repose in the haven of everlasting peace. Their separation from us is not final, the pious dead and the pious living are one family, and shall meet again. The friendships that have religion for their basis, shall survive the changes of earth and time,—for they are friendships of God and His holy kingdom. Let our sorrows then be cheered with hope,—for death is destroyed,—"For, if we believe that Jesus died and rose again, even so them that sleep in Jesus will God bring with Him. For the Lord Himself will descend from Heaven with a shout, with the Archangel's voice, and the trumpet of God,—then we, which are alive and shall remain, shall be caught up together with Him in the clouds, to meet the Lord in the air, and so shall be ever with the Lord.

" Wherefore comfort one another with these words."

REPORT ON AN ECCLESIASTICAL HISTORY OF CONNECTICUT.

At a meeting of the General Association of Connecticut, at Bridgeport, in June, 1861, the following Preamble and Resolution was offered by a committee composed of Rev. WILLIAM C. FOWLER, Rev. E. L. CLEAVELAND, D.D., and the Rev. MYRON N. MORRIS, to wit:—

Whereas, GOD, in His providence, has dealt most kindly with the churches of this Commonwealth, carefully sustaining, until now, the vine which He at first transplanted; thus manifesting His faithfulness to His friends in acts that ought to be recorded for the reverential admiration of future generations; and

Whereas, The FATHERS of this Commonwealth, through many generations, have manifested the power of Christian faith in their obedience to the truth as it is in Jesus; thus proving themselves worthy to be held in everlasting remembrance; and

Whereas, Our form of ecclesiastical polity has certain distinctive features which ought to be understood and appreciated by all the sons and daughters of Connecticut; and

Whereas, In the general history of New England, and in the particular history of this State, and in the histories of many towns, and churches, and individuals, and in the records of Consociations and Associations, there are abundant materials for preparing an appropriate memorial of what God has wrought in the years of His right hand, and what man has wrought, under God, in bringing the population of Connecticut to its present high civilization; therefore,

Resolved, That this Association would view with great

favor a well considered and well executed History of Connecticut.

This resolution was passed unanimously, and the subject was referred back to the same committee, to be reported on at some future meeting.

And here your committee would beg leave to say, that all which they aimed at was accomplished by the adoption of this resolution, which presented the subject for the consideration of the churches and of those authors who have taste and talent and leisure for the composition of such a work.

But inasmuch as the Association saw fit to keep the subject alive before the churches by this reference, your committee would subjoin the following additional report for acceptance:

And *first*, then, a well considered and well executed Ecclesiastical History of Connecticut would embrace the forms of church government, especially of the leading denomination.

Among the Puritan emigrants who came to Massachusetts in the early part of the seventeenth century, was one class called Non-conformists, who cherished an attachment to the Church of England, though in certain externals they would not adopt her forms and ceremonies. There was another class called Separatists, who, besides rejecting the forms of worship, abhorred both the Episcopal and Presbyterian churches. They regarded each local and religious society as a separated and independent church, and not accountable to any Bishop or Presbytery. HIGGINSON, a Non-conformist, but not a Separatist, in 1629, on taking his last look of his native land from the stern of his ship, exclaimed: "We will not say, as the Separatists were wont to say at their leaving England, 'Farewell, Babylon! farewell, Rome!' but we will say, farewell, dear England! farewell, the church of God in England, and all the Christian friends there! We do not go to New England as Separatists from the Church of England."—YOUNG'S *Chronicles*, page 398.

The two colonies, namely, the New Haven and the Connecticut, had a generic agreement in this respect, but they also had specific differences. Can these specific differences be traced to the specific differences between the two colonies, Plymouth and Massachusetts?—or must they be traced for their parentage to the mother country, namely, to the differences between the Separatists and the Non-conformists there? And after the two colonies in Connecticut became one, and the two colonies in Massachusetts became one, these two colonies thus formed have had distinctive features of church government down to the present time; though as members of the same ecclesiastical family they strongly resemble each other.

Connecticut was settled after Massachusetts, and the fathers of the colony, therefore, could avoid the errors and adopt what was good in the civil and ecclesiastical polity of Massachusetts. JOHN COTTON, the personal friend of THOMAS HOOKER and JOHN DAVENPORT, had become disgusted, somewhat, with certain democratical tendencies. Governor WINTHROP wrote a letter to those "who had removed to Connecticut, who were about forming their government, warning them of the danger of referring matters of judicature to the body of the people," in these words: "The best part of a community is always the *least*, and of that best part the wiser is still *less;* wherefore the old canon was, 'choose ye out judges, and thou shalt bring the matter before the judge.'" RICHARD SALTONSTALL was one of the patentees of Connecticut, with Lords SAY and SEAL and BROOK, and was a principal associate in the settlement of the colony. He addressed a letter to some friends in Massachusetts on the subject of the bigotry and persecution in that State. In it he says, "It doth not a little grieve my spirit to hear what sad things are reported daily of your doings, as that you fine and whip and imprison men for their consciences."

With such facts in view, we need not be surprised that THOMAS HOOKER, of Hartford, "the light of the Western churches," and "the rich pearl which Europe gave to America," should, instead of leaning to Separatism and Independency, be "a hearty friend unto the consociation of churches," and that he should make the declaration, "We must agree upon constant meeting of ministers, and settle the consociation of churches, or else we are undone." We need not be surprised that "he would have nothing publicly propounded unto the brethren of the church but what had been first privately prepared by the elders." We need not be surprised that Samuel Stone, the teacher of the church in Hartford of which Hooker was pastor, and afterward the successor of Hooker, should define Congregationalism as "a speaking aristocracy in the face of a silent democracy."

Connecticut more than Massachusetts inclined to a stable, regular, representative church government. Besides having in some churches ruling elders or teaching elders, or seven pillars, Connecticut more than one hundred and fifty years ago established the Consociation of Churches, each Consociation being expected *to keep permanent records of its own doings for future inspection*, in cases of ordination or dismission of ministers or of discipline. Thus in Connecticut the ecclesiastical government has conformed somewhat more to the civil government than in Massachusetts. It is not arbitrary and discretionary, but representative and constitutional. In the civil government representatives are chosen, and delegated rather than original powers are employed, and continuous records kept by an officer statedly appointed. There is a near approach to this in the organization and functions of Consociations. Connecticut has a written ecclesiastical constitution for the Congregational denomination, just as it has a written civil constitution for all the inhabitants. The reasons for adopting the one were similar to those for adopting the other.

It is true that all the Congregational churches in the State are not consociated under this constitution. It might be profitable to investigate the historical reasons why they are not. It might be instructive to investigate the causes why certain churches in Connecticut, which were once inside of that constitution, are now outside of it. In other words, it might be useful to learn what were the grounds and reason of their secession; whether those reasons were the excessive love of liberty; or an unwillingness to submit themselves to censure, when to blame; or an unwise self-esteem, which led them to measure themselves by themselves and commend themselves among themselves; or the influence of demagogues, who are apt to make light of constitutions, whether political or ecclesiastical, as interfering with their own schemes; or some better reasons.

Again, what were the relations of Connecticut to the several Synods anciently convened in Massachusetts? These Synods appear to have grown out of the conscious weakness of independency, or out of certain movements of Presbyterian Puritans who were disgusted with that weakness. The one convened in Boston in 1662 recommended the consociation of churches. What are the historical reasons why Connecticut adopted the consociation of churches and Massachusetts did not?

One or more of the Synods recommended the baptism of children under what was called the half-way covenant. Under that practice, for many years there was a strong desire on the part of those who were in full covenant to offer up their children in baptism. That practice ceased. What relation does the cessation of that practice bear to the present great neglect of that beautiful and impressive ordinance? Why do the Episcopalians perform the duty of offering up their children in baptism more faithfully than Congregationalists?

Why did Connecticut more largely than Massachusetts become Episcopalian? Why did Massachusetts become Unitarian, and Rhode Island become Baptist, more largely than Connecticut? What causes conspired to produce the secession of the Separatists or strict Congregationalists? What were the origin and progress of other Christian denominations in the State? As compared with other denominations, is Congregationalism as strong as formerly? What relation do the churches and ministers of Connecticut, at the present time, sustain to Presbyterianism, compared with what ministers and churches in Connecticut sustained to it when the *heads of agreement* by the united ministers, formerly called

Presbyterian and Congregational, were assented to in 1708? —or what they sustained to it when the "plan of union" was adopted by the General Assembly of the Presbyterian Church, and by the General Association of Connecticut?—or when President Stiles, and President Dwight, and Dr. Strong of Hartford, spoke of the churches of Connecticut as *Presbyterian* churches? In the instructions given by His Majesty, the King of Great Britain, to certain commissioners that were directed to visit Connecticut in April, 1664, it is declared, "We conceive those of Connecticut to contrive themselves under the most rigid Presbyterian government." Is Connecticut more Presbyterian, or less so, than formerly?

Secondly, a well considered and well executed Ecclesiastical History of Connecticut would embrace the doctrinal opinions and the correspondent conduct which has prevailed in the successive eras. Under this particular, it would be seen that our beloved Commonwealth, in comparison with any other New England State, is worthy of praise for orthodoxy and moderation in opposition to extreme views. If there are those who are accustomed to think of Massachusetts as the venerable Mother State of Connecticut, we can say to them, with the most kindly feelings towards that ancient and excellent Commonwealth, *pulchrior filia, pulchra matre.*

Thirdly, a well considered and well executed Ecclesiastical History of Connecticut would embrace the several controversies, both external and internal, which have agitated the Congregational denomination from time to time.

Fourthly, a well considered and well executed Ecclesiastical History of Connecticut would embrace the results of the system and usages of Congregationalism, namely, the inner life of piety, and the external manifestation in worship and in morals; the revivals in the churches; the labors, the influence, and respectability of the clergy; the schools and the colleges; the Sabbath schools and domestic missions; the orderly habits and Christian courtesies in social intercourse; those virtues and graces that have prevailed in private and public life, which make men but little lower than the angels; the transmitted influences which make us what we are to-day.

Connecticut has her historic institutions and her own individuality; should not those institutions be distinctly described, and that individuality be faithfully portrayed by some of her admiring sons? Is it enough to have them faintly pictured in the background of a History of the United States, or of New England, or of Massachusetts? Is it enough that she should be placed in the constellation of American States?—or even in the New England pleiades?—or as a satellite of Massachusetts? Is she not herself "a bright particular star," to be gazed at as she moves on in her orbit?

Nor are materials and helps wanting for preparing an Ecclesiastical History of Connecticut. The several historical societies in Massachusetts, Connecticut, Rhode Island, and elsewhere, have not only inspired a taste for historical studies, but have collected large stores of historical helps. Among the books which furnish valuable materials, two especially should be mentioned. One of these was prepared under the direction of the General Association, and is entitled, "*Contributions to the Ecclesiastical History of Connecticut.*" This does great credit to the Association in the facts which it contains and in the spirit which it breathes. The other, namely, TRUMBULL'S *History of Connecticut*, has everything to recommend it to our confidence, so far as the honesty and industry of the author are concerned. It should, however, be remembered that he prepared the work under great disadvantages. He had been invited by the General Association to write a "History of the United States." While he was engaged in this work, he turned aside to write a History of Connecticut, as a kind of experimental effort. The following are his words: "Had the history been written more leisurely and with fewer avocations, it might have been more perfect; but as it was desirable to make as short a pause as possible in writing the 'History of the United States,' it was judged inexpedient to employ more time upon it. The author is under great disadvantages for historic writing. He can command no time for himself. The work of the ministry, which is his chosen and beloved employment, after all his application, so engrosses his time, that sometimes for weeks and months he cannot find a single day for the composition of history. When he has attempted it, he has been able scarcely to write a single page without interruption. Often has he been so fatigued with other studies as to be in circumstances not the most favorable for composition."

He also remarks, "that about the middle of December, 1796, he began to look over and arrange his papers and compile the following history." The first volume was published in 1797, so that he could have spent but a year in arranging and presenting that part of his work. It need not, therefore, seem strange that it should bear evident marks of haste, of deficiency of materials, and crudeness in their composition.

It should be added that when the whole work was given to the public in 1818, it was objected to on the ground that the civil history is mingled with the ecclesiastical, when they ought to have been published in separate volumes. Indeed, the author himself remarks, "It will be observed that the ecclessiastical part of the history is kept by itself in distinct chapters, and comprises about a third part of the history. It would make a volume by itself, and might be printed separately, without derangement of the narration."

It should also be stated that Trumbull's History is out of print. It took one of your committee two years to obtain a complete copy, at the price of eight dollars, though he sought for it in the principal cities. Nor is there a probability that it will soon be republished. HOLLISTER's would come in competition with it.

Moreover, TRUMBULL's *History*, in the ecclesiastical part of it, comes down only to 1760, so that there are now one hundred and four years not covered by it which require illustration. Evidently, then, from these considerations, it is not adequate to the supply of our wants, as an ecclesiastical history.

There are three divinity schools in the State; ought not the students in these schools to be able to take into their hands a volume which will furnish them with a continuous and connected statement of ecclesiastical affairs in this Commonwealth for the last hundred years? There are three religious colleges in the State; cannot the same question be asked in regard to the students in them, though, perhaps, with less emphasis? There are several hundred Christian ministers in the State; do they not feel the want of such a book? Are there not many thousand intelligent Christians in this State, and elsewhere, who would welcome it?

If such a work should be extensively read, would not its influence be to render men more inclined to substitute the inductions of the past for the dreams of the present, to repress the overweening self-conceit which leads to a removal of ancient landmarks? Would it not help "to correct that cold selfishness which would regard our day and our generation as a separate and insulated portion of man and time; and awakening our sympathies with those who have gone before, make us mindful also of those who are to follow, and thus bind us to our fathers and to our posterity by a lengthening and golden cord"? Would it not help to raise some minds, which live only in the present, up to the full dignity of man, "able to look before and after"?

The General Association has already taken more than one step in the right direction. It has appointed a *Statistical Secretary*, who has collected valuable materials which are the pledge and earnest of future stores for the muse of history. It has patronized the "Congregational Quarterly," which is replete with historical facts and associations. It has had a *historical commemoration* at Norwich, and published a volume which does honor to itself, and contains important contributions to the religious history of the State. Will it not proceed to encourage still further a well considered and well executed Ecclesiastical History of Connecticut?

In behalf of the committee,

WILLIAM C. FOWLER.

ENGLISH UNIVERSITIES.

(From the Theological and Literary Journal, Vols. V. and VI.)

THE UNIVERSITY OF OXFORD is a corporate body, known by the title of "The Chancellor, Masters, and Scholars, of the University of Oxford." It possesses the power of conferring degrees which are necessary to the attainment of many of the places of honor and emolument It is one of the principal avenues to the ministry of the Episcopal church. It takes part in the legislation of the country through its representatives in parliament. It is possessed of immense wealth, has a large patronage, and, in its press, has a large interest in a valuable monopoly.

It seems to be generally admitted that this institution does not meet the wants of the British nation at the present time, and that in its constitution and laws, and course of study, it belongs to a by-gone age. It seems to be admitted also that it ought to be so modified that it shall be not only what it has claimed to be, "one of the eyes of England," but also that it shall speak what it knows to the British nation and to the world.

The question, therefore, has naturally been raised, where does the power to reform it lie? Does it lie with the Queen, with the advice of her ministers; or with Parliament; or with the University; or with the particular Colleges? There are evidently great difficulties in making any radical changes. But of this more presently.

Oxford University is composed of nineteen colleges and five halls.

University College, said to be founded or restored by King Alfred in A. D. 872. In 1851 the number of undergraduates and commoners was 60, and about 55 reside within the walls. There are now twelve Fellows recognized by the statutes with equal privileges and emoluments. The Fellowships are worth about 190*l.* a year. The Mastership is said to be worth about 600*l.* a year. The number of tutors, assistant-tutors, and lecturers, was five. About fifty lectures were given weekly. The average amount of battels, provisions taken from the buttery, in 1847, was 103*l.*

The course of studies for candidates for Honors, included Thucydides, Herodotus, Livy, Tacitus, Aristotle's Ethics, Rhetoric, Politics, and Organon, Homer, Æschylus and Aristophanes, Juvenal, general Lectures on Greek and Roman History, and, occasionally, on Modern History. That prescribed for candidates for an ordinary degree, included Sophocles, Herodotus, Thucydides, Plato's Phædo, Virgil, Livy, Cicero's Tusculan Disputations, and Sallust. There were also lectures for all the undergraduates on the Old Testament, the Gospels, the Acts, the xxxix Articles, and, occasionally, on the Epistles.

Balliol College, founded about the year 1262. The number of undergraduates in 1851 was 80: the total number of scholars was 334. The total revenue of the college was 5,896*l.* 9*s.* 11*d.* This college enjoys the singular privilege of electing its own visitor. The total income of the Master or Head of the College is about 800*l.* a year. There are ten Fellows. A Fellowship is worth about 220*l.* a year.

Merton College, founded in 1270. It consists of a Warden and 24 Fellows, and two Chaplains. In 1851 there were 35 undergraduates. The Visitor is the Archbishop of Canterbury. The annual income of the College is 7,220*l.* The present emoluments of the Warden, in money, are 1,050*l.* a year. The Fellows are elected by the Warden and thirteen Fellows.

Exeter College, founded in the year 1315. The corporation consists of a Rector and 25 Fellows. The number of undergraduates in 1851 was 133. This college educates one-twelfth part of the undergraduates.

Oriel College, founded in 1324. There are 18 Fellows who receive 200*l.*, and 21 Scholarships. The number of undergraduates in 1851 was 87.

Queen's College, founded in 1340. The officers are a Provost, who receives 1,000*l.*; and 16 Fellows, who receive 300*l.* annually. The number of commoners in 1851 was 51.

New College, founded in 1379, by William of Wykeham. He bound all the members by an oath to observe his statutes, and "all and singular the things therein contained, according to the plain, literal, and grammatical sense." The Fellows are 10 in number; the undergraduates were 8. The college presents to 37 benefices.

Lincoln College, founded in 1427. There are a Rector, 12 Fellows, and 9 Scholars. In 1851 there were 40 commoners.

All Souls' College, founded in 1438. There were to be 40 Fellows. Of these 24 were to study the Arts, or Philosophy, or Theology; and 16 the Canon or Civil Law.

Magdalen College. (Pages wanting in the Report.) It was founded in 1459 by William Womfleet, Bishop of Winchester.

Brasenose College. (Pages wanting.) It was founded in 1515, by William Smyth, Bishop of Lincoln.

Corpus Christi College, founded in 1506. The number of Fellows is still 20. The number of undergraduates 6 or 7. The Head of the College receives 1,000*l.*, and the Fellows 200*l.* The income of the College is 8,500*l.*

Christ-Church College, founded in 1526. It is governed by a Dean and eight Canons. The students are 101 in number. Forty-one juniors receive 25*l.*; 40 receive rather more than 30*l.*; and the senior twenty 45*l.* The number of undergraduates in 1850 was about 190.

Trinity College, founded in 1554. There are now twelve Fellows and thirteen Scholars. In 1851 the number of commoners was 67. There are 10 benefices in the gift of the College.

St. John's College, founded in 1555. In 1851 there were 63 undergraduates, of whom 54 were commoners. Thirty benefices are in the gift of the College.

Jesus College, founded in 1571. The number of Fellows is now 19; the number of Scholars 18. In 1851 there were 40 undergraduate commoners. The battels, including tuition and all college dues, range between 50*l.* and 80*l.*

Wadham College, founded in 1610. There are fifteen Fellowships and fifteen Scholarships. In 1851 there were 84 undergraduates.

Pembroke College, founded in 1629. The total number of undergraduates in 1851 was 73. There are fourteen Fellowships and fourteen Scholarships.

Worcester College, founded in 1714. The number of Fellows is 21. The number of Scholars is 16. In 1851 there were 28 undergraduate commoners; 8 undergraduate Fellow-commoners. There are four tutors. There are nine benefices in the gift of the College.

There are five Halls, which differ from colleges in that they have no charter, are not incorporated societies, are subject to statutes framed by the University, and have no endowments except their buildings, with a few Scholarships and exhibitions, which are held in trust by persons not necessarily connected with the Halls. In academical matters they, however, enjoy the same privileges nearly as the Colleges. They are allowed to receive undergraduates, and their emoluments are almost wholly derived from this source. The principals are, indeed, subject to the authority of the Hebdomadal Board, like the Heads of Colleges. The present Halls are—

1. St. Mary's Hall, which, in 1851, had 52 undergraduates.
2. Magdalene Hall, which, in 1851, had 108 undergraduates.
3. New Inn Hall, which, in 1851, had 33 undergraduates.
4. St. Alban Hall, which, in 1851, had 7 undergraduates.
5. St. Edmund Hall, which, in 1851, had 23 undergraduates.

The Administration of the University was anciently in the hands of—

I. *The House of Congregation.* This was the real representative of the primeval Legislature of the literary republic of Oxford. The Legislature of the University in early times consisted of one house only, in which all the masters and teachers had a seat, called "the Congregation." The House was summoned by the sound of a bell, and met frequently. It confers all ordinary degrees which are now in form, what they were once in fact, licenses to teach.

II. *The House of Convocation.* This was composed of all who had attained a certain academical rank, whether they were or were not teachers. This body, called the "great Congregation," met only at intervals. This House was summoned by beadles. The House of Convocation, as comprehending the ever increasing number of those who were not teachers, and also as determining questions which were of interest to the whole academical community, became the more important of the two.

III. *The Chancellor*, elected by the Masters of each College.

IV. *Two Proctors.* They were elected by the whole body of the Masters of Arts.

This was the constitution of the administrative powers formerly.

At the present time, the administration is in the hands of—

I. *The Hebdomadal Board.* This consists of the Vice-Chairman, the twenty-three other Heads of Houses, and the two Proctors. The Heads of Houses had, as such, no statutable power in the University before the middle of the sixteenth century.

II. *The Chancellor.* He is elected by Convocation, from political considerations chiefly.

III. *The Vice-Chancellor.* He is nominated from the Heads of the Houses.

IV. *The House of Congregation.* Of the right of legislation, nothing now remains but that in it must be promulgated all statutes three days at least before they are proposed in Convocation.

V. *House of Convocation.* This consists, as formerly, of all Masters of Arts and Doctors, who have taken out their regency, and who are members of a College or Hall. It possesses the power of debating on the measures proposed by the Hebdomadal Board, and by its acceptance these measures become statutes. It elects the Chancellor, the representatives of the University to Parliament, many of the Professors, and various University officers, while, on certain other appointments, it exercises a veto. To it belongs the ecclesiastical patronage of the University, and the right of conferring degrees out of the ordinary course.

The present constitution gives to the Vice-Chancellor singly, and to the two Proctors jointly, a veto on all the measures brought before Convocation.

Such, briefly, is the constitution of the University, as it was finally confirmed by King Charles the First and Archbishop Laud, and such it has ever since remained.

The Commission propose that the Congregation should be remodeled, and have its powers increased, so that it should be more nearly what it once was. They propose that the members of this remodeled Congregation should be the Heads of the Houses and Proctors, who would sit there as the Administrative powers of the University, together with the Professors and the public Lecturers, who are the authorized teachers; and that, in addition to these, the senior Tutor of each College shall have a seat. The Congregation, as thus constituted, would consist of more than one hundred members, and would be allowed to hold its deliberations in the English language, and not in the Latin, as at present. The duty of conferring degrees would still remain with the Congregation.

It also proposes that the Hebdomadal Board should remain and transact the ordinary business and maintain discipline, and that it should have the right, but not the exclusive right, of initiating measures to be submitted to the Congregation.

It also proposes that the House of Convocation, constituted as at present, should have the right to veto all the measures passed by the Congregation, and retain the right of electing the Chancellor of the University and the Burgesses.

It also proposes to lessen the powers of the Proctors, by taking from them the veto power, and the right of appointing examiners.

The number of students actually residing at Oxford at the present time is 1,300. The annual number matriculated averages about 400. The number of persons who have passed the first examination for the degree of A.B. averages 287. The total number of members of the University in 1850 was 6,060. The number of undergraduates resident and non-resident in 1850 was 1,402. The number of members of Convocation was 3,294. The remaining 1,364 members were either graduates who had not yet acquired the franchise, or graduates who, having once lost it by removing their names from the books, have not yet recovered it by statutable means. The number of graduates, of all ranks, residing at Oxford, is about 300.

That the number of students educated at Oxford is not larger, is owing to the fact that, in the three learned professions, it furnishes a preparation to not very many, except to those who study theology. The great bulk of those who resort to Oxford are destined for the ministry of the church; and the number of students intended for holy orders would be much greater if the expenses were considerably reduced. The number of students at Cambridge is greater than at Oxford, though at Cambridge the accommodations within the College walls are more limited, and the endowments are much less considerable. This may be owing, in fact, to the greater facilities for admission into a good and popular college at Cambridge, together with the greater advantages thus afforded by open Fellowships and Scholarships. Another reason may be, that the examinations in that University can be more easily passed by persons who have not gone through a classical education. The absence, also, of a religious test at matriculation may sometimes cause a preference to be given to the sister University.

There is one practice in the instruction given in Oxford, as also in Cambridge, which deserves a passing notice. We refer to private tuition. "Private tutors are not recognized by name on the statutes of the University or of the Colleges. They are selected by the students. They often become their advisers and friends. The care, or at least the time, bestowed on each student by the private tutor, is greater than that which is bestowed by the College tutor. It is stated, upon good authority, that the sum annually spent for private tuition at Cambridge amounts to 50,000*l*. At Oxford, the practice of resorting to private tutors is less general. Still, the annual sums thus spent must be large."

The following is a statement of the good and of the evil of such tuition :—

Of the system of private tuition the advantages are manifest. "The power of selection has great efficacy in attaching the pupil to the tutor, and I can speak from experience, that the tendency is strong to overrate the abilities and industry of a private tutor, a leaning not generally observed in the case of public tuition. The unfettered intercourse, the power of stating a difficulty without incurring ridicule, the greater equality of age and position, all tend to give the system efficacy. The system of private tuition is a necessary and unavoidable concomitant to any examination. No sooner were examinations established for the masters and mates of merchant ships, than there arose a class of men whose business it was to *cram* the candidates."

"The system of private tuition has, however, its defects. The persons into whose hands it principally falls are young men of unformed character, knowing little of the world, or probably of anything except the course of study by which they have gained distinction. Such is their influence from their position, that they are really forming the minds of the undergraduates before they have formed their own. As for the private tutors themselves, the practice is probably bad for them, since, as soon as they have taken their degrees, they are placed in a position which will tend to narrow the mind and generate habits of self-conceit."

The Commission expresses the belief that reliance must be

placed mainly upon a return to the plan contemplated by the Laudian code, for improving the instruction in the Universities, shaping its application so as to meet the wants of the present time.

Colleges are defined as charitable foundations for the support of poor scholars with perpetual succession, devoting themselves to study and prayer, administering their own affairs under the presidency of a Head within, and the control of a Visitor without, according to statutes which were to be neither altered nor modified, and which were sanctioned by solemn oaths. Colleges were intended to be what they are still, in the eye of the founders, Eleemosynary Foundations. William of Wykeham states, that next to his kinsmen, poor indigent clerks are to be admitted, because Christ, among the works of mercy, hath commanded men to receive the poor into their houses, and mercifully to comfort the indigent. In Queen's and New College, the Fellows are forbidden to keep dogs, on the ground that "to give dogs the bread of the children of men, is not fitting for the poor, especially for those who live on alms."

Colleges were founded for the purpose of affording to students a home in which they would be preserved from the turbulence and the licentiousness which in ancient times were almost always prevalent in the University. Fellows of college were to live together as members of a community. Founders intended that each of their Fellows should be improved by all in their daily intercourse. The rule of life in the earliest colleges was comparatively simple. It included, generally, common meals, during which the Bible was to be read, and silence kept; the use, in private as well as in public, of the Latin tongue, for which in Oriel and Queen's French, in Corpus Greek, in Jesus College Greek or Hebrew, might be substituted; uniformity of dress; strict obedience to the Head and college officers; terminal scrutinies for the purpose of inquiring into the life, modes, progress in learning, of the Fellows and other members of the college; and a system of surveillance to be carried on night and day by the seniors over the juniors. Celibacy was strictly imposed on the members of most colleges.

The purposes for which the indigent students were thus formed into a community, may be generally stated in the words of the older jurists, as related by Blackstone, to be *ad orandum et studendum.* The first purpose was that the Fellows should offer prayers for the living and the dead.

Moreover, each Fellow was bound, after completing his course in college, to proceed to one of the superior professions, generally that of theology. A few exceptions were made in favor of common or civil law; a still smaller number in favor of medicine, and at New College in favor of astronomy. To receive, then, and not to give instruction, was the business of the Fellows.

The founders of colleges sought to procure the perpetual observance of their statutes by placing them under the patronage of some great personage otherwise not connected with the college, who bore the name of Visitor. The Visitors are empowered, and in some cases earnestly entreated, to inspect the societies committed to their care from time to time, and to reform all abuses.

An examination of the condition of the colleges will show that there have been wide deviations from the purposes of the founders. The colleges are no longer eleemosynary. The Fellows are no longer bound to live as members of a community, subject to a strict rule of life. Since the Reformation, the legislature has prohibited masses and prayers for the dead. The main object of the endowment of colleges, namely, to support persons actually engaged in study, has been almost entirely set aside. The number of Fellows who reside for the purpose of study is very small. The Visitors of colleges have long since ceased to inquire into the condition of the communities committed to their care, and the observance of the statutes.

As already mentioned, the authorities of the University refused to give an account of the revenues to the Commissioners. It appears, however, that the colleges are in the receipt of about $750,000 annually, exclusively of what is paid by the students.

In regard to the state of discipline, the Commissioners are of the opinion, 1. That the University should receive indemnification in case it has exceeded its power in altering the Laudean code, and should henceforth have full authority to make, abrogate, or alter the statutes with the exception of a few fundamental articles not to be altered without the consent of the Crown or some superior authority. 2. That the right of initiating measures should be confided to a body comprising the academical teachers as well as the members of the Hebdomadal Board. For this purpose it may be expedient that the body called the Congregation should be remodelled so as to consist of all Heads of Houses, the Proctors, all Professors and public lecturers, together with the senior tutors of all Colleges and Halls. 3. That the standing delegacies intrusted with executive functions, should be composed partly of members approved by the Congregation on the nomination of the Vice-Chancellor and Proctors, and that the Professors should be formed into a standing delegacy, and not liable to alteration, for the supervision of studies, the appointment of exercises, and the management of the public libraries. 4. That the Vice-Chancellor should be appointed absolutely by the Chancellor from the Heads of Colleges. 5. That the tenure of the Proctor's office be extended to two years, and that their power of veto on acts of Convocation be abolished, and some of their other powers be limited. 6. That the imposition of promissory oaths for the performance of certain academical duties, should be prohibited. 7. That the distinction between noblemen, gentlemen commoners, and commoners, should be discontinued. 8. That certain legal checks be placed upon obtaining credit. 9. That the Vice-Chancellor's court for the recovery of debts conform to other courts. 10. That the provision by which the students shall be required to belong to some College, or Hall, and that they shall all enter at a common gate, should be annulled, and that in some cases members of the University shall be permitted to live in private lodgings.

That as to the studies, 1. That there should be a public examination for all the young men before matriculation. 2. That during the latter part of the academical course, the students should be left free to devote themselves to some special branch or branches of study. 3. That the Professors should be distributed into four Boards for the regular studies: I. Theology. II. Mental Philosophy or Philology. III. Jurisprudence and History. IV. Mathematical and Physical Science. 4. That restrictions on the appointment of Professors should be removed. 5. That the appointment of newly-created Chairs should be given to the Crown, but that the appointment to existing Professorships should be left in the same hands as at present, except that those vested in Convocation, in the graduates of Divinity, and in the Heads of Houses, should be transferred to Congregations. 6. That, to assist the Professors, assistant Professors or lecturers should be appointed, whenever necessary, by Boards to which they would respectively belong, subject to the approval of Congregation; that in case independent endowments cannot be furnished, a limited number of Fellows of colleges, if appointed to such lectureships, should retain their Fellowships though married; and that Congregation should authorize the establishment of new Professorships, when they are wanted, or the suspension of those which may have ceased to be required. 7. That Professors and lecturers should be allowed to receive fees. 8. That the long vacation should commence and terminate on fixed days. 9. That the examinations should be conducted, as far as possible, in the vacations. 10. That steps should be taken to remove the restrictions which limit the usefulness of the University scholarships and prizes. 11. That the Bodleian library should be placed under the management of Professors; that the Professors be authorized, on special occasions, to grant permission that printed books and manuscripts be taken out of the building; that a reading room be provided with due accommodations. 12. That arrangements be made for transferring the department of physical science to the Radcliffe library. 13. That a catalogue be prepared of such books as are in the other libraries, but not in the Bodleian library. 14. That the University proceed with the plan lately brought forward for building a large museum of natural history, and that the trustees of present collections of various kinds should be empowered to transfer their collections to this museum.

That as to the revenues, 1. That there should be a balance-sheet of the revenues of the University printed annually, for the use of Convocation, and that the account books themselves should be accessible. 2. That the table of fees exacted by the University should be revised so as to equalize all fees demanded for the same purpose, and to abolish those which are demanded for no service, or which are unnecessary. 3. That the funds at the disposal of the University should be applied to University purposes only. 4. That the stamp duties levied on matriculation, on degrees, and on certificates of degrees, should be remitted.

That as to the Colleges, 1. That all oaths imposed by College statutes, and all declarations against change of statutes, should be prohibited as unlawful. 2. That all Fellowships should be thrown open to all members of the University, wherever born, provided they have taken the degree of Bachelor of Arts, and can produce a proper certificate of character. 3. That persons elected to Fellowships should be released from all restrictions on the tenure of their Fellowships arising from the obligation to enter holy orders, or from that of proceeding to degrees in the faculties of Theology, Law, or Medicine; but that it would be expedient to modify rather than to remove the restrictions arising from the possession of property, and celibacy should still continue to be the necessary condition for holding Fellowships, with certain specified exceptions. 4. That steps should be taken in the various Colleges, to prevent the annual value of any Fellowship from amounting to more than 300*l*., or falling below 150*l*. 5. That no part of the funds of Colleges, except those specifically given for that purpose, should be applied to the purchase of advowsons. 6. That in Colleges where there is more than one foundation, all Fellows should be placed on the same footing, both as to rights and duties. 7. That for the election of Fellows and Scholars in the larger Colleges, Boards should be formed, consisting of not less than twelve, and including the Head and all Fellows engaged in education. 8. That a certain number of Fellowships should be, for the present at least, appropriated for the encouragement of the new studies introduced into the academical system. 9. That if necessary, the Visitor should have power to issue a commission, for the re-examination of candidates for Fellowships, on appeal from rejected candidates. 10. That all Scholarships should be thrown open to British subjects under the age of nineteen, of whatever lineage and birth-place. The only exceptions to this are, that certain Scholarships in Jesus College should be reserved for persons born and educated in Wales, and that certain Scholarships in Colleges connected with particular schools should be reserved for persons educated at those schools. 11. That no Scholarships or exhibitions in the gift of Colleges, should be tenable for more than five years, and that in no case should a Scholarship lead to a Fellowship without fresh competition. 12. That College revenues should be made, to a certain extent, available for the education of the University, and that by the appropriation of funds given for Lectureships or Fellowships, Professorships should be endowed, in Corpus Christi, in Magdalen, Merton, Queen's, and New College. 13. That these Professor-Fellows should not be elected by the College-electors, but that such Fellowships should follow the Professorships to which they may be respectively attached. 14. That the Heads of Colleges should be selected from any persons who have taken the degree of Master of Arts, and that the election to these offices should, if possible, be left to the Fellows of the College. 15. That in all cases the Visitors should be empowered to visit their Colleges and to correct abuses, and that the Visitors should be called upon to lay a copy of a report to be received from the Head of the College on the state, discipline, studies, and revenues of the College before the Sovereign, with such observations as he may think fit to make. 16. That the

Head and Fellows in each society shall have power, under such control as may be thought expedient, to alter or abrogate statutes, and to frame new statutes as occasion may require.

These are the alterations which are proposed by the Commission.

The question naturally arises, where, if anywhere, does the power lie to make these alterations?

Does it lie with the College, or with the University, or with the Visitors, or with the Sovereign, or with Parliament?

The Colleges of Oxford were founded from the end of the thirteenth century to the beginning of the eighteenth, fourteen of the nineteen by Roman Catholics. As already remarked, they were founded for literary and religious purposes, and largely for the support of "poor and indigent college clerks, who are bound to apply themselves to the study of philosophy and theology according to the ordinances of the statutes." The celebration of prayers and masses for the souls of founders and benefactors, was, no doubt, an important collateral object with some of the Roman Catholic founders, but it does not appear that it was the chief object. All persons on the foundation previous to the Reformation were *clerici.*

But to return to the question asked above. According to the legal opinion expressed by Mr. Dampier, one of the Commission, "the power of allowing college statutes which exists elsewhere than in Parliament, is conjointly in the Sovereign, the Society, and in the founder's heir. If the Sovereign be the founder, or if there be no heir of the subject founder, the Sovereign and the Society are sufficient."

That some mode should be adopted, by which changes may be made in the administration of the University, appears to be the general wish of the intelligent portion of the people of Great Britain. And we are inclined to the opinion, that, notwithstanding the difficulties in the case, a way will either be discovered or made for accomplishing some of these changes. Our views on this point we reserve for another place.

Having presented our readers with a brief abstract from the Report of the Oxford University Commission, we proceed now to the second work at the foot of this article. Mr. Bristed, after graduating with honor at Yale, and spending one year at New Haven as a resident graduate, entered the University of Cambridge, England, as a student in Trinity College, where he took one of the Scholarships, and where he remained five years. He thus had the best opportunities to form a correct opinion of the system of education in Cambridge. In his preface he remarks that he " writes this book for three reasons:

" First, very little is accurately known in this country about the English Universities.

" Secondly, most of what we have respecting those institutions, comes through the medium of popular novels and other light literature, frequently written by non-University men, and almost always conveying an erroneous and unfavorable idea of the Universities.

" Thirdly and principally, there are points in an English education which may be studied with profit, and from which we may draw valuable hints."

We introduce this book to our readers, not for the purpose of criticism to which it is open, but to carry out the object of the writer, and assist our readers to form a correct idea of education as carried on in an English University. Many of the statements contained in this article in respect to Oxford, will apply to Cambridge with certain specific differences, so that the second work may serve as a comment upon the first.

On the second page we have a description of a college structure :—

" You enter, then, by a portal neither particularly large nor very striking in its appearance, but rather the reverse, into a spacious and elegant square. There are neat grass plots and walks, a fountain in the centre; on one side stands a well proportioned chapel, in one corner you catch a glimpse through a tantalizing grating of a beautiful garden, appropriated to the delectation of the authorities. In a second court you find sounding and venerable cloisters, perhaps a veritable structure of monkish times; if not, a satisfactory imitation of that period. And as you look on the walls, here rich with sculptured ornaments, there covered with trailing and festooning ivy, the theory and the idea of a college edifice begin to strike you: its front is inside for its own benefit; it turns its back upon the vulgar outside. But you have not yet fathomed and sounded the spirit of seclusion. The entries are narrow and low; the staircases narrow and tortuous; the iron bound doors closed by some mysterious spring; or open only to show another door within, look like portals to a feudal dungeon. But up those breakneck staircases, and inside those formidable doors (sometimes with the additional preliminary of a small dark passage), are luxurious suites of rooms, not exactly like those of a Parisian hotel, or a 'double house' in the Fifth Avenue, but quite as beautiful and much more comfortable. The apartments and the entrance seem made in inverse proportion to each other; a mere hole in the wall sometimes leads you to half a house of rooms; and most cosy rooms they are, with their prodigiously thick walls, that keep out the cold in winter, and the heat, when there is any, in summer; their impregnable *sporting doors* that defy alike the hostile dun and the too friendly 'fast man,' and all their quaint appurtenances, such as book-cases of the true scholastic sort, sunk into and forming a part of the wall, so that it would not be easy to appropriate them or the space they occupy to any other purpose; queer little nooks of studies, just large enough to hold a man in an arm chair and a big dictionary; unexpected garrets which the very occupant of the rooms never goes into without an air of enterprise and mystery, and which the old priests used for oratories—perhaps; the modern Cantabs keep their wine in them."—Pp. 2, 3.

"Studying in vacation? Even so; for you may almost take it for granted as a general rule that college regulations and customs in England are just the reverse of what they are in America. In America you rise and recite to your instructor who is seated; in England you sit and construe to him as he stands at his desk. In America you go sixteen times a week to chapel or woe be to you; but then you may stay out of your room all night for a week together, and nobody will know or care. In England you have about eleven chapels to keep, and may choose your own time of day, morning or evening, to keep them; but you cannot get out of college after ten at night, and if being out, you stay till after twelve, you are very likely to hear of it next morning. In America you may go about in any dress that does not outrage decency, and it is not uncommon for youths to attend chapel and 'recitation room' in their ragged dressing gowns, with perhaps a pretext of a cloak; in England you must scrupulously observe the academical garb while within the college walls, and not be too often seen wearing white great coats or other eccentric garments under it. In America the manufacture of coffee in your room will subject you to suspicion, and should that bugbear, the tutor, find a bottle of wine on your premises, he sets you down as a hardened reprobate; in England you may take your bottle or two or six with as many friends as you please, and unless you disturb the whole court by your exuberant revelry, you need fear no annoyance from your tutor; nay expand your supper into a stately dinner, and he will come (public tutor or private) like a brick as he is, and consume his share of the generous potables, yea, take a hand in your rubber afterwards. In America you may not marry, but your tutor can; in England you may marry, but he can't. In America you never think of opening a book in vacation; in England the vacations are the times when you read most. Indeed, since vacations occupy more than half of the year, he who keeps them idle will not do much work during his college course. Then in vacation, particularly the long, there is every facility for reading—no large dinner or wine or supper parties, no rowing men making a noise about the courts, no exciting boat-races, no lectures (owing to the private-tutorial system, the public lectures, with some happy exceptions, are rather in the way of than any help to the best men), the chapel rules looser than ever, the town utterly dull and lifeless."—Pp. 77, 78.

"The private tutor at an English University, corresponds, as has been already observed, in many respects to the *professor* at a German. The German professor is not necessarily attached to any specific chair; he receives no fixed stipend, and has not public lecture-rooms; he teaches at his own house, and the number of his pupils depends on his reputation. The Cambridge private tutor is also a graduate, who takes pupils at his rooms in numbers proportionate to his reputation and abilities. And although while the German professor is regularly licensed as such by his University, and the existence of the private tutor *as such* is not even officially recognized by his, still this difference is more apparent than real;

for the English University has *virtually* licensed the tutor to instruct in a particular branch by the standing she has given him in her examinations. But the private tutor's office, is somewhat peculiar in the details of instruction, owing to the causes which first called the system into being, and now perpetuate it.

"The publicity given to College and University honors, and the importance assigned to them, have been already more than once alluded to. They exceed anything of which we have any conception in our academical institutions. True, the publicity does not come in the same way; there is no crowding of commencements to hear the young men make speeches; but if a comparatively small number of the public come to gaze at the successful student, his name goes forth to all who read the papers—for in every newspaper not only the results of the degree examination and the University prizes, but all the College examinations, and College prizes, are conspicuously reported. When I was elected Scholar of Trinity, Dr. Whewell thought it worth while to write express to Mr. Everett, announcing the fact in advance of the press; as if our minister would be justified in regarding it as a national matter. When an acquaintance of mine, who was related to a member of the cabinet, wished for a start in the diplomatic line, the statesman's first advice to him was, be sure to get a wranglership! As to the first men of the year there is no end of the celebrities for the time being."—Pp. 146, 147.

But besides the reputation, success in Scholarship brings with it "solid testimonies in the shape of books, plate, or money." A Trinity scholarship is worth from £60 to £40 a year. Some of the small College scholarships are worth £100 a year. A Fellowship gives an income of from £200 to £400. "A friend of mine was during his third year, between school exhibitions, College scholarships and prizes, and the University scholarship, in the receipt of more than *seventeen hundred* dollars." "Indeed, it is a common saying and hardly an exaggerated one, that a poor student, by taking a high degree, supports, not only himself, but his mother and sisters for life."

"The purpose served by a private tutor is to assist a student to supply any deficiencies in his preparation for entering the University; and to direct the study so that it shall not be wasted. An ordinary tutor takes five or six pupils a day, giving an hour to each. One of great celebrity will take twice as many, if a classic, or four times as many, if a mathematician."

"The student reading with a classical tutor translates to him from some (prepared) author, brings him composition prepared at home, and writes out in the tutor's rooms, examination fashion, both translations and compositions, which after being corrected, are compared with the tutor's models. As much of the pupil's reading must be done by himself, the great object of the tutor is composition, but he also serves as a general commentator, and last resort in difficulties; it is also his business to make selections of hard passages from authors whom the student may not have time and inclination to read the whole of, and to point out the proper books for 'cram,' and philological information."—P. 149.

The regular fee of a private tutor is £7 a term, if you go to him on alternate days, or £14 if every day.

The following is the account which he gives of Eton College:

"It is a singular spectacle for an American to see numbers of youths eighteen or nineteen years old, who, in his own country, would call themselves and be called young men, leaders of fashionable society, perhaps—going about in boyish costume, and evidently in the *status* of boys. What increases the singularity of the appearance is, that the Englishman's physical development is more rapid than that of the American, of the Northern States at least; thus the Etonian of nineteen is as old in appearance as the New Yorker and Bostonian of twenty-one. They all wear white cravats and black beavers; caps are forbidden, otherwise there is no uniformity of costume, and the juvenile round jacket is as common as the manly coat upon strapping young fellows nearly six feet high. Still, however you may *dress* persons of that age, it is not possible to confine them fully to the discipline of boys; the upper forms *will* walk out into the town of Windsor, and should one of them meet a tutor, he takes refuge in a shop, the tutor, by a long established fiction, making believe not to see him."

"There are always several hundred boys at Eton; at that period (1845) it numbered more than seven hundred. About one-tenth of these are Collegers. The Collegers are the nucleus of the whole system, and the only original part of it, the paying pupils (*oppidans, town boys*), being, according to the general belief, an after-growth. They (the Collegers) are educated gratuitously, and such of them as have nearly, but not quite reached the age of nineteen, when a vacancy in King's College, Cambridge, occurs, are elected scholars there forthwith, and provided for during life—or until marriage."—P. 262.

We have the following account of Dr. Whewell. "Dr. Whewell's accession to the Mastership of Trinity might well have been an era in the history of that royal and religious institution":—

"The new head was a gentleman of most commanding personal appearance, and the very sound of his powerful voice betokened no ordinary man. He was a remarkably good rider even in a country of horsemen, and the anecdote was often told and not altogether repudiated by him, how in his younger days, about the time of his ordination, a pugilist, in whose company he accidentally found himself while traveling, audibly lamented that such lusty thews and sinews should be thrown away on a parson."—P. 87.

"A young man who enters there (Cambridge), and is disposed to find a *truly* 'good set,' can find one, or indeed form his choice among several sets of really virtuous and religious men. It was my comfort to know many right worthy of the name of Christians according to the highest standard that was ever lived up to; men of no particular clique or theological school, but holding various opinions and coming from various places and teachers; pupils of Arnold from Rugby; Evangelicals from King's College, London; other King's College London men of the eclectic stamp, followers of Professor Maurice, who, looked at from a Presbyterian point of view, might be called high churchmen; Eton men, who were yet more eclectic, and had trained themselves *nullius jurare in verba magistri.* Men who differed in many things, but agreed in being sincere Christians, whether you regarded their faith or their practice; and whose conduct strikingly exemplified that common sense of religion, which is so conspicuous in the writings of Whately, Arnold, and other liberal Churchmen, and of which a really good Englishman, when you find one, presents the very best specimen in his life. They seemed every day to solve that most difficult problem of 'being in the world, not of it.'"—P. 352.

The Universities of Oxford and Cambridge have been called the "two eyes of England." They were long the instruments of vision for the nation at home and abroad, in the British isles, and in the four quarters of the globe. What they saw was communicated in appropriate voices to the world. They were considered as the supreme arbiters on all questions relating to science and literature, morals and religion. To them kings and statesmen resorted for a solution of their doubts. In them was concentrated a learned order, who, in succession, received, as it were by inheritance, the theoretical and the practical knowledge of the times, as well as learning proper. From each went forth into active and professional life, men of cultivated minds, scholars, divines, jurists, acquainted with political truth in its elements, who carried with them a controlling and a salutary influence into Church and State, enlightening the understanding, purifying the heart, and refining the manners of the nation. We see these worthies through the mists of ages "in long procession calm and beautiful," with their eyes raised towards the fountain of truth, with a prayer in their hearts for heavenly guidance. In the middle ages, during the rise of classical learning, during the Reformation, during the turbulent times of the first Charles and of the Protectorate of Cromwell, and, indeed, down to the present day, these institutions have been the conservators of sound learning, and of the orthodox faith. They were the light of the world; they were the salt of the earth. And thousands even now look to the one or the other as their Alma Mater, from whose nourishing bosom they derived the "sincere milk of the word," until they grew up to the stature of intellectual manhood.

But an opinion hostile to the universities, as at present constituted, has grown up extensively in England, especially among Dissenters and Roman Catholics. It is openly asserted, that they do not accomplish the purposes for which they were founded; that being established to meet the wants of former generations, they are not adapted to the present, inasmuch as the present differs from the former; that they have grown into the decrepitude of age ; that though they have been called the "eyes of England," she sees none the better for them ; that though "the light of the body is the eye," yet the light that is in them is but darkness, or, at best, only sufficient to render the "darkness visible ;" that instead of moving on with the age, they are stationary ; that, in the language of Dugald Stewart, in his remarks concerning some of the religious and academic institutions of some parts of Europe, "immovably moored to the same station by the strength of their cables and the weight of their anchors, they enable him (the historian) to measure the rapidity of the current by which the rest of the world is borne along."

In view of the present condition of the universities, questions like the following naturally suggest themselves : Ought changes to be made ? if so, what changes ? and how should they be made ? These questions are now before the British people, as most important questions in their bearing upon learning and religion.

I. Ought any changes to be made ? That there ought to be any radical changes in the organic structure, or in the working functions of the universities, we are not disposed to admit. Such changes can neither constitutionally nor righteously be made. They would be a violation of duties owed to the founders of the colleges, to the personal incumbents in office, to those who have been educated at the universities, and to the whole nation, whose faith and honor are pledged to the maintenance of chartered rights.

It would, moreover, be bad policy to make such changes, inasmuch as it would be virtually a declaration either that the government would not keep faith with the universities, or that the universities, having accepted a valuable trust from the founders, under the sanction of the government, will not keep faith with the dead. It would be virtually a declaration to those who are disposed, by their will or otherwise, to bestow their treasures upon institutions of learning, that these treasures may, after they are in their graves, be applied in other ways, or for other purposes than those which they should prescribe. The consequence would be that no prudent man would dare to endow institutions of learning for special purposes.

But that some changes can be constitutionally and righteously made there is no doubt. Many changes, indeed, have already been made, in which all were agreed, and these may be regarded as the pledge and the earnest of other important changes. Every literary institution is to greater or less extent empirical, and is not found, from experiment in its working processes, to be incapable of improvement. Every such institution is found, on trial, to be defective in some of its arrangements, in other words, is not perfect, and, therefore, can be improved by changes judiciously introduced.

II. The second question, namely, what changes should be made? it is not so easy to answer. They must evidently be such as will help to accomplish the purposes of the founders in the way pointed out by them. They must be such as pertain to the accidents, and not such as pertain to the essential principles of their structure and functions. In ascertaining what were their purposes, we are to interpret their language in a liberal spirit, and feel bound not more by the exact letter than by its general scope.

On a former page we have stated with great particularity the changes which have been proposed, especially in Oxford. The object aimed at by the changes proposed is to bring the university of Oxford into harmony with the spirit of the age in which we live, and enable the graduates to go forth to their several posts of duty to supply the wants of the present time. What is said of Oxford is likewise, to a great extent, said of Cambridge, though not with the same emphasis. The universities, it is asserted, established as they were in former ages, were, in their spirit and form, in harmony with the ages in which they were established. But the spirit of those ages no longer exists, but has given place to another spirit in the British nation and the world. Hence arises the necessity of introducing such changes as shall make them the same to the present age that they were to those ages in which they were established.

Now, in this reasoning there is a fallacy as well as a truth. The fallacy is found in the assumption, that the universities were, when they were established, the exponents of the spirit of those ages; whereas, in fact, they were the exponents of a few leading minds, but not of the ages generally. They were the exponents of men like Alfred, and Baliol, and Walter de Merton, and Walter Stapleton, and others, who in succession, established the several colleges of Oxford. They were the exponents of men like Hugh Basham, and Richard Baden, and Henry of Monmouth, and others, who in succession established the several colleges of Cambridge. But they and other founders differed very widely from the great mass of the British nation in their spirit.

And moreover, the founders took measures in the very establishment of these institutions, that those who frequented them, should be sequestered from society for the very purpose of making them *differ* from the masses. They evidently intended that the universities should rear up the highest style of scholars, the highest style of Christians, the highest style of men, by excluding them from society in general, and bringing them into association with the best specimens of humanity. Indeed, in some of the colleges express rules were enacted, that no student should be permitted to enter into the house of a layman resident in the town of Oxford. It was evidently the design of the founders, that the universities should take promising young men away from the turbulence and corruption of the times, bring them into communion with everything that is pure, and noble, and manly, and afterwards send them out into the world to regenerate and reform it.

When, therefore, it is asserted by the root-and-branch men, that there ought to be radical reforms in the universities in order to bring them into harmony with the spirit of the age, we say in reply, that the assertion is based on an assumption that is not strictly true. The founders did not design that the universities should be conformed to the spirit of the age, which largely was a bad spirit, but that the spirit of the age should be conformed to the spirit in them, which was a better spirit. We cannot believe, then, that they would wish them to be conformed to the spirit of the age now, any more than they wished them to be conformed to the spirit of the age then. But there is a sense in which the reasoning we are considering is sound. In order to accomplish all the general purposes of their creation, they must be adapted to those purposes, as means to an end. Now it must be conceded that they are not thus entirely adapted to supply the wants of the church and the state, the nation and the world. There is in them a vast amount of learning strictly so called, and of science in the proper meaning of the word, of talent and of piety, which are stagnant. There are in them noble libraries, the treasured stores of knowledge, the works of the great ones in the earth's history, of the sages, the historians, the philosophers, which are not read, much less studied, by any considerable number. There are wise men and good men, eminent scholars and eminent Christians, congregated in them, who are as a light shining in a dark place, and the darkness comprehending it not. There are collected in these institutions, something like three thousand young men, who come from some of the best families, and some of the best schools in the United Kingdom; from Eton, and Westminster, and Rugby, and Harrow. And having been nurtured in them, they then go forth, into the learned professions at home, or into the colonies, to give a character to those professions; or into rural life to refine, and dignify, and adorn it; or it may be, into the House of Lords, or the House of Commons, to control and direct the energies of the most enlightened and powerful nation on the globe. And yet there are complaints apparently well founded, that these universities do not, in their religious or their literary polity, exert their appropriate influence upon the masses of the people. We have already specified the changes which are proposed, on a former page. These changes relate, 1, to the state of discipline; 2, to the studies; 3, to the management of the revenue; 4, to the condition of particular colleges.

III. We have now come to the third question, How shall these changes be made? The literary institutions of each civilized nation have a character of their own, and are so related to the other institutions of the country, that we cannot speak confidently as to the manner in which changes should be made in them, without being well acquainted with those other institutions. In making any of the changes proposed by the Commission, as stated in the article in our former pages, regard should be had to the prescribed purposes of the founders, to the views of the visitors, of the sovereign, of Parliament, and to the rights of the several colleges, and to those of the universities at large. The wise men of Great Britain are, we doubt not, perfectly competent to take care of the whole subject, and to determine without our aid, whether any changes should be made, what those changes should be, and how they should be introduced. These questions we have brought forward, not so much for the purpose of answering them, as for that of laying them before our readers for their consideration.

We cannot reason very conclusively from American colleges to English universities. There are several points of difference between the two classes of institutions. An English university is strictly a religious institution, and belongs, in a sense, to the national church. The American colleges, which were first established, were, in like manner, consecrated to "Christ and the church." But those more recently established, have shown some tendency, like the primary schools, to lay aside their religious, or at least, their sectarian type.

An English university is national. American colleges are not national. Most belong to some particular religious denomination; some are State institutions.

English universities have foundations for the support of fellowships, which keep a body of able and promising men together under the most favorable circumstances for prosecuting their studies, and thoroughly preparing themselves for eminence, whether as authors or in professional life. American colleges have no such provision.

English universities include in them the idea of a well arranged government, of an exact code of laws, of an active police, a diligent supervision of the students. They were framed on the idea that education includes government as well as instruction; "both the nurture and the admonition of the Lord;" subordition to authority, as well as the acquisition of knowledge. American colleges, the earlier ones, like Harvard and Yale, and Princeton, and others, were established upon the same idea, and long acted upon it, borrowing their notions from England. Indeed, most or all, still to some extent act upon the same idea. But it must be confessed that many of them act upon the French or the German idea, namely, that the "young gentlemen must govern themselves." Indeed, the young gentlemen sometimes have produced the impression, that, not content with governing themselves, they aspire, in their democratic tendencies, to the control of the faculty or trustees in some of their functions, and even to the giving shape to the organic structure of the institution; as if they were the third estate, the popular, and the most important, because the most numerous branch of government.

In English universities young men are placed under their guardianship, that they may be sequestered from the world, and not be governed by its spirit, whether as seen in mercantile pursuits, in war, in politics, or in moral reform. It seems to have been the design of the founders, at least some of them, that the under graduates should not mingle much in society at large. In American colleges, the young men are not so much sequestered from general society, and conform more to its spirit, live less in the past in communion with men of former generations, and more in the future; are prophetic rather than historical in their association of thought. Many act as teachers of the primary schools. A considerable number take an interest in politics, and exercise the right of suffrage in the elections, even though they are obliged for this purpose to give up some of their college exercises and visit their homes. Some of them, in their eagerness to let their light shine before others, are in haste in their early and precocious maturity to be moral reformers, and mingle in society as religious teachers, or exhorters, before they have finished their academical education.

English universities are, to a large extent, from their great wealth, their ancient renown, from the influence of their alumni, independent in their condition, and are, therefore, under little temptation to lower the standard of scholarship and discipline to court popular favor. American colleges, on the other hand, are comparatively poor, and have to depend chiefly on the payment of the term bills for their support, and are thus dependent on the number of students which they can attract and retain. They are, therefore, in their competition with each other for students, under temptation to underbid each other in some way, either by lowering their requisitions, or by shortening the term of study necessary for obtaining a degree, or by abolishing honorary appointments, so that there may be no distinctions which will mortify the proud and lazy, or the diligent and dull, or by granting larger liberties to the students, or by the introduction of parallel popular courses for the masses.

While English universities differ from American colleges in these and in other respects, they likewise agree with them largely in the end aimed at, in the means employed, and in the results accomplished. We propose, in the following remarks, to examine the importance and value of those results; inasmuch as they are doubted by a large class of men, both in the United States and in Great Britain.

Whoever has carefully examined the progress of human improvement in the discovery and application of truth, must have noticed the fact, that questions which, in one age, seemed to be forever settled, are in another agitated with as much zeal as if they had never before been investigated. In the intellectual war between the children of light and the children of darkness, the champions of learning will, on some occasion, go forth and win, with their arms of proof, wide regions of thought from the dominion of error. What they thus win with their good weapons, they regard as their own, to be transmitted to their successors in perpetual right. But their successors find that what they have thus received by inheritance they cannot enjoy in peaceful possession, but that they too, in their turn, must fight over the same battles which others have fought before them.

The questions which are thus litigated from age to age, are not those which are connected with the mathematics or the physical sciences. The discoveries in these branches of knowledge, made in ancient times, have been transmitted from generation to generation, as a patrimonial inheritance entailed and undisputed. From the time that these have fairly been annexed to that intellectual empire, over which cultivated human mind presides, they have been considered as belonging of right to that empire. Out of the tossing ocean of theories and opinions they rose in their solid strength at the call of philosophic genius; as Delos of old in the broad Ægean, at the command of the father of gods, became fixed and immoveable.

The class of questions to which we referred are those that more directly come home to men's business and bosoms. They are practical in their nature, whether they relate to religion, to government, or to education. It is, indeed, mortifying to the pride of knowledge, that after the principles of these important subjects have been settled by a thorough examination, there should still be so many false systems of religion; so many oppressive forms of government; so many absurd plans of education. And still more mortifying is it, instead of pressing on the cause of original investigation and discovery, and the application of truths long since discovered, to hear these truths questioned, and to be obliged, therefore, to spend time and effort in proving what has been proved, and in doing over again what has been well done by others. To this mortifying condition are the friends of learning sometimes brought by those from whom we ought to hope better things, who question the value and the importance of a liberal education.

By a liberal education, we mean what is generally understood by the phrase: viz., such an education as it is the object of the more respectable universities and colleges to communicate. Originally the term meant that kind of education which is suited to a *free man*, in distinction from that which was suited to a slave. It included a knowledge of what were called the liberal arts. These arts were seven in number, viz. Lingua, Tropus, Ratio, Numerus, Tonus, Angulus, Astra, which may be translated Grammar, Rhetoric, Logic, Arithmetic, Music, Geometry, and Astronomy. As new discoveries have been made in science, and as new arts have been invented, endeavors have been made to introduce these discoveries and inventions within the scope of a liberal education, as additional subjects in the regular course of study. Ethics, Physics, and Metaphysics, were soon added.

It may help us the better to understand the meaning of the phrase Liberal Arts, to bring into view, for a moment, the Mechanic arts with which they were contrasted. These were likewise formed into a Latin Hexameter verse,—

Rus, Nemus, Arma, Fabri, Vulnera, Lana, Rates,

which may be translated, Agriculture, Hunting, War, Smithcraft, Surgery, Manufacture of Cloth, Navigation. Besides these there were many others.

Having said thus much on the origin and meaning of the term, liberal education, we can easily understand why the titles, Bachelor of *Arts* and Master of *Arts*, should be given to students to indicate the degree of their advancement in the course of a liberal education.

In order adequately to understand the value and the importance of a liberal education, I would inquire what should be the end of education? If this is settled, all that we have then to do in determining the general question under consideration, is to ascertain how far a liberal education contributes to the legitimate end of education.

The chief end of education, then, is to strengthen, elevate, and refine the soul, in its intellectual and moral faculties, so that, as nearly as possible, it shall resemble God in knowledge, holiness, and happiness.

According to this view, education, as a whole, is the business of life, which we are sent into this world to perform. It is to commence with our intellectual existence, and to be continued until our eyes close in death. Indeed, this world is to be considered as but a school, in the large sense, in which instruction is communicated, discipline administered, and rewards are bestowed; and of which, God is the great teacher.

A liberal education, therefore, is only a part of the whole education which we are receiving in the school of this world; its value and its importance can be proved by showing that it contributes to the legitimate end of our whole education.

We know there are some who seem to consider education to be little more than merely training the bodily powers to employment in some branch of professional industry. The parent seems to suppose that if he has made his son acquainted with some business, in which little more is necessary than a skilful hand and a practiced eye, so that he is called a good workman, he has done for him all that is necessary. Others regard a good education as consisting merely in the cultivation and furniture of the intellect. They make great efforts in their studies, mainly that they may be the better prepared to engage with success in the practice of some of the higher professions. Others still regard a good education as consisting mainly in the cultivation of a graceful expression of the social feelings in the civilities of life; or, in other words, of those polished manners which qualify him who has them to have intercourse with the world as a gentleman.

We apprehend that great practical evils have arisen from such narrow and erroneous views in regard to the chief end of a good education. To this circumstance it is owing that so many have regarded their education, whatever it may be, as valuable only as a means of personal advancement. They regard their education as another would an investment in trade, as the means of making money, or of gaining influence, or of being useful in a particular way. Now an education gained for such a purpose, and adapted to such a purpose, may, in the issue, prove instrumental in accomplishing such an end. It may enable a man to become rich, or influential; it may be useful in a certain sphere. But it does not make good, or wise, or great men. It may make men distinguished in certain professions, but it will cause them to view everything in its relation to these professions, and not in its relations to man or the universe. It will cause them to be blind worshipers of the idols of the Den, and not the enlightened worshipers of the great Divinities.

For the attainment of a liberal education, it is expected that a young man, after going through a certain preparatory course, shall spend four years at college in disciplining his mind by study, and furnishing it with knowledge. During this period it is intended that he shall, in a good degree, be withdrawn from all professional pursuits; that he shall, if need be, leave his father's roof, associate mainly with those who are engaged like himself in the acquisition of knowledge, and in the improvement of their minds. He joins them, at first, as a timid stranger. He is among them, but not of them. By degrees he becomes interested in his companions, in his teachers, in his pursuits. He catches the spirit of the place. If he makes a good use of his opportunities, he finds that, in the course of the four years during the forming period of his character, he has undergone a great change in his tastes, in his associations, in the frame-work of his mind, and in its furniture. And he is never more sensible of this than when he pays a visit to the village or the hamlet where he spent his early years. As he converses with his youthful comrades, who have been stationary while he has been making progress, he perceives, with some little feeling of vanity it may be, on his part, and of envy on theirs, that he has left them far behind in the improvement of his mind. Remember that we are speaking of him who, fired with a generous love of learning, has dedicated days and nights to mental discipline and acquisition: and not of him, who, having assumed her livery, is ever ready to escape from her service as from a drudgery.

In order to understand how it happens that this improvement is made in pursuing a course of liberal education, we would notice, with some particularity, the studies to which he attends during his connection with the college.

The Latin and Greek languages constitute a large and distinctive part of the course in a liberal education. In defence of these we would remark, that men the best qualified to judge have agreed in exalting them to the high standing which they now occupy in collegiate studies. Their opinion of them has resulted from observation and experience. One of them has said that classical literature was the "ark in which all the civilization of the world was preserved during the deluge of barbarism." The revival of learning, after the night of the dark ages had begun to pass off, was chiefly but the increased cultivation of classical literature. Hence it has happened that, in every civilized nation of Europe, its literature is formed upon classical learning as a basis. As we are best acquainted with English literature we can easily understand that the remark is true so far as it is concerned. Classical literature enters into its very structure, and makes a constituent part of it. Classical learning has furnished it largely with words, phrases, allusions, illustrations, sentiments, opinions, reasonings. If from any piece of elegant English composition we should, by any analysis, be able to take away whatever of form and spirit was derived from classical learning, we should, by so doing, take away all its beauty. We should leave only the *caput mortuum*. No one could write a history of English literature, springing as it does from classic fountains, without a knowledge of those languages. No one can adequately understand such a history without the same knowledge. No one can appreciate the higher branches of English literature, unless he has been trained in the school of classic literature.

Hence, it has happened that the literati of all civilized nations of both continents agree in their attachment to classical literature, and insist upon an acquaintance with it as a prerequisite qualification in a candidate for admission into the republic of letters. And, if any should endeavor to get himself enrolled as a free citizen in that republic without this qualification, he would find, as he mingled with the real literati, the *free born* citizens, that he was still, in fact, a stranger and an alien. Thus they would view him; and thus would he view himself.

Besides the fact that classical literature is interwoven in the modern literature of our country, and in that of other civilized countries, it should be remembered that it can be defended on the ground of its own separate and independent merits. The Greek and Latin languages, in prose composition and in poetry, present a standard of taste to which the student can refer his own productions, and those of others, in estimating their excellence. By a standard of taste, we mean what the human mind, when thoroughly instructed and improved, approves. Let the student become familiar with these models of composition, let him learn to admire their structure, their order of thought, their graceful forms of expression, the beauty of their allusions, and the distinctness of their illustrations, and he will, as a matter of course, find his taste elevated and refined. If it is asked, why not go immediately to nature for the improvement of taste, rather than to these? We will give several reasons, if need be, whenever it shall cease to be the approved practice for modern genius to resort for the cultivation of taste to the models of Grecian architecture and Grecian sculpture, and not merely to nature.

Besides the improvement of the taste, every faculty of the mind is invigorated by the study of the Latin and Greek languages. The memory is constantly exercised in learning the rules, and in retaining the meaning of words. The reason is employed and strengthened by applying the rules, by discriminating between the meaning of a word in one place and its meaning in another. Indeed, it is impossible to arrive at the meaning of a single passage, without having reasons pass through the mind. It is impossible to satisfy a competent teacher when reciting to him, without alleging reasons for the construction that is given to a passage. It is impossible to arrive at the general signification of any important word, without going through a course of inductive reasoning; that is, the word must be seen in a number of different connexions of thought, and a general signification adopted, that will include the variety of cases.

We need hardly say, that the habitual contemplation of the many grand and beautiful objects which are addressed to the imagination in the classics, can hardly fail to impart to it activity and vigor.

Such is the advantage of the study of the languages, that it was justly said by the emperor Charles the Fifth, "to learn a new language is to acquire a new soul."

Moreover, it should be remembered that the Latin and Greek are the most perfect languages—unless the Sanscrit is an exception—ever employed by the human voice for the communication of thought. Lord Brougham says of the Greek language, "It traces with ease distinctions, so subtle as to be lost in every other language. It draws lines where all the other instruments of the reason make blots. Nor is it less distinguished by the facilities which it affords to the poet."

Moreover, in the act of translating from the languages, there is a constant effort at composition, so that the pupil thus acquires a more accurate knowledge of his own language than he could in any other way, and learns to express himself in it with perspicuity, precision, and force. President Dwight once remarked, that he never knew but one man who could write the English language correctly, without having studied the classics.

Besides, in order to understand thoroughly the history of a nation, it is necessary to become acquainted with its language. There is such an affinity between language and character, that if one would understand the language of a nation, in its origin and derivation, he must understand the history of that nation. A history of human language is a history of human nature, in the development of thought, feeling, motive, and action. Language is the index of character, and it is recognized as such, not only by men in their intercourse with each other, but likewise by the omniscient judge of all. Even the vocabulary of a nation, independently of its combinations, shows something of the national character; as, for instance, the great number of weapons of attack and defence found in the columns of a Latin dictionary, proves that the Romans were a warlike people.

Finally, the classics are of service to the student in the lofty sentiments of patriotism which they contain. "The public obligations stood in the foreground of all the ancient morality. The idea of the commonwealth as the supreme object of his duty and his solicitude, attracted to itself the strongest emotions in the breast of every virtuous man." This cannot but have a favorable effect in counteracting that supreme selfishness which is the fashion of the present times.

We know it is said that translations will answer every important purpose. This can be said only by him who knows not the difference between the original and the translation. A translation—to borrow an illustration from Don Quixote—is to the original what the wrong side is to the figured side of the tapestry.

An objection is sometimes made, that the influence of the classics, in their exhibition of vice, is corrupting. In reply, we would say, that the evil, whatever it is, is open and undisguised, and, therefore, is not as injurious as many of the novels, much of the poetry, and many of the newspapers of the present day.

It is said that, in the study of the classics, too much time is wasted upon words. In reply, we would say in the language of the French minister, "words are things."

These are a few considerations which go to show the importance of the classics in a course of liberal education. Opposition has been made to them at different periods, only in the issue to show their excellence, and to increase the study of them.

The mathematics make a part of the course in a liberal education. Opposition has been made to them, though not with the same violence as to the classics, for the reason that the various applications of this science to the practical arts of life manifest its importance even to those who see no value in it for the discipline of the mind. Still, however, the question is asked, Why should a student be compelled to devote years to the acquisition of a species of knowledge which is useful only as it enables him to become acquainted with astronomy, navigation, and other sciences, into which mathematics enter, when he expects neither to calculate eclipses, nor to take an observation, nor to make any practical use of those sciences? What has stereographic projection to do with law, or geometry with physic, or conic sections with divinity? Questions like these betray great ignorance of a superior education, and likewise of the relation of one branch of knowledge to other branches. The truth is, "everything throws light upon everything." It is a remark of Fontenelle, quoted with approbation by Dr. Thomas Brown, that a work of morals, of politics, of criticism, and even of eloquence, will, if other circumstances have been the same, be the more beautiful for coming from the hand of a geometrician. Such is the connexion of every science with every other, that the more thoroughly a man is acquainted with any one of them, the better is he qualified, *cœteris paribus*, to think, to write, and to speak on any of the others.

But the grand argument for the study of the mathematics is found in the discipline it affords to the mind. "By the consent of all who have had a good opportunity for judging, it is especially adapted to sharpen the intellect, strengthen the faculty of reason, and thus prepare the mind for the successful investigation of truth." Lord Bacon mentions a writer who, "reflecting that mathematicians being the only set of men who either maintained no controversies, or, at least, soon come to a determination of them, hence apprehended that mathematicians alone were possessed of the right method of inquiry." Accordingly, he endeavored to apply the mathematical method to other subjects. Whether it can be thus advantageously applied, we are not now inquiring. At least it is true, that minds that have been trained in the study of the mathematics are better prepared than others for the investigation of other subjects. It was upon this ground that Plato said, in reference to entering his school, "Let no one enter here who is unacquainted with geometry." Indeed, it is said, that Plato declared that he would have his disciples apply themselves to the study of arithmetic, "that they may learn to withdraw their minds from the ever-shifting spectacle of the visible and tangible world, and fix them on the immutable essence of things."

The physical sciences occupy a portion of attention during the college course. Less opposition has been made to these, and, therefore, less is demanded in the way of defence. We need not say how desirable it is that the sympathies of the soul should be touched into harmony with external nature. The subjects connected with these sciences are valuable, as tending to produce a habit of observing the various phenomena and the general laws of nature. In connexion with natural theology, the study of nature tends to repress a spirit of arrogance, and produce simplicity of character.

The practical application of these sciences to the arts of life, in the increase of the products of agriculture, mechanical and commercial industry, is attended with so many obvious advantages, that even the opposers of colleges make very little opposition to them. We speak of them now only as what should be known by every man who pretends to a superior education. The composition of matter disclosed by chemistry, the laws of motion disclosed by mechanical philosophy, the various forms of vegetable, animal, and mineral existence, as disclosed by natural history; the present state and the past history of the globe we inhabit, as disclosed by geology; the condition and laws of the planetary and stellary systems, so far as they are understood, are appropriate subjects of inquiry for every rational mind; and no man unacquainted with them can be considered as liberally educated.

The study of ourselves, considered as individual and social beings, makes a part of the course of a liberal education.

The study of the laws of the human mind, of human obligations and relative duties, of our individual character, and of the structure of society, deserves the attention of every man who aims at a superior education, as the bare mention of them must show. Γνῶθι σεαυτὸν *e cœlo descendit.* Who would willingly remain ignorant of what the great masters of reason have written on the character of the understanding, on our speculative and our active powers, on the laws of association, on the will, on conscience, on the affections and passions? Who would willingly remain ignorant of what the great teachers of morals have written concerning man as a member of society, and the obligations which he owes to the family, to the community, and to the nation with which he is connected? Who would be willing to have all such books as Locke, and Stewart, and Paley, struck from the list of studies?

In our estimate of a collegiate course of study, we are to bear in mind that it is the object of that course to lay the foundation, not to raise the superstructure; to give a *liberal*, not a *professional* education. Undoubtedly many studies might, with advantage, be added to the list; still we should consider, that though many more should be added, there would many remain behind. All cannot be included. "Life is short, and art is long." There must, then, be a selection, and the only question is, what studies should be prescribed? In reply, we would say, that such studies should be prescribed, and such modes of instruction adopted, as are best adapted to fix the attention, to direct the train of associations, to guide the judgment in the investigation of evidence, to awaken and control the imagination, to arrange the stores of memory, and to animate the powers of genius. And if the studies are properly used which are prescribed in most of the colleges, these results will be produced.

The students, as they meet together two or three times a day, to recite and to hear recitations; to hear lectures and to see experiments, as well as to attend upon text-book instruction; as they pursue their studies at one time alone, at another with their room-mates; as they are forced to give reasons in the recitation-room as well as to make statements; as they have intercourse with those who are in the same circumstances with them, who meet with the same difficulties, or who have passed through them; as they discuss subjects in classes, or before the societies—do, as a matter of fact, learn to study, learn to think, learn to speak. We never knew of an individual who made a good use of his advantages during a four years' residence at any respectable college, who was not ready to say that he had derived great benefit in the improvement of his mind. We could summon, if need be, a cloud of witnesses, both of the living and the dead, to bear testimony in favor of a collegiate education. "They would tell us of those powerful correctives of singularity and frowardness which are found in the attrition of mind against mind, on a spot where different classes live together under a system of general discipline; of the force of established rules in producing early habits of regularity and decorum; of the strong though easy yoke that is thrown over the impetuosity of youth; of the propensity of the heart, unassailed by care, to form the best friendships and from the best motives; of the efficacy of oral instruction diligently communicated; of the competitions that will arise among numbers whose judgments on their respective qualifications are too frequent to be eluded and too impartial to be resisted."

Thus Dr. Parr, speaking of Bishop Lowth, says: "He had been educated in the university of Oxford; he had spent years there in a well regulated course of discipline and study; and in the agreeable and improving commerce of gentlemen and scholars; in a society where emulation without envy, ambition without jealousy, contention without animosity, incited industry and awakened genius; where a liberal pursuit of knowledge and a genuine freedom of thought was raised, encouraged, and pushed forward by example and by commendation." These are the natural feelings of a son towards his alma mater. "A liberal mind will," says Gibbon, "delight to cherish and celebrate the memory of its parents; and the Teachers of Science are the parents of the mind."

A similar feeling we entertain, almost as a matter of course, towards certain favorite authors with whom we became acquainted during our connexion with college. And here we cannot do better than to quote a passage which we lately met with in an article on a different general subject. "Nothing can be more natural than that a person of sensibility and imagination should entertain a respectful and affectionate feeling towards those great men with whose minds he had, in their works, daily communion. The debt which he owes to them is incalculable. They have guided him to truth. They have filled his mind with noble and graceful images. They have stood by him in all vicissitudes. They have been his comforters in sorrow, nurses in sickness, companions in solitude. Time glides by. Fortune is inconstant. Tempers are soured. Bonds which seemed indissoluble, are daily sundered by interest, by emulation, by caprice. But no such causes can affect the silent intercourse which we hold with the highest of human intellects. These are the old friends who are never seen with new faces, who are the same in wealth or in poverty, in glory or in obscurity."*

Having spoken of the importance and value of a liberal education, chiefly in regard to its influence upon the individual, in elevating his intellectual, and ripening his moral nature ; we proceed to inquire concerning its value and importance in qualifying him to be useful to his fellow-men, in the relations of society.

In order to do justice to this subject, we would remark that the opposers of learning have said that a philosopher is one who studies everything and does nothing ; that he is an intellectual miser, who hoards up his stores of knowledge, without any disposition to impart them to others. They have said that the tastes and habits of a literary man disqualify him for acting his part in the drama of crowded life, with pleasure to himself or with advantage to others. There is a fascination, say they, in literary pursuits, which is apt to make men forget the duties they owe to society. While reposing in the soft

* Review of Bacon, Edin. 1839.

shades of retirement, and inhaling the fragrance of the balm diffused around them, they are in danger of giving themselves up to a sort of luxurious indifference, and to think very little of the part God calls them to act in the busy scenes of life. Or, if they are not so much absorbed in the pleasures of these pursuits as to forget that man, as an active being, has important duties to perform, they are still prone to look upon these duties as somewhat irksome and unworthy of their elevated and refined regard. They attach a sort of vulgarity and repulsiveness to the every day business of a man who is going through the drudgery of active life. When the mere man of letters sees the statesman, for instance, toiling amid the dry documents of finance, and projecting schemes for the promotion of mere national wealth, how apt is he to be disgusted with the employment, as destitute of everything that can charm the taste, or quench the thirst for knowledge. Here are no shady groves, nor winding rivulets, no Castalian fountains nor Arcadian landscapes; the rugged paths of business are not the creation of fancy. They call for the sober toils of intellect, working its way through a long process of thought and calculation, and putting to flight the images and delights of classical associations.

In some such language as this, the opposers of learning and of literary men, have expressed their opposition. Or they will select such an instance as Gray, the poet, who spent his life in the enjoyment of the luxuries of literature, in seclusion from the busy world, as a fair illustration of the injurious effects of learning.

Now we are ready to grant that some who have distinguished themselves in the walks of learning, have proved that they were entirely unqualified for the duties of active life. It may be true of the proud, shy poet, just mentioned, that he was no better qualified for the duties of active life, than he was to excel in horsemanship, having never, it is said, in his life, mounted a horse. It may be true that Bacon, the great philosopher, never ought to have been Lord Chancellor, and that Addison ought not to have been Secretary of State. It may be true that Gibbon never distinguished himself in the House of Commons, nor Byron in the House of Lords. It may be true that some have plodded in their closets until, like the "great owl, or the little owl," they cannot bear the strong light of public life. But for these few, we can point to thousands who have drunk copiously from the fountain of learning, and, like a "giant refreshed by wine," have felt themselves invigorated by the draught.

It hardly needs to be mentioned, that the great points to be gained in the course of a liberal education, are the *discipline* and *furniture* of the mind; expanding its powers, and storing it with knowledge. And the question at the present moment is, whether a person who has disciplined his mind by exercise, and furnished it with knowledge, is better prepared to bless mankind by his efforts than one who has not? This question resolves itself in the very statement of it. According to the views already presented, a liberal education, as obtained at college, is only the foundation of a superior education, the superstructure of which is to be raised and finished by the individual himself, in subsequent life.

Then a liberal education is important as a preparation for professional education, and is in this way valuable as a means of usefulness. We do not mean that this is true in regard to every profession. Some professions in the minute sub-divisions of labor, instead of demanding much mental discipline, require little besides bodily strength and activity. Some professions, however, on the other hand, require, in order to excel in them, all the discipline and all the knowledge that a liberal education can furnish.

This is true eminently of what are called the learned professions. This is true of the profession of law; which requires, in order to understand its distinctions and to comprehend its principles, an intellect sharpened by exercise, and enlarged by study. It requires a mind trained to the analysis of thought; trained to the interpretation of language; trained to a correct and graceful expression of opinions and sentiments.

Moreover, if great thoroughness of legal education is desired, a knowledge of the Latin language is indispensable; inasmuch as a thorough legal education is unattainable without the study of Civil Law, which is the term used for Roman Law.* No one can successfully study Roman Law, without an acquaintance with the Latin language. Roman Law, it is acknowledged, affords the example of a completer and more self-connected system than the jurisprudence of any modern nation can exhibit. Evidently a minute and comprehensive knowledge of that system, in its principles and their application, cannot be acquired without a philological knowledge of the language in which this law is written; and an historical knowledge of the circumstances under which it was developed.

Besides, many of the law maxims, and moreover, the decisions of the English courts, which are Common Law, were made by men whose minds were intimately conversant with classical literature, and trained to habits of mathematical demonstration, logical precision, and rhetorical illustration; the most of them were made by men educated at the universities. To enter fully into their labors, it is necessary that the mind of the student should be trained as theirs were. So beneficial are the mathematics which contribute to this training, that many have been ready to say, that they learned how to state an argument extemporaneously from being obliged to give demonstrations of mathematical propositions, while in college. Indeed, one of the most distinguished and successful advocates in our land was accustomed immediately before going into court to make some great plea, to demonstrate a difficult proposition in Euclid as a mental preparation.

It should be remarked, in this connexion, that such is the advantage of a liberal, in the way of preparation for a professional, education, that in some of the states and in some of the courts a longer period of study by two years was required for admittance to the bar, for those who have not, than for those who have been graduated at a college.

---

* Many of the terms used are expressed in the Latin Language.

What is true of the profession of law, is, to a large extent, true of that of medicine. "Among the most illustrious scholars, since the revival of letters, no inconsiderable number of them have been physicians." Formerly, indeed, all medical works were written in Latin. Though this is no longer the case, still traces of this language are frequent in all valuable medical works. But the intellectual training in colleges will be of great service to the physician in teaching him to reason upon correct principles, concerning the nature of various diseases and the modes of their cure. Moreover, in the natural sciences, he becomes acquainted with facts and principles that are of great value in their immediate application in the practice of his profession. Thus, in the discipline of mind and in the knowledge furnished by a liberal education, will he, when called to exercise the divine art of healing, have resources, which will supersede the necessity which some feel themselves to be under of resorting to the arts of quackery and imposture. We have never heard of a physician, liberally educated, who adopted the Thomsonian practice, though it is possible that there are those thus educated who have done so, inasmuch as there are quacks in all professions.

The profession of theology peculiarly demands the preparation furnished by a liberal education.

What is Protestant theology but certain doctrines and precepts drawn from the Bible, by the application of philology and criticism? And how can this philology and criticism be applied without a profound knowledge of the language and history of the ancient world? Learning is necessary in order to discover the evidences of Christianity; to examine the miracles that were performed; the prophecies that have been fulfilled; the correspondence between sacred and profane history; the harmony of the doctrines revealed with each other and with nature. Revelation being conveyed to us in written language, cannot be understood in its import without a knowledge of the laws of interpretation. To understand the laws of interpretation, as applied to the Bible, an intimate acquaintance with language generally, viz., in those points in which all languages agree, is necessary. Besides this, there are interpolations, and omissions, and various readings in the text; there are conjectural emendations; and profound learning is necessary to judge of these. Moreover, a man's mind, who enters the ministry, must be disciplined by study to take in a wide view of divine truth, so that he shall be consistent with himself in his statements.

And, besides all this, it should be remembered that, in the Greek church and in the Roman Catholic church, men of learning have taken care of the sacred codes; have defended them; have examined them; have enforced their truths on the consciences of men; have transmitted them to us; and no one can adequately understand the history of the doctrines of the church, or church history in general, or the lives and characters of good men of past ages, or enter into their labors, without having disciplined his mind and stored it with knowledge.

And in addition to this, it should be remembered that "in Germany the Reformation proceeded from, and was carried through by, the *Academical Divines;* the princes, the cities, and the people only obeyed the impulse first given and subsequently continued from the universities. In its origin, the religious revolution was, in the empire, a learned revolution, and every permanent modification and every important movement had some learned theologian for its author. From this circumstance, the determination of religious opinions then was naturally viewed as a privilege of erudition—as more the function of the universities than of the church, the people, or the State."

In order to understand the history of the Reformation and the doctrines of the great Reformers, in order to appreciate the value of their labors and the excellence of their character, in order to accord to such men as Luther and Melancthon the admiration which is their due, it is necessary to enter into their spirit, to drink at the same classic fountains at which they drank.

The great lights of the English church were men who had

enjoyed the advantages of an education at either Oxford or Cambridge. The divines who gave a character to the religion of New England, were men liberally educated.

It was originally intended that the priest's lips should keep knowledge, and that the people should seek the law at his mouth. The great and important subjects that he was required to investigate, pertaining as they do to the character of God and his moral government, and the duties and destinies of men, require the best human talents, improved by the highest cultivation. Besides this, he is required, in his official duty, to come in contact with his people at many points; and, therefore, at all points should he be armed with the truth, that he may give to every one a portion in due season.

It has long been a favorite opinion of ours, that ministers should take an active part in the great cause of popular education; and in order to do it successfully, they must themselves be thoroughly educated.

As we attach importance to this opinion, we shall dwell on the arguments in support of it with some particularity.

Our first argument is derived from the *nature of Christianity*. It is a religion which addresses accountable beings through the medium of their intellect; and just in proportion as you improve their intellect, will you enlarge their capacity of being influenced in their moral nature by the power of divine truth. Now, as we know that Christianity is a general provision for the spiritual wants of all mankind we may be sure that all classes of the community ought to experience so much of intellectual cultivation as shall qualify them to receive the benefit of that provision.

Other religious systems were designed, at least in some of their parts, for only certain privileged orders in the community; while the many, the οἱ πολλοὶ, as they were styled by the Greeks, were excluded from a participation. Those systems had their exoteric doctrines, which were communicated to the common people; and their esoteric doctrines, which were communicated only to the few, to the initiated, as they were styled.

But among Christians it is not so. To the poor the gospel is preached; to them it is given to know the mysteries of the kingdom. Now, in order that this preaching be effectual in any high degree, in order that these mysteries be understood adequately, mental cultivation is necessary. Evidently it is the duty of the minister to endeavor to promote the intellectual improvement of those who may come within the sphere of his influence; for, in accomplishing this, he is preparing them to understand and appreciate the truths and duties of religion.

Our second argument is derived from the *character* of *Protestantism.* The right of private judgment, in opposition to all human claims to a dictatorial authority in matters of faith, is an essential article in Protestantism. Now, this single fact that we call no man master, is proof that the followers of Christ are regarded as being capable of forming an opinion for themselves; and, in order to form a correct opinion, some degree of mental cultivation is necessary.

The Roman church, on the other hand, acted on the principle that ignorance is the mother of devotion; as well she might, since an implicit faith in her decisions was enforced on all her adherents. Indeed, in certain periods of that hierarchy, when men seemed to consider religion and philosophy as mortal enemies of each other, that what is philosophically true may be theologically false, *carbonaria fides*, or implicit faith, was, in fact, the faith of a large part of that church.

But the Reformers, in opposition to this, took the ground that the Bible is the religion of Protestants; and, in doing this, they virtually declared themselves in favor of elevating the condition of the great mass of the people up to such a level that, in the exercise of the right of private judgment, in the formation of their religious opinions from the Bible, they would not wrest it to their own destruction. It is true, that what is now understood by the term popular education, was not then thought of as practicable. But they adopted such principles, and pursued such a course in diffusing intelligence among the people, as justifies us, so far as their authority is concerned, in promoting the cause of popular education. Romanists might commit the error of opposing revelation to reason, and in so doing, might extinguish the light of both; but Protestants, if they are true to their principles, must bestow the greatest possible cultivation on reason, in order that the truths of revelation may be the more distinctly seen and the more deeply felt.

Our third argument is derived from the practice and principles of our *Puritan forefathers*. Besides the general principles of Protestantism, they adopted extensively the opinion that the people were capable of self-government in political and religious affairs, and this implies that they should be educated. In accordance with this, they adopted measures for the establishment of common schools and a college. In eleven years after the settlement of Massachusetts the foundation of Harvard College was laid; and in seventeen, the system of free schools was organized. The clergy of those times were active not only in procuring the establishment of these institutions, but likewise in sustaining them. As teachers, as patrons, and visitors of the schools and the college, they exerted a controlling and salutary influence.

Our fourth argument is drawn from the example of some excellent ministers in our own recollection. They avowed and acted on the principle that they were under the same obligation to lend their aid in fitting young men for college that they were to preach the gospel. Many of them taught school during the winter for the young people of their congregations. The consequence was, that these thus became acquainted with their minister, esteemed him, respected him, and in subsequent years sustained him. This was the course of some of the best ministers of the land.

If, then, it is the duty of ministers to promote the cause of popular education, and generally to elevate the public taste and to refine the public sentiment, they ought to qualify themselves to do it by educating themselves as thoroughly as possible.

For professional education and for success in all the higher professions, a liberal education is a most valuable preparation. Unless a man learns to look abroad upon the wide fields of literature and science, before he engages in professional life, he probably never will do it. And even though he should become somewhat eminent in his profession, still this will only show his ignorance on other subjects the more.

Now and then there are splendid exceptions to this general remark. Such a man as Franklin, or Patrick Henry, or Nathan Smith, can be cited to show that a man may, by the force of his native genius, by industry, and by the power of concurring circumstances, raise himself to a high standing in influence and respectability among his fellow-men without the aid of a collegiate education.

But it should be remembered that these men would never have been what they were, if there had been no colleges in the country. " When an elevated standard of education is maintained by the higher literary institutions, men of superior powers who have not had access to them, are stimulated to aim at a similar elevation by their own efforts, and by the aid of the light that is shining around them. They catch the thought, the spirit, and the language of those with whom they are conversant, and thus, perhaps, through them, receive some of the advantages of a collegiate education."

Besides, the general fact has been that these very men who have thus risen, have been deeply sensible of the disadvantages under which they labored from the comparative deficiency of their early training, and have been the advocates of a liberal education. Henry Clay, in some of his passages at arms with John Randolph, when taunted by him on his incorrect use of a certain word, referred with tears to the difficulties he had experienced from the want of a liberal education such as the other had enjoyed. General Washington left a legacy for the establishment of a national university.

But it is alleged that all that we have said is the mere offspring of prejudice in favor of a system that is old and which ought to be given up for something new.

On this point we cannot do better than to quote a passage which had a somewhat different application :—" One of the most foolish whims of this age is to deride the old. Those who are absurd enough to do so, forget, or perhaps never knew, that there lies deep in the human heart an inextinguishable reverence for the past. As time goes on, all the meannesses that encompass human life disappear, and the grand features in the characters of the ages alone remain as objects of our contemplation. The venerable forms of antiquity stand before us in severe relief, and we bow down in a willing homage of the heart to their unutterable majesty. The past is sacred. It is set beyond the revolutions of nature and the shifting institutions of man. He who would destroy this treasury of the human heart and mind, by rudely assailing our reverence for the old, would rob human life of half its charm and nearly all its refinement. Let no enthusiastic student, then, permit his ardor to be chilled by the fear that his love has been wasted on an unreal thing; that he has been bewildered by an idle dream; and that he has lost much precious time which ought to have been given to the stirring interests of the present; for he may rest assured that the study of antiquity has a noble power to elevate his mind above the low passions of the present, by fixing its contemplations on the great and immortal spirits of the past "

Go on, then, we would say to every student in college, go on with good courage and not be troubled because, while in college, you are required to study some ancient authors, contemplate some ancient truths, and because collegiate systems of instruction are ancient. Let your minds be well disciplined and well furnished, and you need not fear but that you will have abundant opportunities for usefulness and success. Never was there a fairer field for enterprise than that which lies before you. And, as you look out from the retreats of science upon the sunny fields, the green valleys, and broad plains of your country, you hear a thousand voices inviting you to come forth and apply the mental stores which you may gain here to increase the stock of human virtue. A thousand hearts will welcome you into professional life, if you carry with you the desire to be useful.

In the mental history of many of the most useful and successful, who have distinguished themselves in the way of benevolent action, it appears that they formed their principles of action while in college as well as acquired those means or qualifications for usefulness. In forming your moral and religious principles of action, you enjoy great advantages in the quiet and calm of your situation. Your interests here do not interfere with the formation of correct principles, as they will when you come into the employments of professional life. Let your desire to serve God and bless mankind grow up under your cultivation, in your hearts, as a permanent principle of action. Carry out into the world with you, when you go, a benevolent heart, what stores you can acquire, and a philosophic spirit. Having learned in the retirements of collegiate life to scale the high abode where truth has reared her awful throne, having consecrated your acquisitions, at the foot of the cross, to the service of Him who hung thereon, you will in your earthly progress move in a halo of glory brighter than that which encircles the hero's brow. And, when coming years shall have gathered you to the great home of the dead, to rest from the toils both of studious and of active life, you will, with enlarged capacities and with stores of heavenly knowledge, enter into a brighter scene of action, where you will forever "drink the spirit of the golden day and triumph in existence."

Having spoken of the value and importance of a liberal education; first, in its influence in elevating and refining the intellectual and moral character of the individual; secondly, in its influence in preparing him for a professional education, that he may act his part among men usefully and successfully; we are next to speak of it in reference to the practical application of the truths communicated during the course. We have dwelt hitherto chiefly on its value and importance as a discipline to the mind; we shall now speak of the knowledge communicated to the students, and through them to the community at large.

This knowledge is frequently underrated in some such language as this: "one ounce of common sense is better than a pound of college learning;" "one grain of mother-wit is better than a bushel of book knowledge." And in illustration of the truth of such assertions, the visionary schemes of learned men are collated with the practical skill of self-taught men, for the sake of throwing contempt on the former.

Now, we have no disposition to underrate "good sense," "mother-wit," or "practical skill;" but, besides these, scientific principles and systematic rules are necessary. And here we would introduce a quotation from Whateley's Logic, to show our views of the case: "The generality have a strong predilection in favor of common sense, except in those points in which they respectively possess the knowledge of a system of rules; but in these points they deride any one who trusts to unaided common sense. A sailor, *e. g.*, will despise the pretensions of medical men, and prefer treating a disease by common sense; but he would ridicule the proposal of navigating a ship by common sense, without a regard to the maxims of nautical art. A physician again, will perhaps contemn systems of political economy, of logic, or metaphysics, and insist on the superior wisdom of trusting to common sense in such matters; but he would never approve of trusting to common sense in the treatment of diseases. Neither, again, would the architect recommend a reliance on common sense alone, in building, nor the musician in music to the neglect of those systems of rules which, in their respective arts, have been deduced from scientific reasoning aided by experience. And the induction might be extended to every department of practice. Since, therefore, each gives the preference to unassisted common sense only in those cases where he himself has nothing else to trust to, and invariably resorts to the rules of art wherever he possesses the knowledge of them, it is plain that mankind universally bear their testimony, though unconsciously and often unwillingly, to the preferableness of systematic, to conjectural judgments." According to this view of the matter, "common sense," and "mother-wit," and "practical skill," are not underrated, while science and systematic rules are exalted to their proper station.

In every age of the civilized world, the conduct and character of the great mass of the community depend on the moral and intellectual influences which operate upon their minds, and these influences descend originally from high sources. They descend from the minds of philosophers, speculating in their closets, to the minds of those leading men in the community who have the more immediate control of the popular sentiment; and from them they go down, as from so many distinct fountains, to the great level of the common people. Those who are thus engaged in active life cannot, indeed, be expected to devote much attention to original investigation in science and literature, yet they may serve as the medium to transmit to the community the intelligence that comes from the great lights of the world. We cannot stop to speak of those bright constellations which, at different times, rose in the hemisphere of Greece, and shed their choicest influences upon the great men who in public life governed her destinies. Whence was it that Lycurgus was qualified to compose that code of laws which laid the foundations of Spartan greatness? It was from Thales of Crete, the learned and the wise. Whence was it that Solon was qualified to give laws to Athens? "I grow old," said he, "in the pursuit of learning." Whence was it that Pericles became so distinguished as to merit and receive the name of Olympius? From Anaxagoras the philosopher.

From the lyceum, the porch, and the grove, there came forth those statesmen and heroes, furnished with the philosophy of Zeno and Aristotle, who thus, by their superior knowledge, swayed the minds and directed the energies of the Grecian states.

Thus has it ever been. Knowledge is power both in the application of the laws of nature to useful purposes, and in influencing the minds of men. The abstract principles taught in ancient schools or in modern colleges have been diffused more or less extensively through the surrounding communities.

In this way the whole mass of the people becomes more or less enlightened.

In order to show that abstract principles, such as are taught in colleges, are actually diffused through the community, and applied to practical purposes, we will refer to the principles taught by Bacon, the father of experimental philosophy. This great man received his education at Trinity College, Cambridge, where, it has been asserted, he conceived the idea of the inductive mode of philosophizing. The end aimed at by Bacon was, to use his own language, "fruit," which means the mitigation of human suffering, and the increase of human enjoyment. He was willing that the tree should be judged by its fruit. Of the method which he pursued, and which he proposed to others, for the interpretation of nature, and entitled Novum Organon, this is the fundamental axiom, "As man is but the servant and interpreter of nature, he can work and understand no farther than he shall either in action or contemplation observe the proceedings of nature, to whose laws he remains subject." This mode of philosophizing was adopted by Newton, both when a student and when a professor at Trinity College, Cambridge, with great success; as it has been since by multitudes of teachers in colleges, academies, and common schools. Thus it has happened that almost every intelligent man in the community understands something of what is termed the Inductive Philosophy of Bacon. Reflect, for a moment, upon the value of the fruits of his philosophy in every science, whether physical or moral; in every art, whether liberal or mechanical. Think of what it has done in the investigations of the heavens, in the sublime science of astronomy, and in the application of that science; of what it has done in the investigation of the crust of the planet we inhabit, and of the various tribes of animate and inanimate existence. Think of what it has done in mechanical and chemical philosophy; how it has guided the thunderbolt to the earth; how it has enabled man to descend into the depths of the sea, and to soar into the air; to traverse the land in cars that whirl along without horses, and the ocean in vessels which are propelled against the wind. These are some of the fruits of his philosophy, in its application to science and to art. The abstract principles which he brought forward into notice being adopted by kindred minds, and by them communicated to others, or applied to practical purposes, have revolutionized the world in philosophy and the arts.

In illustration of the same fact, we may take the instance of the Newtonian philosophy. At first it was taught, in its general principles, in the universities of Great Britain, and from them was introduced into the universities of the Continent. In the progress of time, a knowledge of these principles was diffused through the community in many parts of the civilized world. This has been done, for the most part, by those who have enjoyed the advantages of a liberal education, as teachers, or as the writers of popular works; and what is true of this is true of the physical sciences generally.

As a further illustration of the same general fact, we may take the instance of the philosophy of Locke. This philosophy has had a powerful influence in forming the opinions of men in regard to the laws of the human mind; in regard to government, morals, religion, and education. He was educated at the university of Oxford, and was distinguished there as a scholar. His works have been studied in the universities and colleges of Great Britain and this country, and in this way have exerted a controlling influence upon the minds of men.

To take another case. It is now, perhaps, forty years since the president in one of the colleges in South America conceived the design of spreading through the province in which it was situated, correct principles of civil liberty. Accordingly, with the injunction of secresy, he put into the hands of the most promising scholars in each class in succession, one of whom related to us this fact, certain books, which were proscribed by the laws, on the ground that they were hostile to arbitrary power. These scholars, carrying with them the principles of liberty derived from this source into active life, have since kindled the watchfires of revolution, which burned so brightly among the hills and valleys of the Andes. And they are now engaged in establishing the civil institutions of the country in accordance with those principles of liberty which they imbibed during their residence at college.

The results of ethical and metaphysical speculations are equally obvious and striking. They have, in like manner, through the colleges as their appropriate medium, a powerful influence in forming the mind and coloring the intellect and moral principle of all thinking men. The works that came forth from the universities of Scotland, in rapid succession, from such men as Reid, Stewart, Brown, and Hamilton, have effected a revolution in intellectual philosophy no less important than that which was produced by the writings of Locke. Rousing themselves from the lethargy that had long reigned, they awoke the slumbering intellect also of Great Britain, and excited a spirit of investigation, and gave an impulse to knowledge, that continue to the present day. They were a light kindled in the North, which, like the glorious emanations on a summer's night, spread far and wide over more southern latitudes.

Our limits do not allow us to show how the systems of philosophy, as adopted by men liberally educated and taught in universities and colleges, have, in successive ages, influenced the faith of the Christian church. Nor can we find room to show the great value of an acquaintance with the laws of nature, in their application to the useful arts; how it prevents us from attempting impossibilities; how it enables us to accomplish our ends in the easiest, shortest, and most economical manner. We need not appeal to the triumphs of practical mechanics, which, for the most part, is a scientific art, nor to the wonderful transformations wrought by chemistry, nor to the application of the science of astronomy to the art of navigation.

But it is said that many of the most successful and important applications of science to the arts, were made by men who were not liberally educated. This was readily admitted;

but still it is true that colleges and men liberally educated must come in for their share of honor and merit for these applications. For instance, Fulton had not enjoyed the advantage of a college education, and yet he was the inventor of the application of steam to propelling boats. But it should be remembered that Fulton was upon intimate terms with the celebrated Duke of Bridgewater and with Lord Stanhope, both of whom had a superior education; that he resided some time in Paris with that elegant scholar, Joel Barlow; that he made himself acquainted with the French, Italian, and German languages; that he acquired a knowledge of the high mathematics, physics, chemistry, and perspective; that he was associated with Chancellor Livingston,—whose mind was enlarged by education,—in the enterprise of employing the steam-engine in navigation. It is said of Watt, who brought the steam-engine to a high degree of perfection, that, though he had not received a liberal education at a university, he was conversant with all the wonders of natural philosophy, and was the pupil and intimate friend of Professor Black. And he often acknowledged that his first ideas on this subject were acquired by his attendance on his lectures, and from the consideration of his theory of latent heat, and the expansibility of steam. In this way, universities and colleges may claim the honor of having educated indirectly, through the medium of their alumni, many who have been the benefactors of their race, by the application of science to the arts.

Colleges have thus, directly or indirectly, changed the whole circle of mechanical employments, from the condition of empiricism to that of scientific art. And, besides furnishing a vast amount of important inventions, abridging human labor, increasing human comforts, they have thrown a clear and strong light upon those processes which had been studiously concealed under the veil of mystery.

Nor are the services which learning has rendered to morals and religion of less importance. It has derived from the Bible, in harmony with nature, a system of pure morals and elevated piety. It has ever sympathized with the truth, and has ever been ready to detect and expose the arts of men who depend for their success on popular delusions. The history of colleges in our own country shows that they were not the patrons of witchcraft, when that was rife in the land; that they did not promote the delusions of Mrs. Hutchinson or of Davenport; that in them mesmerism, and spiritual rappings, and the transient follies of the day find but few votaries.

Let the colleges, then, in our country take their proper position in the public estimation, in connexion with academies, high-schools, and common schools, as the popular and conservative institutions of the land, to be sustained by public sentiment and public contributions.

---

1. Oxford University Commission.—Report of Her Majesty's Commissioners, appointed to inquire into the State, Discipline, Studies, and Revenue of the University of Oxford, together with the Evidence and an Appendix; presented to both Houses of Parliament by command of Her Majesty. London: Printed by W. Clowes & Son, Stamford Street, for Her Majesty's Stationery Office. 1852.

2. Five Years in an English University.—By Charles Astor Bristed, late Foundation Scholar of Trinity College, Cambridge. *'Αλλ' ἀπ' ἐκθρῶν δῆτα πολλὰ μανθάνουσίν ὁι σοφόί.*—Aristoph. *Aves.* 376. Second edition. New York: Putnam & Co. 1852.

OBITUARY NOTICE OF PROFESSOR ALEXANDER METCALF FISHER.

Through the medium of the public prints, our readers have been apprised of the loss of the packet ship Albion of New York. We have seldom known an event of this kind, occasion a wider or deeper sorrow. The line has been celebrated for its regularity and success; and on the first of April, nearly sixty persons, of various character and pursuits, presented themselves on the deck of the ship, and in the gaiety of their feelings, as she was getting under way, shouted forth the customary animating cheers for a prosperous voyage. On the 22d they all, with the exception of nine, met with their common fate, as awful as it was unexpected, on the coast of Ireland, near Kinsale.

No very distinct account of the particulars has been received. It appears that their passage had been pleasant until the 21st, when the ship encountered and weathered a severe gale, and the tempest-tossed mariners were cheering themselves with the hope, that in less than two days they should reach Liverpool, the port of their destination. Early in the evening she "shipped a sea, which knocked her on her beam-ends, swept her deck, and her main-mast went by the board." From not being in possession of proper instruments, they were unable to clear the deck; and as she consequently became unmanageable, they drifted along at the mercy of the waves, and subject to all the agonizing agitations of mind, produced by the alterations of hope and fear, until about twelve o'clock, when the light of Old Head hove in sight—now the beacon of their danger, for it told them that they were drifting rapidly ashore.

About four o'clock, as the day dawned, Capt. Williams, who

had made every exertion to encourage the men and preserve the ship, communicated the dreadful certainty, that no efforts could possibly save her, and in about five minutes she struck, and shortly after went to pieces, within a few rods of land. The shore was rocky and precipitous, rising to the height of 150 feet, and prevented those who were collected on its brow from rendering much assistance; and amid the confusion and remaining darkness, which took from them the means of safety, or the presence of mind, to use these means, the billows, in their fury, burst in upon their victims, and bore down to destruction the brave and the beautiful, the man of business and the man of science!

But the ways of Jehovah are mysterious. He hath his path in the deep waters—and in this awful calamity, involving the death of so many individuals endeared to their kindred and acquaintance, and sending mourning into other lands as well as our own, we would view the hand of the Almighty, though raised in anger; and even while we are looking upon the blasted joys of friendship and love, and the withered hopes of science, we would invite the numerous and widely scattered bereaved friends to repair with us for consolation to that God who may hide his face for a moment, but whose loving kindness is everlasting. Yes, we would invite them to go with us to the mercy seat, and in the language of christian submission, to say, "Father, thy will be done."

While we would mingle our sympathies with the sorrows that flow from so many hearts, we may be allowed to dwell more particularly on the fate of one, who contributed to adorn the pages of this work. We allude to ALEXANDER M. FISHER, Professor of Mathematics and Natural Philosophy in Yale College. He was a native of Franklin, (Mass.) where his parents now reside. Though in the sadness of bereavement, they may remember him with feelings of exultation, as a dutiful and affectionate son, who gave early indications of those talents which were afterwards developed and matured. At the age of fifteen he entered Yale College, and was distinguished for his punctual performance of all College exercises, for the delicacy of his moral feelings, and for his success in the various departments of classical knowledge. The activity of his mind, and his unwearied application joined to his success, attracted the notice of the faculty and of his fellow students, and led those who best knew him, to form pleasing presages of his future distinction in science.

After taking his degree in 1813, he spent one year in Franklin and one in Andover, in attending to the study of Theology in its direct and collateral branches.

In 1815 he entered upon the office of Tutor ; and he performed its duties with ability, and a spirit that shrunk from no self-denial, either of instruction or discipline.

In 1817 he was appointed Adjunct Professor of Mathematics and Natural Philosophy ; and two years after he became sole professor in the same department.

His course in science had been as rapid and successful as the fondest wishes of his early friends and instructors presaged ; and as he had gradually risen in his attainments, and could thus command a wider and wider field of vision, with pleasure we beheld him casting his eyes to Europe, the home of the sciences, and forming the design of going thither to promote his own improvement, and the welfare of the Institution, and the cause of learning generally in our country—by travel and study, and intercourse with the good and the great of other lands. After making the necessary preparations to facilitate the attainment of the various objects proposed, and completing his arrangement in such a manner that the college would not materially suffer by his absence ; we saw him in all the excitement of departing, with buoyant spirits and animated countenance, and active step—and followed him with our wishes and our hopes to the ship—little apprehensive that we 'should see his face no more.'

Multis ille bonis flebelis, occidit.

The general sentiment of sorrow, expressed by his personal friends, and the larger circle of his acquaintance, and the sympathy of the public, bear ample testimony to his high intellectual and moral endowments, and an accurate analysis of a character of so much worth and promise, would be useful in furnishing fresh motives and facilities to those who are aiming at the acquisition of learning and virtue. An exhibition of only a few traits must now suffice.

A prominent trait in his character was a love of investigation. He valued truth, and he sought for it not in the current opinions of the day, or under the sanctions of illustrious names. He ascended to first principles in his researches, and having with cautious diligence ascertained the legitimate scope of the human intellect, and the proper objects of a rational inquiry, with independence of mind he advanced to his own conclusions, and with confidence in his perceptions, he trusted to these conclusions, even though they might clash with received opinions. He had a taste for whatever is beautiful or grand in science, and a spirit that was alive to every intellectual excellence, and a fondness for the exercise necessary for its attainment. In the career of learning it was not merely the applause of the spectators, or the bright prize at the goal; but it was likewise the effort and animation of the race itself that he loved. From his connexion with the college, it became his duty, as it was his inclination, to bestow peculiar attention upon the *exact sciences*, yet he never suffered them so to absorb his mind, as to become magnified beyond their relative importance: and instead of undervaluing other branches of knowledge, he urged, with a generous warmth, their importance, and rejoiced in their advancement, and seconded this opinion, expressed to others, by giving variety to his own pursuits.

In his application he was constant and assiduous. He neither changed his objects of pursuit, nor relaxed from the necessary efforts. We often see men of fine genius wasting their powers, and failing of success by a too frequent change of their studies. The ease with which they gain one victory after another, tempts them to press on to universal dominion, instead of staying to gain complete possession of a single region. They are diligent, but at the same time desultory. We often see others failing, not from fickleness, but from a relaxation of effort. Under the influence of some strong, but transient excitement, they make very rapid intellectual progress; and then the excitement being over, they yield to a natural love of ease, or to the languor of exhausted health. Both of these evils he avoided; and preserved an unshaken attachment to the same objects, and an unremitted exertion to gain them. Believing that there is no *royal road* to learning, and ambitious rather of the possession, than of the reputation, of excellence, and not finding it necessary to put himself under the influence of strong feeling, in order to render his perceptions vivid, and therefore not led to any imprudent expenditure of spirits and health; he continued a series of untired efforts, making every day contribute to his stock of knowledge: and not suffering himself to be led away by the influence of surrounding objects, or to sink down from indolence, he went on from one conquest to another, gaining fresh strength from every new acquisition. His mind, which was highly gifted by nature, by being trained in this course of habitual application, received a high degree of improvement, and acquired great facility in its operations.

One of its most striking atributes was logical acuteness. At the same time that he possessed sufficient comprehension in his views, and was able to examine great subjects in their extensive relations, he was more distinguished for that acute discrimination which enabled him to perceive and adopt proper distinctions of thought; to detect a fallacy, though brought forward with all the parade of argument; and to trace with the rapidity of intuition a succession of premise and conclusion, through a long train of subtile disquisition.

He used sometimes to complain that his memory was treacherous, and failed him in his need. This however was the case only with respect to some insulated fact, which was not connected by some scientific association. But with respect to facts or truths ranged under a philosophical classification, or founded on the relations of cause and effect, premise or conclusion, his memory was retentive, and prompt in assembling the stores thus arranged.

His imagination, if we consider it as that faculty that is conversant with the lovely or the grand in the world of nature or of fiction, and graphic skill in describing the objects of conception, was neither very active or vivid. But if it be considered as that faculty which discovers analogies and relations, though remote, and the power of summoning with judgment and taste, the materials of knowledge—furnished not so much by the senses as by reflection—and of arranging them with beauty and harmony, for the elucidation of truth—he was distinguished for the possession of a vigorous and fertile imagination.

Though accustomed to abstraction and retirement, he still was remarkable for his talent for philosophical observation. His mind was habitually attentive to external objects, and from his own inspection of men and things, he was constantly collecting useful facts, and connecting the speculations of the closet with the common business of life, and thus he dignified the pursuits of philosophy by the high moral aim of rendering them subservient to the happiness and virtue of our race.

Without remarking upon the variety and extent of his acquisitions in his peculiar province, or in the several departments of natural science, or in metaphysics and ethical philosophy, it may here be mentioned that, in addition to his regular instruction in the recitations, and his course of experimental lectures, he likewise prepared a course of written lectures that evince great ability. Averse to hypothesis, and adopting the severity of inductive reasoning, his philosophy consisted of a just comprehension of facts; and without departing from the dignity of true science, he demanded all the vigor of attention from his audience; and as he delivered his lectures, though somewhat rapidly, in a clear medium of thought, perspicuous language and lucid arrangement, though the listless and the ignorant found little to interest their feelings, those who were prepared by previous study, and who were willing to bestow the necessary attention, always carried from the lecture-room clear and distinct views of the subject.

He was very much in the habit of using his pen as an instrument of thought; and though he died at the early age of twenty-seven, has left behind him a large collection of writings on various subjects, as a monument of his industry and talents. He contributed to several periodical publications. It does not come within the compass of our design to enumerate his productions. This, it is hoped, will be done by the hand of another. As a specimen of his writings we would refer our readers to the Review of Dr. Brown's Essay.*

His manners in his intercourse with others were unaffected and pleasing, and while he was not very attentive to the courtly accomplishments and etiquette of fashionable life, which result from extensive commerce with the world, he at the same time showed himself possessed of genuine politeness,—in his regard for the feelings of others, in his attention to the wants and wishes of his friends, not occasional, but constant, and in the ready surrender of his own convenience. He had that good will towards those around him, which is manifested, not so much by a compliance with the mere forms and ceremonies of the world, as by a continuance of generous and kindly acts, intended to make them happy.

He was social in his feelings, though his habits did not lead him extensively into promiscuous society. Possessing neither those overflowing spirits, nor that desire for display, which are so favorable to copious conversation, and at the same time, well acquainted with all the usual topics of elevated discussion, he knew both how to talk, and how to listen. He was observed very seldom to introduce the topics of his own profession; his language, however, and his illustrations, and his arrangement of ideas, showed the influence of his habitual studies upon his mind.

In his intercourse with his intimate friends, he was companionable and interesting. He was animated and sprightly in his communication, and in his interchange of thought and feeling, he manifested great purity of purpose, and freedom from those evil passions that are often repressed in the presence of the public, while in the private circle they are uncontrolled. He indeed appeared to be habitually under the influence of conscience. His daily business or the common avocations of life, he performed, not as the task of a hireling, but as a labor of love, springing from a high-minded and generous sense of duty. He took a lively interest in whatever con-

* Christian Spectator, Vol. I., Page 414.

cerned the welfare of the College, and cheerfully and unceasingly did his part towards its advancement; and produced on those around him a strong impression of his singleness of purpose, and integrity of motive, in all his actions.

His constitution was delicate, but by regular exercise and rigid temperance, he preserved his health and mental vigor and cheerfulness of temper. In addition to his other modes of relaxation, he attended habitually to music, which he cultivated both as an art and as a science. He found pleasure in it, not merely from the agreeable associations it awakens, but from a nice perception of the relations of sound. He entered deeply into the principles of the science, and contributed to its advancement, by an essay on *Musical Temperament*, which appeared in the American Journal of Science, and called forth expressions of admiration, from such as were able to appreciate its merit, both in this and foreign countries.

He bestowed great and systematic care in the formation of his religious opinions, and was very watchful that his conduct should correspond with his principles. He was accustomed to ascend to first truths in the formation of his opinions, and it would therefore sometimes happen that even when he came to the same result with others, he would not always adopt the same arguments, or pursue the same course of reasoning. He was not however of that class who find reason in all opinions, and truth in none: for though he was apprehensive of danger in believing too much, as well as in believing too little, he held with a firm grasp the fundamental doctrines of christianity. Nor did he consider christianity as a mere system of speculative doctrines, which is to be admired for its symmetry, and for the grandeur of its subjects, and to be defended with animated zeal against the open attacks of its enemies, and the insidious designs of its professed friends; but as a collection of practical truths, that should be present to the mind and influence the conduct in all the common hours of life, that should shed a sanctifying influence over the whole character, send the glow of holy and constant love into the heart, direct the imagination in its wanderings, curb the violence of the animal propensities, and ascending to the intellect, should repress its proud aspirings, and thus elevate and improve the whole nature by enlisting all its powers in the service of the Redeemer. Forming this high standard of christian character, and accustomed in everything to look rather at his defects than at his good qualities, he was not in the habit of expressing a strong confidence in his personal piety. Yet his friends may console themselves in their affliction with the hope, that he has gone to a brighter world, where his delight in duty will be consummated, and his aspirations after moral excellence will be gratified. We will believe that though the surges of the ocean may continue to sweep over his remains, that "He who rides in the whirlwind," took his spirit to himself, as it rose from the billow, and conducted it to the abodes of the blessed.

His body lies on a Foreign strand beneath the dark waters which chant his dirge first in the wild notes of the storm, and repeat it in the sullen murmurs of the calm. But remembrance of it will haunt that rugged shore of Kinsale to weep over his early death and gather inspiration for the high purposes of this life and the life to come.

It is remarkable that Prof. Fisher had a great dread of a sea voyage. While the subject of going abroad was pending, in his daily walks he would express his fears, often in strong language, and when I attempted to quiet those fears by the usual arguments, to which he always candidly listened, he would very often close the conversation by saying: "Well, this is all very true, but a certain percentage is lost."

The following lines, at my request, were composed by the poet James G. Percival:

We ask no flowers to deck thy tomb,
Thy name in purer light shall bloom,
When every flower on earth is dead
And all that bloom below are fled.

To thee, the light of mind was given,
The center of thy soul was heaven;
In early youth, the spirit came,
And wrapped thee in its wings of flame.

The lambent light that round thee flow'd,
Rose to its high and bright abode;
And bore thy restless eye afar,
To read the fate of sun and star.

Fain would we think the chain is broke,
That bound thy spirit to its yoke;
That now no mist of earth can bind,
Thy bright, thy pure, and perfect mind.

Thy grave is on a foreign strand,
Thy tomb is in a foreign land;
No kinsman came, no friend was near,
To close thine eye and deck thy bier.

But friends shall gather round thy tomb,
And long lament thy early doom;
And thither science oft repair,
To plant thy choicest laurels there.

The following lines were written by the young lady to whom Professor Fisher was engaged:

SUNDAY EVENING, 1822.

Where shall the mourning heart find peace,
  Whose every throb is filled with woe,
When shall the aching heart find rest
  And bitter tears forget to flow?

Wisdom with kind, inviting voice,
  Directs the way to paths of peace,
And points to Heaven th' o'erflowing eye
  Where pain shall end and sorrow cease.

But vain her call—the wayward heart,
  Its best hopes wrecked—its comforts o'er—
Wanders unhappy and unblest—
  To Erin's cliffs and dismal shore.

There, while the dark and troubled wave
  Hides the dear form for ever lost;
Still hovers 'round uncomforted,
  Afflicted, lone and tempest tost.

Oh Saviour! at whose sovereign word,
  The winds and waves of sorrow cease,
Thou see'st my tears, and hear'st my sighs,
  Speak but the word and all is peace.

Be thou my trust, while I resign
  The dearest boon thy mercy gave,
And leave my ruined earthly hopes
  To Erin's cliffs and Ocean's wave.

MEMOIR OF MR. RUFUS WOODWARD.

This sketch of the life and character of Mr. Woodward has been delayed, in the hope of receiving from Edinburgh, some farther account of his last sickness and death. With the best materials, it is sufficiently difficult to write the mental history of any one, in such a manner that exact justice shall be done to the deceased for the instruction of others. Especially is it difficult to unite the faithfulness of a biographer with the affection of a friend: a multitude of mingled feelings come thronging upon the mind, and fix the attention too exclusively on those features in the character of the deceased, which won and secured his affection; a crowd of recollections rising up, demand the recording pen for those passages of his life only, connected with the scenes in which they moved together. His intimate friends cannot, in this delineation, find a portrait distinct and glowing like that which memory has drawn upon their own hearts; it is hoped that they will find a correspondence with truth, and with "that which they themselves do know." Others, and especially those whose path may lie in the walks of contemplative life, may find something to gratify a rational curiosity, and some incentives to the attainment of kindred excellences of character. The lamented subject of this memoir, was not anxious for the praise of men while he was among us; and now, so much respect shall be paid to his memory, as not to bestow unreserved eulogies upon him when dead, that would have pained his modesty when living.

Rufus Woodward, the son of Dr. Samuel Woodward, was born in Torringford, (Conn.) July 16th, 1793. Residing at home, he had the advantage of spending his early years in a family much respected for their good sense and amiable disposition; and to this circumstance, as an active cause, must be referred many of those valuable traits in his character, which, in subsequent life, were matured by his own exertions. It appears, that during this period, he showed little of that precocity of mind which sometimes indicates genius, but which, perhaps, more often, is the harbinger of intellectual impotence. He entered on the studies of childhood with little interest; as is not unfrequently the case with those whose mental habits, so far as they are formed, lead them to prefer ideas to words, until from use, the latter, by suggesting trains of thought in the mind, fully assume their representative character, and become nearly identified with the former.

When he entered upon the period of youth, he gradually acquired a fondness for study. It was only at the vestibule of the temple of learning that he discovered any reluctance, for soon after it appears that he became a confirmed votary. Mr. Goodman, in his funeral sermon, says of him, 'while other youths were regaling themselves, during the long winter evenings, with their sports and pastimes, he was often found no less eagerly engaged by the fire-side, in the acquisition of knowledge. Study was his pastime from early youth, and intellectual pleasures the pleasures for which he had the highest relish.'

Having completed his preparatory studies under the Rev. Dr. Backus, of Bethlem, he entered Yale College in 1812, with the reputation of an accurate scholar. Describing himself at this period, he remarks: 'I was addicted to no gross vices. My prejudices against religion were strong. Among the most obstinate early habits with which I had to struggle, was that of speaking and thinking rapidly and confusedly. I had also an early habit of loose and wandering thought which I have taken great pains to correct. On account of this habit and that of thinking rapidly, my conversation was rather abrupt, broken, and deficient in connexion and ease.' Facts, like these, in his intellectual history deserve notice, because they correspond with the mental defects of which many are conscious, and which from discouragement they do not attempt to remove. He attempted with success, and the masters of mental science tell us, that what has been done once may be done again.

In a very concise account of his college life, after mentioning his successive Tutors with feelings of gratitude, in high terms of commendation characteristic of each, he proceeds: "I come now to a man who has been the means of doing me more good than any individual on earth, except my parents. Dr. Dwight was a father to us. His instructions formed a sort of chart for the voyage of life. His example furnished the sublimest lesson of morality and religion that I had ever seen. His manners were those of a refined and accomplished gentleman. He was particularly distinguished for possessing a vast fund of practical information, and for an ability, as well as inclination, to communicate it to his pupils. He had arranged his ideas in such a manner, that when he had occasion for one, all that related to the same point, followed after in quick succession. Perhaps his reliance upon facts was such as to lead him occasionally into credulity and dogmatism. But take him all in all, he was a very superior and a very excellent man. Never while I live and breathe, shall I cease to remember with gratitude, the benefits I received from his instruction and example. I attended a course of excellent lectures on natural philosophy, by Professor Day; and of chemistry and mineralogy, by Professor Silliman. I was exceedingly fond of physical science, and the result of my attention to it has been a total change of my views of the material world. The charm of this study consists in witnessing constantly a wonderful adaptation of means to ends. This is particularly true of some parts of chemistry and vegetable physiology. My views of many other subjects, experienced no less change in the course of my college life. The tendency of the college honors in which I shared, was to teach me the emptiness of such pleasures, and of human applause in general. The example of the officers of college, and the instructions of Dr. Dwight, gave me new views of the subject of religion. Instead of associating with it the idea of vulgar ignorance, of austere manners, and of a gloomy life, it assumed an air of cheerfulness, of refinement, and of an enlightened regard to the welfare of man. An examination of the evidences of Christianity, by Dr. Paley, had also a powerful influence on my mind. At one time, I hoped I was a Christian; at another, doubted. * * * On the whole, I was graduated at college, a very different person from what I was when I entered; and I rejoice exceedingly that I did enter. The advantages of a college education, do not consist principally, in attainments and habits that are completed; but in commencing habits for life—such for example, as a habit of reflection, of observation, and of study. A habit of reflection, particularly, was one of the most valuable that I acquired in college. It has led me to examine subjects for myself, and especially to study a subject elementarily.

He was as a student distinguished among his class-mates, for his diligence and solid attainments; and he drew their eyes upon him, not as one superior to all others as a scholar, but as one, who in his love of truth, whether found in speculative, or practical principles; in his admiration of intellectual excellence, and in his determined pursuit of all the high objects of a liberal education, showed that he had within him the elements of a character, which, if brought into contact with favorable circumstances, might be moulded into a form of intellectual strength and moral dignity. Though remarkably punctual in preparing the required exercises, he seemed to be governed, rather by a desire to furnish himself with materials in the acquisition of knowledge, and instruments in the cultivation of his mental faculties, for usefulness in life, than by any present advantage in the applause of others. Being actuated by such a desire, he applied himself to study under the influence of a motive that is constant in nature; while those who are governed only by a desire for a high reputation at college, though they may make themselves distinguished as classical scholars, act under the influence of a motive that is evanescent in its nature, producing no excitement after the individual has left the scene of his classic triumphs.

His deportment was exemplary. Having taken the station of a pupil, he had the feelings of a pupil. Having nothing refractory in his temper, he was not inclined to oppose the requisitions of the government, merely because they were requisitions. He was not inclined to regard with a jealous eye, every change of measures growing out of the necessary change of circumstances, as an encroachment upon the rights of the students. He sought for no distinction as the self-appointed guardian of these rights, by flying in the face of authority. Nor did he merit the praise of ingenuity, by his skill in evading the laws of the institution. Nor did he belong to that class of students, who delight in disorder, but have too much caution to engage in it; and who generously countenance the thoughtless and excitable ones in those violations of propriety which they dare not commit themselves. He had no taste for the beauties of disorder and moral deformity.

" After I was graduated," he says, " I taught an Academy in Stratford nine months; and one in Wethersfield a year. It is a very useful employment, and were it not for that consideration, I hardly know what would have supported me through such labor. No single effort in the business is very laborious; but it is a constant succession of petty efforts, which are gradually exhausting the mind of its energy, and wearing down the constitution.

" I devoted my leisure hours in Stratford, almost exclusively to study. I occasionally visited the Rev. Mr. D. and Dr. Johnson." Of the latter, he remarks, that he is a venerable sage of the age of ninety. " He is, on the whole, as venerable an object as I ever beheld. View him at a short distance, and you would suppose he must be in the last stages of decrepitude. Sit down by his side and talk with him, and you would indeed find him deaf enough, and trembling with age over the grave; but you would see something within that looks very much like divine. A mind refined, rich, clear, comprehensive, benevolent, and astonishingly eloquent. His very voice is eloquence—clear, trembling, deep-toned, soft, musical, and perfectly expressive of the internal workings of his mind. * * * * * * My plan of study was as follows:

20

—the evening I devoted to the study of some elementary work of science, such as Stewart's Philosophy, Smith's Wealth of Nations, &c. I devoted two hours in the morning to the business of thinking. At noon, and after school in the afternoon, I read some leisure book, like Shakespeare, Johnson, Goldsmith, &c. On the whole I think my attainments made this year were greater than those of any other year of my life. The habit of reflection, which I commenced at that time, (and which perhaps I never should have commenced, had it not been for what I had heard from Dr. Dwight,) I regard as one of the most valuable that a man can form. I am convinced too, that the course I then began to pursue, for the acquisition of valuable knowledge, is the best, viz: the *study*, and not the *mere reading*, of elementary works. It is to no very valuable purpose that we read works of detail, mere matters of fact, unless we form some general conclusions and principles as we go along; and these conclusions or principles are already formed, and by masterly minds too, in elementary works. We should be careful, however, not to adopt these general principles without due examination. A man, for example, would know more of the science of politics by studying thoroughly Smith's Wealth of Nations, than by merely reading in the ordinary way, all the history that was ever written.

"This year I lost a dear brother. This was the first time I ever realized how strong are the bonds of natural affection. I had, it is true, lost a sister; but I was then young, and she had not, for that reason, taken so strong a hold of my affections. My grief on this occasion was exceedingly great; though I hope it was mingled, in some degree, with that submission to the divine will which is so becoming the weakness and dependence of man.

"My time passed away, much in Wethersfield as it had done in Stratford; though during the latter part of my residence there, I mingled much more in society. It was at this time that I began to keep a common-place book, or at least such a one as I think on the whole profitable. In one of these, I put down the most important general principles of a science,—leaving room under each, for those details which would illustrate the principles, and which I was to put down in a very abridged form of expression, as they occurred, either in the course of my reading, observation, or conversation. My common-place on political science is an example of this kind. In another, I put down the synopsis of an argument scattered through an octavo of 300 pages. My common-place remarks from Allison on Taste, is an example of this kind. In another, I put down a train of thought, which I had made chiefly from my own reflections, as in my common-place book entitled 'Religious.' My school was an agreeable one; and my acquaintances formed during my residence there, valuable and interesting."

"October, 1818. Entered on the duties of my new situation, that of Tutor in Yale College, with great anxiety of mind, under the responsibility laid upon me."

"September, 1821. I am about completing the third year of my Tutorship, and bidding farewell to my class. When I look back, and see how great improvement most of them have made, I feel a degree of satisfaction which cannot be described. I trust I have not been found unfaithful; though like all the rest of my conduct, my services have not been just what they should have been. It requires a great degree of moral firmness, to keep constantly in view one's duty. I have been on the whole much pleased with my situation in college. It opens a field of usefulness, affords much leisure and time for study, access to books and to good literary society."

"November, 1822. I left my Tutorship in college last February, principally on account of ill health. I had not enjoyed good health for six or eight years; having had more or less of the dyspepsia. It originated, I doubt not, in a want of exercise, and of due attention to my diet. Students are very prone to neglect exercise, until they begin to feel the want of it; and then it comes almost too late; for the constitution by that time is usually considerably impaired, and it is difficult to restore its vigor, so long as one lives a sedentary life. They are not sufficiently attentive also to the quality, and especially the quantity of their food. Instead of diminishing the quantity of their food, in proportion to the diminution of their exercise, as they ought, they eat fast, stimulate their appetites by means of condiments, &c., and then overload their stomachs. This falls peculiarly hard upon those who have commenced their studies from an active life."

As he entered upon the office of Tutor with a deep feeling of responsibility, so he performed its duties with a most scrupulous regard to the general interests of the college, to his brethren in office, and to his immediate pupils. In imparting knowledge to his division, while he was sufficiently critical in the stated exercises, he made it an important object to connect together the different branches of instruction, and to show how these are related to the practical duties of life ;—that thus they might make every kind of improvement that would adorn them as mere scholars cloistered in a college, or as men when called to a more enlarged theatre of action. Disposed to act in concert with the other officers, and under the direction of the laws of the institution, he cheerfully did his part, whether of instruction or of discipline. While he valued the affection of those whom it was his duty to instruct and to govern, he at the same time appeared to have very little of that moral cowardice, which shrinks from odium ; for his was the virtuous mind that is ever attended by that " strong-siding champion,"—conscience.

November, 1822, he remarks: "From the time I left college, to the present, I have been devoting my time, as far as has been practicable, to the recovery of my health. But in vain, and I am now housing myself for the winter. Being pretty well convinced that the state of my health will not soon admit of my performing the duties of a clergyman, I have come to a determination to devote what little time I can prudently, for the present, to preparing a course of lectures on political science. If it should be wanted, very well; if not, I shall endeavor to do the best I can with it.

" In the mean time, I hope to be able to do something in

the way of writing on theological subjects, and should it ever be in my power I am resolved at some time or other, to attempt writing a text-book for our colleges, on the science of moral philosophy."

He still persevered under much that was discouraging, in using active exertions for the recovery of his health, residing with his father in Torringford, or with one of his brothers, either in Wethersfield or Middletown, each of whom, by his professional skill, was able to assist him in palliating his disease, as well as by the most affectionate attentions. Having derived some advantage from a voyage to Charleston, it was thought advisable that he should try the experiment still farther, in a longer voyage; and accordingly, in July, 1823, he sailed from New York for Europe, where it was hoped that he might be able likewise to gain some mental advantages in the prosecution of his favorite studies.

August 2, 1823. He writes, "I am at length within a few hours sail of Liverpool. You will unite with me in gratitude to our Heavenly Father that I am now so near the end of my voyage, in safety. My health is somewhat improved."

Remaining but a few days in Liverpool, he visited Glasgow, Edinburgh, and London, in succession, and in each place he received very gratifying civilities, from the highly respectable gentlemen to whom he carried letters of introduction. His health still continued about the same; for a time apparently improving; and then he would be visited by a return of an old complaint that exhausted his strength, and took away the flattering hopes of a recovery that he began to indulge. After beginning to recover from the effects of one of these attacks, he writes to his family friends:

"But I confess it is a little discouraging, and not a little trying to one's patience and powers of resignation. To be sick, too, among strangers—shut up in a little room on the fourth floor, with but one window, and that through the top, and not visited by the sympathetic voice of man, woman, or child, but my chambermaid, for five days, two or three *drops* of a fellow-lodger, and the short visits of my physician, my hostess being sick below—this tends to sadden the soul. But blessed be God, I find I can go through such scenes, though not—no not with so entire a submission as I could wish, or ought. To be entirely resigned amid long protracted and repeated sufferings, is surely one of the last lessons to be learned on this side the grave!"

It being judged advisable, on account of the climate and some other considerations, that he should spend the approaching winter in the south of France, he was proceeding thither, when he was again arrested by his complaint at Montreuil.

"Then," he says, "I was for a week in a French hotel, with a servant to wait on me who understands scarcely anything of the English language, and a chamber-maid who knows nothing at all of it. Indeed, I was pretty much my own physician, my own nurse, and what is about as necessary, you will find, if any of you should ever be sick among strangers, and especially among such strangers as it was my lot to find at that hotel—my own comforter. But blessed be God, I am getting better again. I have to-day got back as far as this place, Boulogne. I hope to-morrow to reach Calais, thence to sail back to London, thence to Edinburgh by the first opportunity. I am, however, a poor, feeble, emaciated creature; and I know not but a few more such attacks will close my eyes forever on all that is on this side the grave. May heaven prepare me for it, and you too—for I think of you abundantly at such times, and I know full well that you also think of me, and would hail my arrival among you once more, with all the sincerity of a long established and deep devoted affection."

Following up his intention, which the improved state of his health enabled him to do, he arrived in Edinburgh about the 1st of November—anxious to avail himself of the advantages of attending the lectures in the University, and, as a friend remarks, "esteeming the warmth of Scottish friendship, in the present state of his health, more than a counter-balance for the rigor of a northern winter."

But his studies, his sufferings, and his life, were now very soon to have their close. The final scene is thus described in a letter from the Rev. Dr. Dickson, of Edinburgh, to Prof. S.

My Dear Sir—How uncertain is the tenure by which our life is held! Your, and I can truly add my highly esteemed friend, Mr. Woodward, is no more. His mortal remains are deposited in a land of strangers; but his spirit has, I trust, been taken to its native home, with God and the Redeemer. This most painful event took place here on Monday, the 24th current, and the distressing duty of announcing it to you, and through you to his relations, has devolved on me. May the God of all grace abundantly sanctify to them this peculiarly severe dispensation of his holy providence, and enable us, my dear friend, to improve it for our progressive advancement in Christian godliness. At what time our dear departed friend's last letter to any of his correspondents in the United States was written, I have been quite unable to ascertain. I shall therefore give you a short statement, gathered from the notes in his traveling journal, along with what is consistent with my personal knowledge. After spending about eight days in Edinburgh, (where I had the pleasure of receiving your letters of introduction, and showing him some slight attentions, for which I felt more than rewarded by the enjoyment I had in his society and conversation,) he left this for London towards the end of August, and remained there until the 19th of October. During that period, he had formed an acquaintance with several excellent and distinguished individuals, to whom he had brought letters of introduction from America; had evidently laid himself out to acquire correct information on almost every subject, whether of science or of religion, and visited several places in the vicinity of the metropolis, though during the whole time his health appears to have been gradually declining. So early, indeed, as the 16th September, I find this entry on his notes: "Am confined to my bed the greater part of my time yet—a very great trial of patience and resignation, to be again prostrated, in a land of strangers, at so great a distance from home, and with the prospect of a speedy approach of cold weather. But may God grant that some good may come out of my afflictions. May they serve to wean me from the world, and to direct my thoughts, and feelings, and motives of conduct, towards him, and that nobler state of existence promised to the good hereafter."

On the 20th October, he reached Calais, rode next day to Boulogne, and on the 23d to Montrueil, when he was confined so as to be unable to proceed. On the 24th, he thus wrote: "This is a severe trial of one's power of resignation. I begin to think I shall not reach the south of France this season, and if I can get as far as Paris, I ought to feel grateful for it, and consider myself happy. God grant, if I am to leave my bones in this foreign land, like the Rev. Mr. Thatcher, I may grow in submission as hope declines, and that I too may be grateful for the kind severity with which death may be conducting me to another, and (it may be) a better world."

With the 28th, on which he returned as far as Boulogne, being unable to proceed on his journey, his notes terminate. Subsequently he returned to London, where he received the most particularly kind and Christian attentions from Dr. Burder, son to the Secretary of the Lond. Miss. Soc., and from whom, on leaving that for Edinburgh, he received a special introductory letter to Dr. Robert Hamilton, a young physician of excellent talents, and distinguished Christian character.

On reaching this about the 10th of November, he wrote me a short note, mentioning his arrival, his intention of spending the winter in Edinburgh, and saying that he should be glad to see me when convenient. Besides being quite unaware of his being seriously indisposed, I had so much unavoidable duty on my hands, I delayed calling from day to day, till on the morning of Thursday sevennight, I received a note from Dr. Hamilton, stating that he and Dr. Abercrombie had been attending him for several days, and that they considered him as very dangerously ill indeed, and that he thought it would be a satisfaction for me to see him. Almost immediately after breakfast I accordingly went to his lodgings, and found him in a much weaker state than I was prepared for, even by Dr. Hamilton's notice. His strength seemed completely exhausted, and his voice so feeble that it was with difficulty I could hear the few words he was able to speak to me. Yet on asking him how he felt, particularly as to the state of his mind, I heard him distinctly say, "My hope rests on the sure foundation laid in Zion." Having spoken a little with him, I prayed beside him, and I never shall forget the emphasis with which, at its conclusion, he said, Amen, or the affectionate pressure of his hand, or the "God bless you" with which he bade me farewell. Along with Drs. Abercrombie and Hamilton, I saw him again in the evening, when he appeared somewhat revived. On Friday I was prevented by indisposition from going out, but I saw him on Saturday, and again prayed beside him, with which he evidently seemed much pleased. On Sabbath I had to preach forenoon, afternoon, and evening, so that it was out of my power to call for him, and about four o'clock on Monday morning his spirit was dislodged from its earthly tabernacle. Nothing could surpass the attention he experienced from Drs. A. and H., who indeed are influenced by the true spirit of the gospel, and who, feeling peculiar interest in him, as a stranger, but who they hoped was a Christian brother, were most anxious to do everything for his comfort as well as relief. His body was interred in the ministers' burial ground here, in a spot immediately beneath a stone tablet in the wall, on which a suitable inscription may be cut, or into which a small marble slab, with such an inscription, may be inserted. * * * *

When a man distinguished in the walks of active life dies, his memory long survives him, because it is connected in the minds of men, with his actions. They have only to look at what he accomplished in the senate, or the field, and his character stands distinctly before them animated and glowing, true to life and nature. His friends, too, can point to a course of successful efforts, or to some brilliant action, and in doing this, they pronounce the best eulogy. But the retired scholar is engaged in none of those brilliant and imposing actions, that in the eyes of the people reflect a lustre on the agent, whatever may be his real worth or demerit. And when he dies, though a few will cherish his memory in their hearts, because they knew him well, and loved him well; others, as they see no train of effects flowing from his efforts, which "come home to men's business and bosoms"—regard him simply as an individual of the human family, and his death only as a " unit withdrawn from the sum of human existence." There is then the more propriety in presenting the character of such a one for a nearer inspection, that others as well as his friends may understand what were the mental and moral qualities that constituted its real worth, and by dwelling on these excellences, may copy into themselves what they admired in him.

In looking at Mr. Woodward's character, we are not so much struck with any one or a few prominent features, as by a happy combination and symmetry of the whole. This is true, whether you regard his intellectual habits, or the active powers which gave rise to these habits, or the acquisitions which arose from them as a joint result. It not unfrequently happens, in men of highly distinguished reputation, that by the side of some very marked and brilliant traits, there are deficiencies equally marked, and faults equally prominent, which when subtracted from their excellences, leave the general amount but small. They may have cultivated some faculties to the exclusion of their other faculties, or they may have placed themselves under the dominion of a particular class of feelings, until these become their master passion ; or they may have sought for eminence in a narrow range of acquisitions. But he, while he sought for none of these brilliant traits, avoided the correspondent deficiencies ; for he wished to cultivate his whole mind to the extent of its capacities, rather than any set of powers at the expense of the rest. He had a quick relish for intellectual excellence of every kind, as seen in others, and he loved to hold communion with those great minds who have been the lights of the world, " by whom the torch of science has been successively seized and transmitted." By intercourse with such minds, introduced to him through the medium of their works, he acquired an increased love for truth, in the various branches of knowledge, speculative and practical, that led him to be unsatisfied with superficial views, and in the diligent investigation of first principles, to seek for her among the innermost shrines of her temple.

The love of knowledge, united with the admiration of intellectual excellence, forming the exciting motive, the mode that he adopted in the prosecution of his studies deserves notice. The first point in his estimation to be gained, was an accurate acquaintance with his own mental defects, both in regard to habits and acquisitions, that he might thus be able to subject his mind to the proper discipline for establishing good habits, and apply to it the appropriate objects for promoting valuable attainments. He had read what Newton said: "If I have done the public some service, it is due to nothing but industry and patient thought." His industry in acquiring knowledge, or in preparing himself for communicating this knowledge, was unwearied. You might have seen it, not only in his regular hours of study, but likewise in his seasons of comparative relaxation; for even then he was employed, either in conversation on some important topic, or in making observations upon men and things, or in committing to paper some train of thought, or in taking an abstract of some book that pleased him. His plan was, not so far to exhaust himself by some great effort, as to require complete relaxation, in order to recruit his spirits and power of attention; but it was by patient thought, perseveringly continued, to possess himself of extensive views of the various subjects of inquiry, and to weave them, as it were, into the very texture of his mind. Even in his hours of sickness, when his body was borne down by lassitude, would his mind rally its powers, not to a nervous excitement, but to a gentle exercise, which at the time appeared salutary, but in the end may have contributed to impair the energies of life.

His attainments, the fruits of his constant and well directed application, though considerably various, should be estimated by their completeness rather than their variety. Here two particulars may be mentioned, and the first is this, that he was very much in the habit of retaining the proofs in his mind upon which his conclusions were founded. This he was able very conveniently to do, because in his investigations he committed the arguments to paper, and by referring to these frequently and passing them through his mind, they became firmly associated with the conclusion, and could be summoned whenever necessary to show that his knowledge was actual, as well as habitual. A second particular is this, that he was well acquainted with subjects and sciences in their relations with each other, and with the various arts of life ; and thus he was able to give a practical character to his speculations, and make them interesting and valuable to men of common attainments. He brought away from college, when he was graduated, a thorough knowledge of the books recited, and a very large amount of the instruction delivered in lectures, and less formally. Soon after that period, he devoted considerable attention to philology and philosophical criticism, which were of great assistance to him in turning his attention to the precise import of language, and enabling him to clothe his conceptions with a graceful drapery. But the studies to which he devoted the largest share of his attention, and in which he made the greatest acquisitions, were the philosophy of the human mind, and political science. The transition from the one, which treats of man as an intellectual and moral being, to the other, which treats of the same being as a member of political society, was natural; and they both furnish, in the mighty mass of facts upon which as sciences they rest, ample scope for a mind of the largest powers. By the exercise of a discriminating judgment, which enabled him to perceive the near differences of things as well as their general correspondence, by a patience of doubting, which enabled him to take a comprehensive survey of a subject, and by rigidly applying the rules of Bacon, *the Prophet of the arts*, which have since been revealed by his followers, he obtained an uncommon degree of acquaintance with the sesciences, not only as they are exhibited by the ablest elementary writers, but likewise as they are elicited by an examination of one's own consciousness, and the details of general history. His pursuits led him frequently into an examination of the causes which conspired to give currency to various opinions, and in doing this he often found by experience the truth of that maxim, "to trace an error to its fountain head is to refute it." A diligent examination and comparison of these writers led him to discover those great principles of philosophy, upon which all are agreed, and likewise pointed out to him the various legitimate objects of inquiry; while the facts collected from general reading and observation, when classified and arranged, would have served him as valuable materials for those original investigations which he hoped to make. He was so much in the habit of using his pen in his studies, that he almost literally obeyed the injunction, *nil sine calamo;* yet considering the amount of his writings, he published very little.*

His style is pure and simple, for the most part of an argumentative tone, yet occasionally rising into a high strain of eloquence and pathos. The force of his reasoning does not consist in its mere formalities, in a succession of carefully wrought syllogisms, nor in the mystical use of general terms, nor in bringing forward artfully constructed paradoxes, to baffle the mind of others, and exhibit his own ingenuity; but rather in a fair and manly exhibition of a subject addressed to the good sense of mankind, and producing conviction, because it is found to agree with their consciousness and observation. The oration which he delivered before the Phi Beta Kappa Society, 1822, "On the practical tendency of the Moral, Political and Metaphysical Philosophy of the present Age," will be remembered by those who heard it, as a specimen of his mode of discussion. A more favorable specimen, perhaps, might be found in a dissertation he prepared for the Connecticut Academy, "On the structure of Civil Society."

His mind showed the effects of the discipline to which it had been subject. From cultivating a habit of reflection, he obtained the power of long continued attention to the subjects of consciousness, while at the same time, he lost little of his

* To the Christian Spectator he contributed the following articles: In the second volume, a Review of Memoirs of Samuel J. Mills, p. 250; An inquiry respecting Conscience, p. 337; A Review of the Means of National Prosperity, p. 358. In the third volume, On Purity of Heart, p. 225; Review of Stewart's Outlines, p. 244.

interest in external objects, and of certain classes of these objects he was a minute observer. His judgment was comprehensive, rather than acute, forming its decisions upon a careful survey of a subject in all its relations, rather than upon verbal distinctions, and dialectic subtleties. His memory, as it had been trained to depend more upon scientific than casual associations, was more distinguished for its retentive power, than its readiness. His taste was correct, and in the latter years of his life very much refined, by the contemplation of the various objects of grandeur and beauty with which his mind was conversant. It was more remarkable for a ready notice and admiration of what is lovely, than for detecting and dwelling on faults.

But it was not merely or chiefly for intellectual excellence that he sought. He wished to devote his improved faculties and acquired knowledge, to the high purpose of benefiting his fellow-men. He was well aware that nothing but moral excellence can meet the favor of God, or gain admission into that high world, for which the present is only a scene of preparation. " It has," he remarks, " sometimes appeared to me to be very strange, that while so much is said of the cultivation of the mind, so little is said of the cultivation of the heart. The moral powers are of a more exalted character than the intellectual; and it would seem that they demand proportionally, a more careful and assiduous culture; so also moral excellence is far more desirable than intellectual, and hence also the superior importance of the culture of the heart to that of the understanding." He always appeared to have a vivid feeling of approbation towards virtuous actions when performed by others, and by dwelling on the character of those who habitually performed them, he acquired a high admiration, not only for the agents, but for those moral qualities that constituted the governing principle of their lives. The same qualities he admired in the benevolent Author of the universe, and in the character of that Holy Being, who came down from heaven, and exhibited to mortals the moral glories of the only begotten of the Father. These qualities he wished to incorporate into his own character. "I am," he remarks, "apt to consider this world as a school, where we are to be disciplined for another state of existence. Almost everything, in the arrangement of things here, seems adapted to promote our progress in virtue and piety. The great means of our discipline are our various temptations. By overcoming temptations, we advance in moral excellence. The impressions they make on our hearts, are gradually weakened; while our habits of active virtue are strengthened, and our power of self-command increased.

Having this high admiration for moral excellence, he devoted himself with the most assiduous care to its attainment, as the grand object of his existence. He entered deeply into the consideration of those relations in which man is placed as a social and dependent being, that thus he might be able to understand his duties to God and man, founded on these relations; and that thus too he might, by enlightening his conscience, place himself more completely under its dominion. In forming his opinions, though he could not perhaps, in all cases, go to the full length of the sentiment of Burke, "that our passions instruct our reason," yet he was very much in the habit of consulting his moral feelings. Such an action, he would say, cannot be wrong, whatever theory it may oppose; for it is consonant with my moral feelings. He likewise in adopting religious doctrines, while he anxiously examined the usual proofs, was accustomed carefully to observe their moral tendency; taking it for granted that truth is favorable to virtue, and that therefore any doctrine that is shown to be unfavorable to virtue, must be false. He was convinced that God has written his will on the heart of man, as well as in his word, and that in the words of Melancthon, "he never meant to supersede by a law graven on stone, that which he had graven with his own finger on the table of the heart." He listened to the holy voice of nature as to the language of God, the more readily because he found that it coincided in its import with the oracles of truth. In examining the truths of Revelation, he was not satisfied with an assent to them, on a superficial view; but he went into an extended investigation of the proofs upon which the canonical authority of each separate important book is established, and then applied the rules of interpretation to the discovery of its doctrines. His mind learned to attach less importance to those points of controversy that have "drifted to the leeward with the change of time," than to those practical truths that can be applied daily and habitually to the heart. He watched his emotions no less carefully than his intellectual habits, that he might repress those that the word of God condemns, and encourage those that deserve cultivation.

The effects of this love of moral excellence, and of this discipline of his emotions, aided as we trust by that good Spirit whose influences he habitually implored, were strikingly manifest in his moral progress. Instead of yielding himself, as most do, to the influence of passive impressions from surrounding objects, and changing in feelings and opinions as these objects change; he was governed by that class of motives which have very properly been denominated rational principles of action. What is my duty? What is the will of God? What is best on the whole? These were the questions that seemed to be constantly present to his mind, and in searching in his conduct for the answer he gave to these questions, we are very seldom able to discover that his understanding was under the blinding influence of passion, or confused by the complex nature of the subject, or deceived by the power of association. A friend says of him, "he was more under the control of principle, and less under that of impulse and feeling, than any man I ever knew." This habit of deciding upon mature reflection, may have taken away somewhat of boldness and apparent energy from his character, while it gave him the qualities of consistency and uniformity in a very high degree. There are minds, especially those formed in the scenes of active life, in which, "on each glance of thought, decision follows, as the thunderbolt pursues the flash." The decisions of his mind resembled the silent and regular laws of nature, whose operations can always be predicted. You had only to determine what would be his opinion of duty in given circumstances, and you would know what course of conduct he would pursue.

United to this habitual subjection of his emotions to a sense of duty, was a strong feeling of good will towards men, which seemed indeed plainly to comprise in itself that scriptural virtue, charity, so far as it fulfills the second table of the law. It is sometimes the case, that men of retired habits, who have attended for some years to the abstract pursuits of science, have perceived in themselves a growing indifference towards their brethren of the human family, which approaches even misanthropy, if they have a keen sense of the follies and vices of mankind. His studies led him to contemplate mankind in their several relations, and towards them in all these relations he appeared to have the appropriate feelings. Whatever concerned the welfare of the human race, he felt concerned him, for he was a lover of his species. Whatever concerned the welfare of the land in which he lived, he felt concerned him, for he was a lover of his country. In his intercourse with general society, which, owing to his feeble health, was not very extensive, he exhibited that Christian courtesy towards others which told them that he would not carelessly injure the feelings even of the humblest human being. Towards the opinions of others, when they differed from his own, he exhibited a uniform candor, which told them that he valued truth more than victory in argument. With his intimate friends, he was frank and confiding in the disclosure of his feelings and purposes; and if it be true that in every man's mind there is an interior circle into which none but himself and the Divinity can enter, all the concealment which he allowed in himself seemed to spring from the best of motives, and not from a regard to any personal advantage. He could perform towards his friends the high duty of kindly admonishing them of their faults, because he sought to promote their excellence as he did his own; but he seemed to dwell with the most pleasure on the bright parts of their character, and thus kept his mind free from suspicion and distrust, and incorporated into his own character the traits which he most loved in them. His temper was uniform. His manners were unaffected and pleasing. In his person he was tall, and apparently formed for strength and activity. His countenance was of a fine order of faces, containing a frank and guileless expression, suiting well with the cast of his mind.

Though unknown by profession as the disciple of Christ, those best acquainted with him believe that piety formed the crowning grace in his character. It may indeed be viewed as the parentof the rest. "How obvious it is," he remarks, "that a religion which is designed to transform us anew, should operate powerfully on our *whole* moral constitution. It should soften our rough dispositions, sweeten our tempers, and make us more amiable as well as more excellent. It should take the acrimonious speech from our lips, and make the voice cease to be a vehicle of unkindness. It will produce this effect—because it will remove the cause—it will dry up the fountain; for the character of our conversation will depend upon the disposition and feelings that are kept alive in the heart." His habitual love to God sprung from the habitual contemplation of him in his word and in his works; perceiving in the magnificent scene around him, the proofs of his attributes, and his superintending providence, he wished firmly to associate in his mind every event and every object falling under his notice with its great author, that thus he might not only behold his presence and his glory, but likewise constantly listen to his voice. Instead of viewing the "great and the little things of this world only as toys spread on the lap and the carpet of nature, for the childhood of our immortal being," he wished to elevate them to their true meaning, and gather from each a serious lesson to prepare him for that being. Kindling his devotion in this manner, by direct views of God as its source, rather than from the variable feelings of others, and guarding it with a zealous care—it burned with a pure and constant flame upon the altar of his heart. As he felt a lively gratitude to God for the bestowment of his mercies, so, when these mercies were removed, he felt a correspondent resignation. Sickness, while it darkened his earthly prospects, seemed to lift his soul into a region of perpetual sunshine. Instead of rendering him selfish by fixing his attention exclusively on his own wants, it seemed to quicken his social sympathies, and increase his benevolence towards others. Scarcely a murmur was heard to escape his lips. On one occasion, during a paroxysm of pain, he was observed suddenly to suppress every expression of anguish. Being asked how he could remain so quiet, distressed as he was,—" Whisper duty in my ear," was his reply, " if you ever again witness in me the least expression of impatience." By previous discipline, his soul was armed with religious fortitude for enduring even the final agony. " As for the conduct," he remarks, " proper in a dying hour—our obligation to the performance of the duties which are still within our power, continues; and among these duties, the most difficult probably is entire resignation to the divine will. Not a word, or action, or look, should be the external sign of an unyielding, and so far as the nature of the disorder will admit, of a discomposed spirit within. All should, if possible, be as tranquil, as serene, as the setting of an unclouded sun." It would be a solace to have been present at his dying hour; but God, we trust his best friend, was present, to calm his fears, and to inspire him with confidence to " rest his hopes on the foundation laid in Zion." He is gone, but he is not lost—he will still live in the virtues which his example called into existence—he will live in the hearts of a numerous circle of friends in his native country—while in the land where his ashes repose, some kindred minds will still think of him whom they now describe as the *amiable American stranger*. He is not lost; he is gone, we trust, to that high world where his thoughts loved to go—where Dwight his father, and Fisher his brother in excellence, had gone—where intellect and moral feeling, which here he cultivated with so much care, will expand forever.

His brother, Dr. Charles Woodward, of Middletown, Conn., through the kindness of Professor More, of Edinburgh University, placed, in the year 1852, a marble tablet to his memory, in the wall mentioned by Dr. Dickson in his letter.

The following lines were written by the poet Brainerd, on the occasion of his death :

Another! 'tis a sad word to the heart,
  That one by one has lost its hold on life,
From all it loved or valued, forced to part
  In detail. Feeling dies not by the knife
  That cuts at once and kills—its tortured strife
Is with distilled affliction, drop by drop
  Oozing its bitterness. Our world is rife
With grief and sorrow ; all that we would prop,
Or would be propped with, falls—when shall the ruin stop.

The sea has one, and Palestine has one,
And Scotland has the last. The snooded maid
Shall gaze in wonder on the stranger's stone,
  And wipe the dust off with her Tartan plaid—
  And from the lonely grave where thou art laid,
Turn to some other monument—nor know
  Whose grave she passes, or whose name she read ;
Whose loved and honored relics lie below ;
Whose is immortal joy, and whose is mortal woe.

There is a world of bliss hereafter—else
  Why are the bad above, the good beneath
The green grass of the grave ? The mower fells
  Flowers and briars alike. But man shall breathe
  (When he his desolating blade shall sheathe
And rest him from his work,) in a pure sky,
  Above the smoke of burning world ; and death
On scorched pinions with the dead shall lie
When time with all his years and centuries has passed by.

REVIEW OF SILLIMAN'S CHEMISTRY.*

If the excellence of a work consist mainly in its adaptation to the professed object for which it was written, this truly is one of the best productions on the subject of Chemistry, that we have ever examined. In the preface, the author informs us, that "the object of this work is to present the science in the most intelligible form to those who are learning its elements"; and the principles laid down, the facts adduced in support of these principles, and the mode of their presentation, are all in keeping with the design. Throughout the whole, he evidently proceeds on the ground that the students for whose use it was prepared, are entirely unacquainted with the subjects of which it treats; that he is writing for the novice, and not for the initiated; and he endeavors, and we think very successfully, "to find his way into the mind of the pupil, and to fix there the knowledge presented to him."

When Sir Humphrey Davy composed his work on Chemical Philosophy, he had a different object in view; namely, to classify and arrange the great phenomena of the science in such a manner, that Chemistry, arrayed in all the glories of his brilliant discoveries, might not fear to take her proper rank with her sister sciences. Though he probably fell short of what was due from his fine genius, he produced a very valuable work for the master, but not such an one as the student wants. Dr. Henry's "Elements of Experimental Chemistry" is in some degree chargeable with the same defect; for it is evident, that his eye is directed rather to the new discoveries

* Elements of Chemistry in the order of the Lectures given in Yale College. By Benjamin Silliman, Professor of Chemistry, Pharmacy, Mineralogy, and Geology. In two vols. New Haven. 1831.

in the science, than to what has long been known; and that in the composition of the work he was thinking more of chemists than of learners; so that while he is careful not to depart from the dignity of science, he has failed of communicating all that interest to his work, which it ought to have to recommend it to those who have but just entered on the study of Chemistry. He is correct and discriminating, and the successive editions present a fair view of the progress of the science. But however excellent the works just mentioned are, the one as showing great genius in generalizing, and the other a sound judgment, they are neither of them well adapted to be text-books in our colleges.

In the preface to the work before us, the author remarks that

"The materials of this work have been gradually accumulating since 1802. They have been drawn from scientific journals, from the transactions of learned societies, and from the principal writers who have flourished since the middle of the last century,—*the Augustan age of Chemistry.* From works of an earlier date, light has been occasionally derived, as well as from notes and recollections of the instructions of the distinguished teachers, to whom the author was formerly so happy as to listen. In this view, he takes particular satisfaction in naming the late Dr. Murray of Edinburgh, and Professor Thomas C. Hope, still a distinguished ornament of the university in the same city.

"Various notices, derived from the author's own experience, and from his personal communications with others, are introduced, with occasional figures, for illustration; and in the notes, many miscellaneous facts are preserved.

"In the immediate preparation of this work for the press, the original memoirs of authors and discoverers have been often consulted, and the abstract has been frequently drawn from them, rather than from the elementary books; but the analyses contained in the latter have not unfrequently been adopted; sometimes even after a careful examination of the original; and for this reason, among others, that the statements contained in them could be often, without injury, still further abridged. In such cases, several eminent elementary writers have been diligently compared on the same subject; and thus omissions have been supplied, and obscurity has been removed, either by the comparison or by resorting to the first record.

"References to the original memoirs have been always preserved, when such memoirs were attainable; and when the books containing them were not at hand, the citations have been copied from the latest systematical writers. Credit has also, in most instances, been given to elementary writers for materials drawn from their pages; but for brevity, and especially when the facts are the common stock of the science, the references have been sometimes omitted, or an initial letter only retained. There are, however, some works, to which a more particular acknowledgment is due. Those of Bergman and Scheele; the lectures of Dr. Black, by Robison; the system of Dr. Thomson, in all its editions, and also his more recent work on the First Principles of Chemistry; the Dictionaries of Nicholson, Aikins, and Ure, the Compendium of Dr. Hare, the Dispensatory of Dr. Coxe, the Technology of Dr. Bigelow, the Operative Chemist of Gray, and the Chemical Manipulation of Mr. Faraday; the System of the late Dr. Murray, and his Elements, ably edited by his son; as also the writings of Mr. Dalton; the works of Lavoisier, Chaptal, Berthollet, and Fourcroy; the System of Thénard, in its most recent edition, and his miscellaneous writings, especially in connection with Gay-Lussac; and those of Dr. Priestley, Bishop Watson, Mr. Parkes, Professor Berzelius, and Sir H. Davy, including also his Elements;—these are among the leading authorities, although it would be easy to increase the catalogue.

"A recent work by Dr. Turner, of the London University, has been of great utility. It is highly scientific and very exact, particularly on the facts and doctrines of definite and multiple proportions, and combining equivalents; and many of its details have been adopted." Preface, pp. 4, 5.

After the preface comes the plan of the work, which we shall again have occasion to notice, and then follows an introduction, containing a spirited sketch of the main branches of natural science, and the connection between them.

"CHEMISTRY. The remaining branch of science relating to natural bodies, begins where natural philosophy and natural history stop. As the gleanings of its early history may be found in the prefaces of the larger elementary works on Chemistry, we shall here omit the vague annals of its infancy, and the delusions of its middle age.

"It would exceed our limits to trace the progress of Chemistry from age to age; to unfold the delusions of ALCHEMY, whose object was to discover the philosopher's stone, an imaginary substance, which, it was supposed, would convert the baser metals into gold or silver, or to speak of the equally delusive pursuit after the GRAND CATHOLICON, or universal remedy, which was to remove every disease; to avert death, and confer terrestrial immortality on man; or to mention the imaginary ALCAHEST, or universal solvent, whose power it was supposed nothing could resist. The alchemists indeed, imagined that these miraculous virtues resided in one and the same substance, and during the dark ages, most of the cultivators of what was then called Chemistry, smitten with the delirium of Alchemy, pursued their occult processes in cells and caverns, remote from the light of heaven, and wasted their days and nights, their talents and fortunes, in a vain pursuit. The alchemist, however, accumulated many valuable facts, which have been employed with good advantage, in laying the foundations of modern Chemical Science.

"Some knowledge of chemical arts is coeval with the earliest stages of human society; and it has happened with this, as with other branches of natural knowledge, that many facts were discovered and accumulated, in the practice of the arts, and in domestic economy, long before any general truths were established, by a course of inductive reasoning, upon the phenomena.

"The arts are all either mechanical or chemical, and not unfrequently both are involved in the same processes. The practices of the arts may be regarded as experiments in natural philosophy and chemistry. The object of the arts is usually gain; but he, or any other person, who views the facts correctly, may reason upon them advantageously, and thus obtain important instruction.

"The *Science* of Chemistry, considered as a collection of elementary truths derived from the study of facts, can scarcely be referred to a period much beyond the commencement of the last century, and its principal triumphs have been achieved since the middle of that period. It would be premature, to detail on the present occasion, the particular discoveries, which, like stars, rising successively above the horizon, have broken forth in rapid succession. Those discoveries, their periods and their authors, will be mentioned, in giving the history of each particular substance. At present, it would not be proper to attempt any thing more than to convey to those to whom the subject may be new, a general conception of the nature, extent, and objects of the Science of Chemistry, reserving the details for the time when they will be both the most intelligible and the most interesting.

"DEFINITION.* *Chemistry is that science which investigates the composition of all bodies, and the laws by which it is governed.*

"Not satisfied with the knowledge of the external properties and the mechanical relations, which are unfolded by natural history and by physics, but taking them into view, and retaining and using their principal discoveries, chemistry proceeds to investigate the hidden constitution of every species of material existence in earth, sea, and air.

"*Earth, air, fire, and water*, were the four elements of the ancient school. They have, however, yielded to analysis, and water, bland and simple as it seems, contains two bodies, whose properties are entirely different from its own and from those of each other: burning, when mingled and ignited in large quantities, with violent explosion; and in a small stream, with a heat, which melts and dissipates the firmest substances. We should never have conjectured that water, whose great prerogative it is to extinguish fire, contains both a combustible and a supporter of combustion.

"*The air*, the *pabulum* of life to the whole animal and vegetable creation, mild and negative like water, is not *simple*, but incidentally contains many bodies,—essentially, however, only two; one of which, and that constituting four-fifths of the whole, is, and was intended to be, in a high degree noxious and even deadly to animal life, and fatal to combustion. The air does not destroy life instead of invigorating our frames, and extinguish instead of inflaming combustion, because the prevalent noxious principle of the air, (nitrogen) is balanced by a life and fire-sustaining principle, (oxygen) too vigorous to be trusted alone, and therefore diluted exactly to the proper degree by the opposite principle; both being, by another extraordinary provision, sustained, in constant proportion, and thus producing a salubrious and unchanging atmosphere.

* "For various definitions the student may see the principal authors, Thompson, Fourcroy, Henry, Murray, La Grange, Thénard, Davy, Brande, Turner, Hare, and others."

"The *earth* under our feet, the soil, the sand, the gravel, the firm substance of the rocks, is not simple. In this ancient but assumed element, we have a double complexness. The one imagined simple earth contains at least nine, and each of these is again complex, containing for one principle, oxygen, the same that exists both in water and in the atmosphere, united to nine or ten varieties of metals or combustibles, none of which are known in common life.

"He who is acquainted with the wonderful effects of chemical combination, will not think it strange that half the weight of marble is carbonic acid, and that metals, when combined with oxygen, resemble very exactly the earthly substances.

"*Light as well as heat*, is contained in common fire, and therefore it is not simple, unless fire and heat are varieties of one and the same thing.

"Modern research has proved that, besides light, which, in its seven prismatic colors, is contained in the solar beam, there is also, in this emanation, an opake, radiant principle, which accompanying light and heat, neither warms nor illuminates, but acts to decompose certain chemical compounds; that there are opake rays which warm but do not illuminate, and illuminating rays which are cold to the sense of living animals, but impart to the universe its splendid drapery of colors; and that, associated with one or more of these emanations, there is a surprising power, which imparts magnetism to a needle, and gives it the properties of the load-stone. But we have used the word element without defining it.

"*An element is an undecomposable body*,—it is therefore simple, or in other words, not reducible to any other form of existence. We must, however, carefully distinguish between *real elements*, and those which are such only in relation to the present state of our knowledge. When modern science speaks of a body as elementary, it intends nothing more than that it has not been decomposed. It is therefore simple as far as we know, but it is possible that by future efforts, it may be decomposed. Although we have no reason to doubt that there are *real* elements, we cannot say that we are certainly in possession of any one element. It is, however, perfectly safe to reason upon bodies as elementary, until they are proved to be compound. Iron is, as far as we know, a simple body; we cannot as yet exhibit it in any simple form; all we can do, is to alter its size and figure, without at all changing its nature.

But iron rust, or the scales which fly off when red hot iron is hammered, are not simple; they consist of iron combined with oxygen, one of the principles of the atmosphere; we can explain these substances in a simpler form; the iron which they contain can be separated from the aerial principle, and both can be exhibited apart, and thus the proof will be complete; red lead and red precipitate are still better examples, because the former can be partially, and the latter wholly, brought back to the condition of metals, by simply heating them.

"The four ancient elements, earth, air, fire, and water, were assumed at hazard, because they are so conspicuous and important; the conception was grand, but it was wholly erroneous.

"Instead of four elements, we have at the present time not less than fifty, nearly four-fifths of which are metals; the remainder are chiefly combustibles and bodies which, combining with combustibles and metals with peculiar energy, are generally called supporters of combustion.*

"Our simple bodies then are,

1. Metals, about . . . . 40†
2. Combustibles not metallic, ... 7†
3. Principles or supporters of combustion, . . 2 or 3
4. One body, or possibly two,‡ of an undetermined character, in all . . . . . 50 or 51
5. Imponderable bodies, light, heat, and electricity; besides the power called magnetism and the other varieties of attraction.

"The principal object of Chemistry is to display, first the great powers upon which its phenomena depend; and, secondly, the properties of the elements, the mode and energy of their action, the combinations which they are capable of forming, the properties of the resulting compounds, and the laws by which they are governed. This statement obviously includes all bodies, natural and artificial. There are many chemical compounds made by art,

* "Some object to this phrase, preferring to consider combustion as being only an example of intense chemical action; this view is philosophical; but combustion is so frequent an occurrence, and involves so many important chemical events, that it is convenient, in accordance with the general practice of mankind, to designate it and the bodies contained in it, by a peculiar phraseology."

† "It is perhaps doubtful, where some of these bodies ought to be classed,—whether among metals or combustibles."

‡ "Perhaps silicon and bromine; we have, however, classed them where they appear to belong."

which, as far as we are informed, do not exist in nature, and there are many natural bodies which art has not yet been able to imitate." Vol. I. Introduction, pp. 14—19.

We have already expressed the opinion, that this work is eminently adapted to the object for which it was prepared, and one circumstance which shows that it is so, is the vast number of interesting facts contained in it, illustrating most distinctly and satisfactorily the principles of Chemistry. They are drawn, not merely from the experiments of the laboratory, but likewise from the shop of the artist, and the grand processes of nature. They are not only such as are found scattered through elementary works and scientific journals, but they are also such as the author himself gathered from his own experience and observation, during the nearly thirty years which he has devoted to the subject. They are also, many of them at least, related in a manner so distinct, graphic, and attractive, as to prove that he is not only a close observer, but a warm admirer of this class of the phenomena of nature.

Now this is just what the student wants, as one said a few days since, who was endeavoring to glean some knowledge from a dry text-book. "I should be very much interested in Chemistry, if I could find *data*." It is peculiarly a science dependent upon facts, which are needed to give a local habitation to its doctrines; and without them, though one should write a system with all the acuteness of Aristotle, and the elegance of Plato, it would not interest a novice any more than would a metaphysical system of divinity, compared with the narrations of the Evangelists. Every science has its metaphysics, and we know there are some who would prefer a cold statement of the abstract principles of Chemistry; just as there are those, who, from their attachment to Anatomy, would feel more interest in a naked skeleton than they would in a form through which life pours its mantling tide, and in which intelligence dwells. And we apprehend that in the progress of investigation and discovery, the tendency is to lay aside facts and to dwell on principles. One chemical philosopher, in all the ardor of original investigation, arrives at certain conclusions, which he publishes to the world with the facts upon which they are built, and the uses to which they can be applied. Another, adopting these conclusions as his premises, while he says little about those facts or those uses, presses on in the field of discovery, and in his turn enlarges the boundaries of knowledge. And it has happened, that some of the late works on this source are very deficient in those interesting phenomena, upon which its great principles are founded, and in the discussion of the practical application of those principles; while they are fuller than the older systems of the doctrines of the science. This is the case with Dr. Turner's recent work; which is worthy of all praise for the philosophical accuracy of its statements, and yet has very little attraction for one who has just entered on the study of the science, as we have had good opportunity of knowing. And here we are happy to fortify our opinions, by quoting the kindred sentiments of Dr. Ure, from the preface of his Dictionary of Chemistry.

> "It must however be confessed, that the listlessness with which chemical systems are frequently perused, is not entirely the fault of the reader. Too many of these books are dry compilations of names, qualities and numbers, in methodical complexity, containing no intelligible examples of chemical inquiry; nay, hardly a trace of the genius of discovery or of the splendid course which it has run."

The same good judgment which appears in the selection of a great number of facts, led the author to dwell on those doctrines that are the most important, and interesting; and this is another circumstance, which renders the work well adapted to the purpose for which it was prepared. When Nicholas Lemery published his course of Chemistry, we are told that it was devoured like a novel, and we are disposed to believe, that by a selection of certain topics, illustrated in a suitable manner, a book might be prepared which would be equally attractive at the present time. Let the grand doctrine of *caloric* be exhibited, with its various phenomena of radiation and slow communication ; in its vanishing and re-appearing forms, according as it becomes latent or sensible, with its several sources and its powerful effects, whether they are seen in clothing the earth with verdure and working into life the tribes that people it; in changing the dimensions and the state of bodies by its expanding and decomposing power ; or as they appear in the steam-engine, the noblest trophy of the conquest of science over nature ; and in the volcano, which sends forth from the interior of the earth its desolating flood. Let the simple combustibles, such as carbon, phosphorus, sulphur, and hydrogen, find a place ; and the grand supporter of combustion, oxygen, in its several states, solid in union with the metals, liquid in the water we drink, gaseous in the air we breathe ; united with one class of bodies to form the alkalies, earths, and oxyds, and with another to form the common acids ; expanded in large quantities to support animal life, and, by a beautiful arrangement of Providence, restored to the atmosphere by the vegetable creation. To these should be added chlorine, some of the more important metals, some of the proximate vegetable principles. It would be highly important not to omit galvanism, with its wonderful phenomena, and the laws of affinity, especially as they are exhibited in the doctrines of definite proportion. Let these and some other topics be selected and presented with sufficient detail in an appropriate form, and in the same spirit with which Sir Humphrey Davy wrote his last work, though in a less ambitious style, and the science could not fail of awakening a deep interest, and of securing more attention than it now does.

Chemistry has become very extensive in its ordinary branches and applications, and we see not why the same course should not be taken in preparing works for the learner, on this as on most of the other sciences. He who prepares a work for schools and colleges, on arithmetic, or algebra, or geometry, does not think it necessary to include in it the theory of numbers, or of analytical functions, or the porisms recorded by Pappus; and for the plain reason, that these investigations would not only be of no use to the student in his incipient course, but from their intricacy, would be actually discouraging and repulsive. But in the larger works on Chemistry, such as for instance, Thompson's, Murray's, and Henry's, there are subjects introduced, with which it is impossible that a student should become acquainted in the time usually allotted to the study of Chemistry in our colleges, and which must serve only as stumbling-blocks in his way.

We are happy to find that M. Lavoisier justifies this view of the subject, in the course which he took in the composition of his work; though the reasons for it, owing to the progress of the science, are much stronger now than they were when he wrote. Having omitted the subject of affinities, he remarks in his preface that he had done so, because he considered the "science of affinities as holding the same place with regard to the other branches of Chemistry, that the higher or transcendental Geometry does with respect to the simple and elementary part."

In the work before us, Professor Silliman, while he has conformed to the common mode of saying something on every substance, has, for the most part, bestowed attention upon each according to its relative importance, presenting some of them in a strong light, and casting into the shade others of less importance.

The next circumstance to be mentioned which renders this work well adapted to the object for which it was prepared, is its arrangement. Had it been prepared for the purpose of presenting to thorough-bred chemists a logical view of the various substances in nature in their relations to each other, perhaps the order in which the subjects are treated, would not have been in every respect the most scientific; while it may be the best that could be devised for those for whose use it was especially designed, and who are supposed to know absolutely nothing on the subject of Chemistry. The problem to be solved was, what is the arrangement best adapted to awaken and sustain an interest in their minds, and communicate to them clear and adequate views of the science? and from his long experience and great success as a teacher, we think that no one is better qualified than the author to furnish a solution. There is an inherent difficulty in the case, which does not exist in the exact sciences, and it is not surprising that a man trained in these, should be dissatisfied with any system that can be proposed.

Bodies are frequently related to each other in themselves, or in their proximate principles, or in their ultimate principles.

For instance, carbonate of potash and carbonate of soda agree with each other in being made up in part of carbonic acid; and after this is removed by lime, the two substances, potash and soda, agree in being made up in part of oxygen; and after this is removed by iron turnings or charcoal, the two substances agree in being metallic. Now let a classification be adopted, founded on either of these relations, and there will be practical inconveniences of one kind or another, if the system be carried through. For particular bodies it would not be very difficult to determine what should be the arrangement, yet a mode that would answer for these, would not answer for all others. Among the British chemists, there is considerable diversity in their systems of arrangement, and which of them has adopted the best, it would be rather difficult to say; we are sure it is not Dr. Thompson, however meritorious he may be in other respects.

We are inclined to believe that too much importance has been attached to a logical system, just as theologians formerly thought lightly of doctrines, which could not find a place in some body of divinity. Instead of entering at large into arguments in support of our opinion, we shall barely allow ourselves space to quote a paragraph from Dugald Stewart's Dissertation on the Progress of Philosophy. Page 248, 1 dis. part II.

"The passion of the Germans for *systems*, is a striking feature in their literary taste, and is sufficient of itself to show that they have not yet passed their noviciate in philosophy." "To all such," says Mr. McLaurin, "as have just notions of the Great Author of the Universe and of his admirable workmanship, all complete and finished systems must appear suspicious."

"At the time when he wrote, such systems had not wholly lost their partisans in England, and the name of *system* continued to be the favorite title for a book, even among writers of the very first reputation. Hence the *System of Moral Philosophy*, by Hutcheson, and the *Complete System of Optics*, by Smith, titles which, when compared with the subsequent progress of these sciences, reflect some degree of ridicule upon their authors."

In the plan of the work before us the author remarks,

"I have not thought it best to describe the simple substances in uninterrupted succession. Such a method does not appear to me to present advantages sufficient to compensate for the inconvenience of plunging at once into the most complex parts of the science; which must be done, if we would draw the elementary bodies from their combinations, and present them in the beginning in a connected view." p. 1.

"The natural process of acquiring knowledge is the analytical, or the progress from the complex to the simple, from the whole to its parts; the shortest is the synthetic, that is, from the simple to the complex; from the parts to the whole; and this is the course now more generally pursued in Chemistry. If our knowledge were perfect, this would be not only the most obvious, but the best process; and perhaps that mode will be found to combine most advantages, which unites them both. With this view, I have therefore sometimes adopted the one and sometimes the other, aiming to present the most important elements and combinations as early as possible." p. 2.

"In teaching, the great object should be, *to find our way into the mind of the pupil, and to fix there the knowledge that we present to him.* He is ordinarily no judge of our theoretical views, with regard to classification and arrangement; he will in most cases even fail to understand us, when we discuss them; and he will be best satisfied with that course, which, in the most interesting and intelligible manner, presents to him the greatest amount of useful knowledge. Both in my public courses of lectures, and in the present work, I have, therefore, considered this object as paramount in importance to every other." p. 3.

Another circumstance which adds very much to the value of the work, is this, that it presents the doctrines of Chemistry in their connection with the practical arts of life. There is enough, indeed, in the grand and beautiful phenomena they unfold, to awaken interest and secure a generous and lasting attachment to the science from its own intrinsic excellence and beauty. But it must be confessed, that the *amor habendi* has gained a place in so many hearts, that even science herself is loved mainly for the dower she brings. You must convince men that Chemistry will enable them to increase their wealth, before they will consider the study of it as worthy of their attention. It was said by one, who had borne the honors of his country, and by his counsels had helped to increase her resources, in speaking of a young lady who was about to commence the study of Chemistry, "Why, if it will help her to make a better pudding, let her study it." Now to men of this class, who value every thing as it contributes to the amount of national or individual wealth, Chemistry, in its application to the arts, presents strong claims, as the experience of France can testify. Formerly, the arts were enveloped in mystery and concealment. They stood separate from each other, and a knowledge of some one of them was frequently transmitted from father to son as a valuable inheritance. But the lights of modern Chemistry have disclosed these confidently treasured secrets; and besides introducing a great many new arts, have shown a connection between those already known, that was not suspected to exist before.

It is in this way that Chemistry, by discovering the laws of nature, has been a source of wealth to those who have applied these laws to the practical arts of life, and enabled them to realize for themselves and their country, that of which the votaries of alchemy only dreamed.

Professor Silliman has generally mentioned the uses to which the various substances described are applied, and not unfrequently, some of the processes by which this application is made. As, for instance, under *silica*, he mentions some particulars concerning the manufacture of glass; under *alu-*

mina, the process for making porcelain and pottery; and under *nitre*, the mode in which gunpowder is made.

This work was needed. It was due from the author that he should promote the science by his pen, as he had long done by his lectures. It was due to the Institution with which he has been connected, with so much reputation to both. The science has undergone almost as many changes as the objects in the vegetable, the animal, and mineral kingdom, which it investigates, though no valuable truth is lost. *Omnia mutantur, nil interit.* Take as an instance the theories of combustion. At one time, the doctrine of phlogiston prevailed, with its successive modifications. In place of this, the views of Lavoisier were brought forward, and his house, we are told, became a temple of science, where the Parisian chemists held a festival, at which Madame Lavoisier, in the habit of a priestess, burnt Stahl's *Fundamenta* on an altar, while solemn music played a requiem to the departed system. Then followed the doctrines of Davy. A science thus constantly changing requires a work suited to its present condition, enriched as it has been within a few years by a succession of brilliant and useful discoveries, and such a work is the one before us.

REVIEW OF THOMPSON'S SERMONS.*

One characteristic of these Sermons is, that they bear internal evidence of having been prepared to meet the *actual wants of the congregation to whom they were addressed.* It is evident, that both in the pulpit and the study, the author felt his mind to be in contact with the minds of at least some who were infidels in fact, if not in name. There is a directness in the arguments, and an earnestness in their application, which could spring only from a mind excited and warmed by a personal intellectual encounter with the enemies of the gospel. Indeed, through the whole of his attack upon them, while he manages his weapons with sufficient gracefulness and dexterity, he bears himself in such a manner as to remind us of some stout warrior, engaged with his whole soul in mortal strife against the foes of his country, rather than of some errant knight showing forth his skill in arms at a tournament.

And from other sources we know that this was the case. At the time when Dr. Thompson commenced his ministrations at St. George's, the leaven of infidelity was fermenting in the mass of the population of Edinburgh, just as it was then, and is now, more or less, in all the large cities in christendom. It was no longer confined to a few speculative minds, but was extending its influence to every class of the community. We are not speaking so much of that open-mouthed, brawling infidelity which we sometimes meet with, as of a secret, indefinite unbelief of the peculiar doctrines of the christian system. When Hume first sent forth into the world his writings in opposition to christianity, they generally met with

---

* *Sermons on Infidelity,* By Andrew Thompson D. D. Minister of St. George's, Edinburgh. First American Edition, with a Preliminary Essay. Windsor, Vt., Richards and Tracy. New York : Jonathan Leavitt, 1833.

a cold reception, even in the country and city of his birth. The Scotch were a cautious, as well as a religious people. We have it on good authority, that the controversy between him and his antagonists, was regarded with interest, rather as an exhibition of the intellectual strength of the parties, than because great interests were staked on the decision of the question. They seemed to have looked upon the struggle between that "prince of doubters," and such a master of reason as Reid, Campbell, or Beattie, as each rushed to attack him in defense of truth and christianity, with the same feelings with which the Roman people witnessed the combat between two accomplished gladiators. Each of the combatants, indeed had his partisans; but the great body of even the higher classes, were interested mainly in the contest itself, and not in its issue.

But, in time, the infidel opinions then first promulgated, were adopted, in part at least, by a class of men, who by their talents and learning exerted a controlling influence upon public sentiment. Indeed, there was a period, when it was to a considerable extent the opinion in England, that the learned men of Scotland were all infidels, and the common people all christians. At least, it was true that some of the most celebrated public instructors and writers were conversant with the works of Hume, and gave currency among their countrymen to doubts concerning the peculiar doctrines and duties of the gospel. Unbelief was rife in certain circles in Edinburgh, and "church-going was a thing comparatively out of fashion in the New-Town of that metropolis, till Andrew Thompson was removed from a church he had formerly held in the Old-Town, and established under the splendid dome of St. George's.

It was for the especial benefit of the intelligent and fastidious unbelievers of his own congregation, that these discourses were prepared; and to this circumstance, they owe much of their uncommon excellence. A minister who fixes his view upon infidelity as it exists among his own people, can see its real form, and describe it more accurately, and argue it down more conclusively, than if he should look all over Christendom to find what infidelity is in the *abstract*, and should then write a book to confute it, which should be so general in its arguments, as to be as well fitted to one age as another.

He who would write a truly effective volume on this subject, must have access to the hearts of reflecting men, who having read the writings of distinguished infidels, and find themselves unable to meet their objections ; and who with some appearance of candor, and some show of reluctance, have become unbelievers. He should have conversed with them freely and familiarly, and thus have become acquainted with their mental history, and the causes of their unbelief. He should have humbled himself to hold intercourse with another class of infidels, whose mouth is full of cursing and bitterness, and who show clearly that they hate the light of truth. He should, likewise, have conversed with still another class, whose opinions are vague and unsettled, and who are carried about by every wind of doctrine ; and with those who are too unreflecting to think much, and too stupid to feel much, either of attachment or dislike on the subject of religion. Besides this acquaintance with individuals, he should have witnessed the effects of infidelity upon communities,—observing how it dries up the springs of the social virtues, withers whatever is fair and lovely in social happiness, and as if it were the hot breath of the pit, kindles into a consuming flame the passions of men. With a preparation like this, he would be qualified to come forth to the world in opposition to infidelity, either from the press or the pulpit ; and without some such preparation superadded to learning obtained from books, what he publishes or preaches must be deficient in many important particulars.

We are strengthened in this opinion, by calling to mind in what year the bible was written. It was written, at least a considerable part of it, not to supply the general wants of the church, but was for some local or individual exigency. Read the Epistle to the Romans, or those to the Corinthians, or indeed any of the scriptures, and you will be convinced, that each one of them was composed for the purpose of instructing and edifying the particular church or person to whom it was addressed, and that from this circumstance is derived its principal excellence. Mere generalities, either in doctrines or in precepts, are not what we want, and are not what we have in the bible. The sacred penmen wrote in view of actual existences. Their language is, "that which was from the beginning, which we have heard, which we have seen with our eyes, which we have looked upon, and our hands have handled, of the word of life—declare we unto you." The bible being prepared by those who were thus intimately acquainted with what they undertake to communicate, for the purpose of meeting the wants of particular individuals or communities, in certain definite exigencies, presents facilities for being understood, like those presented by statute law, when explained by commentaries and the reports of adjudicated cases. And being prepared in this manner, it is found to be altogether better adapted to exert a moral influence upon the great mass of mankind, than if it were made up of ten thousand precepts delivered in an abstract form.

The additional circumstance should be taken into view, that in modern times many causes are in operation to assimilate men in civilized countries, to each other, in their sentiments and opinions; so that a work on religion which is adapted to one large town, may be considered as well adapted to almost any other in christendom. The press circulates every new opinion which may be broached on the subject of religion, with wonderful promptitude. We have met with persons from the valley of the Mississippi, who were well versed in the works of Mirabeau the Atheist. Hume is read, more or less, throughout the countries denominated christian. Paine's works are circulated in India, even among the natives. But more than this; many of the popular writers of the present and the last generation, have read these same authors, and not unfrequently have contributed, perhaps in some cases unwittingly, to introduce some of the subtle poison of infidelity into the public mind. A work which is well adapted to unbelievers in Edinburgh, will of course, then, be well suited to unbelievers elsewhere. But unless written with a distinct reference to *some* people, and some actual state of public opinion, it will be of but little use. An ingenious man by the help of books solely, can prepare a work against infidelity; just as Phormio the Peripatetic, who had never seen military service, spoke some hours in the presence of Hannibal on the art of war and the duties of a commander; but he will expose himself to the ridicule of some thorough-bred infidel, just as the philosopher brought upon himself the contempt of the accomplished Carthagenian general.

Another characteristic excellence of these sermons, is that they are evidently *the result of close observation*, on the part of the author. He was not only placed in favorable circumstances, as we have seen, for preparing this work, but he was qualified by his mental habits, to avail himself perfectly of these circumstances. In other words, he had that acquaintance with men and things which is usually denominated a knowledge of the world. Many learned theologians, we need not say, have been wofully deficient in this kind of knowledge; and, as the necessary consequence, have exerted less influence than they would have otherwise done, upon men of cultivated minds who were accustomed to fashionable life. This, we suppose, was to some extent true in the case of the great theologian of our country, President Edwards. Until the time when he entered Yale College, he was educated at home in company with his sisters; when a member of that institution he was very greatly devoted to his books; and in subsequent life he was occupied almost constantly by his preparations for the pulpit, and by the works which he published. He seems indeed, not only to have avoided intercourse with general society, but also to have considered himself in some degree as unqualified for it. Undoubtedly his heart was full of love towards "being in general;" but a perusal of his life will show, that this love was not manifested towards individuals out of the circle of his personal friends, by any strong interest in society at large. And in correspondence with this, his works do not show an acquaintance with men. With the general features of the human mind, he was intimately acquainted.

He knew man in the abstract, and he reasons upon some of the faculties of our nature, with surpassing strength and clearness. He knew man as sinner or a saint; and he describes him as the one or the other with great exactness, in the more prominent traits of his character. The truth seems to be, that as subjects of thought, God and his moral government, his plan of redemption by Jesus Christ, and man as a voluntary and accountable being destined to happiness or misery, so absorbed his powerful mind, that he felt no disposition to descend to the varieties of individual character. At least, he does not show that minute acquaintance with those varieties which some other great men have manifested in their writings. And though we are professed admirers of his genius and moral excellence, we have often regretted, that he did not share in such opportunities for observing the varieties of character, as those which were enjoyed by Barrow and Berkeley. Had he occasionally stooped from his contemplations, to hold converse with more of his brethren of the great human family, he would have accommodated the truths which he discovered, more persuasively to their hearts.

A retired theologian may have fastened his mind on some truth like this, "the heart is deceitful above all things and desperately wicked," and may insist on it in his reasonings with great ingenuity and force, and yet, if he happens to go abroad into society, may be the dupe of the first man he meets. Like some others, he may be inclined to worship the "idols of the den," and to seek for truth in the "lesser world and not in the greater and common one." He may be very ingenious in reasoning from the objects of his own consciousness and experience, or from the abstract principles of theology; but in the one case he may be told, that it is dangerous to take the "a priori road," and in the other, that his consciousness and experience are not the measure of the intellect and moral feelings of others.

We admit, that the writer who describes his own experience and the objects of his own consciousness, will often by so doing waken some of those feelings of our common nature, in the

25

heart of many readers. This was the secret of the success of that class of poets, who have been styled the "Egotistical school." Going on the ground that "face answereth to face in water, so the heart of man to man," they painted their own feelings with great distinctness and strength of coloring, and thus found their way to the hearts of others.

So in religious experience, some eminent christians have in their diaries, or their letters to friends, or their sermons, or their published works, unfolded their own hearts in the description of the graces of holiness, or of their trials and temptations; and have thus afforded consolation and encouragement to other christians, especially if they belonged to the same section of the church, and were conversant with the same doctrines. But the difficulty is, that the christian and the infidel have so little in common, that if the christian minister attempts to reason from his own consciousness, in order to convince an unbeliever of his error, he will do it to little purpose. Neither abstract principles, nor his own experience, will answer any very good end. He must by actual intercourse with men, have enjoyed the advantage of making external observations; and then will he understand what are the prejudices and prepossessions, the associations and the dullness which exist among even baptised infidels. And from pursuing a different course, and trusting to the power of christian truth, as they feel it operating on their own hearts, to the neglect of this course of observation, some preachers, and able ones, have addressed men who are shrewd, worldly, and sceptical, only to provoke a smile at their ignorance of mankind.

We are strengthened in our opinion on this subject, by calling to mind the astonishing knowledge of human nature displayed by the great founder of the christian system, and by the great apostle to the Gentiles. The arguments which they use are always exactly adapted to the very men to whom they are addressed. The one with the different sects of the Jews, and the other in his intercourse with the inhabitants of different cities among the nations which he visited, always seemed perfectly to understand the men they had to deal with. Hence it was, that they were able either to convince their opponents, or at least put them to silence.

While we would thus insist upon a thorough knowledge of men, as a necessary pre-requisite for successful argumentation with intelligent unbelievers, we at the same time would guard ourselves against running into the opposite extreme, of neglecting the study of the general principles of theology, and the duty of self-examination in retirement. We are well aware that among the present race of ministers, there are in these bustling times those who are conversant only with particulars, with the doings at anniversary celebrations, and with private history. We do not dwell at any length upon the deficiencies of men of this class, because they will not be very apt to undertake to write a work on the evidences of christianity. This would require study, an employment to which they are not especially addicted. They neglect books as the others do men.

Now the man who would undertake to write a work, or to preach sermons, to convince intelligent unbelievers, ought to be deeply versed in both theological learning, and the knowledge of mankind. He should have attentively studied the great book of human nature, not merely as theologians are apt to do, to learn what relations the several faculties of man have to each other, or to duty and accountableness, but to see the actual workings of the mind. He should at the hazard of being considered " a gluttonous man, and a wine-bibber, and a friend of publicans and sinners," place himself on free and familiar terms with sceptical men, gain their confidence, and then learn what are the true causes which operate to prevent them from receiving the truth. He need not be afraid lest by associating with them occasionally, he shall incur the censure bestowed on the man who countenances their opinions and practices. He need not, from the fear that he shall lose their respect by familiarity with them, adopt the sentiment of the Roman Emperor, " Ex longinquo major reverentia ;" for if he is acquainted with theology as a public teacher ought to be, and if his heart is governed by right motives, he may be sure that neither the cause of truth nor his own respectability will suffer.

In the work before us, the author shows that he is intimately acquainted with human nature, and particularly with the various workings of unbelief in the heart of the infidel. He seems to have been accustomed to look at the various lights and shadows in the characters of men; instead of being satisfied, as some are, with bare generalities. Had he been a mere theologian, he could never have written these discourses. He seems to have collected by observation, a great variety of valuable facts in the mental history of unbelievers, and to have composed these discourses while those facts were in view. Hence it is, that he can "hold the mirror up to nature, show virtue in its own form, scorn its own image," so distinctly that unbelievers of every cast can each see his own shape and color. He does not indeed enter into a minute relation of what he has seen with his own eyes. He is not a story-teller. But having the power of generalization, he presents the results not as common place remarks, but in all the freshness of original investigation and discovery. His thoughts are connected together by some luminous general principle running through them. They are not scattered pearls. They are presented in orderly arrangement like gems on a thread of gold.

Another characteristic of these Sermons, is, that the *argumentation is of a kind that is adapted to produce conviction.*

We have read works which were written to prove that a revelation from God is desirable and necessary, and that therefore it may be presumed, that he would grant a revelation like that which we have. To this the infidel replies, that human sagacity cannot determine what course an infinite being would be likely to take; and that the same reason which leads us to suppose that he would grant a revelation to any, would lead us to expect that he would grant it to all; which he has not done. The reasoning of some theologians on the dealings of God with mankind, seem to go on the supposition, that the race have but one intellect, one conscience, one soul, as if some of the visions of Swedenbourg were true; whereas he deals with them as individuals and not in any federal capacity. Indeed, it seems to be supposed by them, that he deals with the whole race collectively, just as a monarch deals with an organized body of rebels. Now the difference between mankind as a race, and such a body, is just this, that the latter from the circumstance that they are organized, become responsible for what is done by their representatives; while the race have no organization which could make all and every one responsible for the doings of any one man, or body of men. The Bible has not been given either to every individual of our race, or to any body of men who might be considered as their representatives; so that however desirable and necessary revelation may be proved to be, we cannot from this, without other evidence, conclude that a revelation has been given.

Lardner has collected a great mass of historical evidence, which should be thoroughly examined by every minister of the gospel; but his work is not very well adapted to effect the conversion of infidels, not only because it is so voluminous that they will not be apt to read it, but likewise because the arguments are not sufficiently concentrated, to make an impression on an unbelieving heart. Neither Leland nor Lardner, though they open to us treasures of knowledge, is precisely what is wanted. Nor does the eloquent work of Chalmers supply the deficiency. And as to the external evidences, we are disposed to think that ten have been made unbelievers by reading what Hume and Gibbon have written, for one that has been converted to christianity by what Lardner and Chalmers have written, though the one is so learned and the other so eloquent.

Other works have been written for the purpose of defending christianity against some particular attack, as for instance, Watson's Apology for the Bible, and Scott's Vindication of its inspiration, against the Billingsgate abuse of Paine. Now in regard to this class of works, it is to be remarked, that in them christianity acts on the defensive; and if successful, she merely continues to maintain the ground she had previously occupied. She throws off her assailants, but makes no new conquests. Now this course of acting only on the defensive would be fatal to the church. Her course must be "from conquering to conquer." Two of the greatest generals that the world ever saw, the one of ancient, the other of modern times, were invincible as long as they led their armies in offensive war, to attack other nations. But when they were called to act on the defensive, they were conquered.

Christianity was intended by its great author to carry on, without intermission, an offensive war against unbelief and irreligion, such as Jesus and the apostles waged in Judea or throughout the Roman Empire. The assailing party has the advantage of the one that acts on the defensive, for the plain reason that it can always choose the point of attack. Now, we hold it to be true in moral reasoning, on wide and complicated subjects, that unanswerable objections and arguments can often be brought forward on both sides. If one of the parties instead of entering into the merits of the whole question, chooses to confine himself to bringing forward some unanswerable objections, he has the vantage-ground, as long as he can keep his antagonist employed in attempting to answer, what from some peculiar circumstances of the case, is unanswerable. Christians are not to sit still and let infidels select their point of attack, and then confine themselves to the single purpose of defending their cause on that point; but they are to turn the tables on their opponents, and in the character of assailants, carry the war directly into the heart of the enemy's country. It is in this way only, that they can hope to make conquests. They are to let infidels feel that their own bulwarks are weak, and that though they can sound to the attack, and hurl their missiles briskly against the walls of Zion, they have no arms of defense with which they can stand against an enemy in the open field.

Nor should there be in the controversy with infidels, any waste of strength in attempting to defend facts or principles, that are of little consequence. We have sometimes witnessed controversies on some trifling subject, which put us in mind of what is written in an old book entitled, A Discourse of Logomachy, which we recommend to the careful perusal of some good folks who have an itching for controversy. "You are mistaken if you think Scaliger and Cardan two such coxcombs, as to dispute in earnest, which had the most hairs on its back, the kid or the goat! The real question in debate was, which of these two gentlemen was the better scholar and the more ingenious man."

Nor should there be any use made of the *argumentum ad invidiam*, not only because it is disgraceful to the party that employs it, but also because it is powerless in producing conviction. It is, indeed, easy to represent the opinion of an antagonist, as dangerous to the interests of society, and himself as reprobate to every good work. It is easy to use reviling language, and instead of debating a matter fairly, like christian gentlemen, to enter into the contest with him like a prize-fighter in a bear garden. But even if you succeed, by raising a strong popular feeling against him, and thus force him to silence, have you convinced him? Mere human power, let it be exerted in what way it will, whether by inflicting evil on the person or the reputation, is totally unable to obtain the assent of the mind to the truth of any doctrine. This assent can be obtained only on the perception of the truth of such a doctrine. As long, therefore, as you trust to any thing else to produce conviction, and not to that sort of evidence which is adapted to the mind of your antagonist, you labor to no purpose, so far as he is concerned.

We have said, that the author of these Sermons has employed in them a kind of argumentation that is adapted to produce conviction. He avoids, for the most part, the errors which we have noticed. He makes but little use of *a priori* reasoning; he says very little about the external evidences; he neither exhausts his strength upon unimportant points, nor descends to the use of furious declamation, against the motives of infidels, and the tendency of their principles. His great excellence as a reasoner consists in this, that he looks at infidelity in the very shape which it now wears; and then selects his argument to meet it in that very shape. He gives us very little of the history of infidelity. He says, if we remember right, nothing of Hobbs and Shaftsbury, Tindal and

Morgan, and little of Bolingbroke and Hume, and of the mode in which they may be met. He just describes the infidelity of the present age, and plies it with appropriate arguments. The merit of the reasoning consists in the correctness of the observations which he has made of the present character of infidelity, and then in the application of the appropriate truths. We can easily believe, that another kind of reasoning would have pleased some minds better. Lord Bacon remarks that "*anticipations* always have a much greater power to entrap the assent, than *interpretations*; because, being collected from a few familiar particulars, they immediately strike the mind, and fill the imagination; whereas interpretations being separately collected from very various and from very distant things, cannot suddenly affect the mind." If Dr. Thompson had gone through a course of mere common place reasoning, adorning it with the associations of his fine mind; especially if he had dealt somewhat in startling paradoxes, ultimately cleared up by some definition of his terms; and more especially, if he had given his sentences a syllogistic form, and introduced a goodly number of conditional, adversative, and illative conjunctions, such as *if*, *but*, and *therefore*, he might have seemed to some, to reason more powerfully than he now does. But he had to do with men who had been trained to inductive reasoning, or as Lord Bacon calls it, *interpretations*, and who would not be satisfied with what he calls *anticipations*, or hasty conclusions. He might have rung in their ears the language of denunciation, and they would have laughed like Leviathan at the shaking of the spear, and called for proof. He might have amused them with buffoonery and vulgarisms, like some popular preachers, who shall be nameless, and they would still have called for proof. He might have tried upon them the power of all the machinery of a camp meeting, and they would have still called for proof. And so he gave them proof, in language befitting the preacher, the pulpit, and the auditors, dignified yet earnest, pungent and yet decorous.

The infidelity of the present age is not so much distinguished for its opposition to christianity as a whole, as to particular doctrines. The warfare which it wages somewhat resembles Capt. Bobadil's method of defeating an army. It endeavors to destroy the christian system in detail. It comes in the guise of a friend, into the christian camp, and even uses the arms which it finds there, against the true and loyal servants of Christ. It employs certain doctrines which it finds in the bible, against other doctrines which it hates. Thus, some endeavor to destroy the credibility of the endless punishment of the wicked. Some oppose the divinity and some the humanity of the Savior ; or they deny the doctrine of the atonement, or of justification by faith ; or they would desecrate the sabbath, or annihilate the church as a distinct class in the community ; or they ridicule the duties of devotion, and indeed all the peculiar duties of the gospel. Humility they would represent as meanness of spirit, and obedience to the last injunction of Jesus, as a kind of Quixotism. All this and more, they will do, though they claim for themselves the name of christian. They would thus blot out one by one from the christian system, each glorious truth, and leave to us naught but the dark and cheerless waste of naturalism. The time was, when the legions of infidelity, clad in the panoply of a false philosophy, exultingly raised the war-cry, as they rushed into the open field, against "the host of God's elect." But now, they choose to fight under cover, and rely more upon sappers and miners, than upon the prowess and skill of their champions. And their numbers have become astonishingly increased. We are aware, too, that the church generally by means of voluntary associations and the press, has put on a greater show of strength ; and actually exerts a greater amount of concentrated efficiency, than it did forty years ago. Indeed, if you will listen to the speeches delivered on some anniversary occasions, you would almost feel that the great victory over the foes of unbelief and irreligion, is already won, and that the speakers had come together, not to "animate the battle, but to chant the triumph." The managers and agents of these several associations, very naturally wish to present their claims to patronage in their full strength, and accordingly dwell considerably on what they have accomplished, and what they are destined to accomplish. But after you have looked at these bright visions of the prosperity of the church, then go through the length and breadth of the land, and behold the vast numbers that seldom or never visit the sanctuary; that seldom or never read the bible; who seldom or never mention God but to profane his name; and who are able, very generally, to defeat any measure connected with the interests of religion, whether proposed in town meeting, in the state legislature, or in the great council of the nation. Go to the scattered hamlets, as well as to the market places, and learn in conversation, how many are indifferent to the truths and duties of religion; how many are rank opposers, though they may from prudential motives conceal their opposition. Go and see how the fashionable literature of the age is exerting an influence unfavorable to purity of faith, upon all classes, even upon females, teaching them to be doubters, thus falsifying the declaration of Hume, recorded in the life of Beattie, that "scepticism is too sturdy a virtue for woman."

When you have thus by actual inspection seen the extent of infidelity in our own country, as well as in the countries of Europe, you will be prepared to understand the value of such a work as the one before us. It resolves the different forms of infidelity into one radical principle. It shows how exactly adapted the gospel is to man, in all his associations, and desires, and exigencies; so that the inference is inevitable that the same great being who is the creator of the one, is the author of the other. The web of Dr. T.'s argument is not like that of the spider, which entangles the smaller flies, but lets the stronger ones escape, but it is especially designed for strong men, who are of full age; "even those who by reason of age have their senses exercised to discern between good and evil."

Moreover, his argumentation is of such a character, and couched in such language, that any intelligent man can easily understand it. He neither introduces new terms, nor uses old ones in an uncommon sense. He has no mysticism, no wire drawn speculations, no hair splitting distinctions: every man who understands the English language can understand him. Some men seem to be fond of trying to make their argumentation resemble a chain, each premise and conclusion successively corresponding to the several links, from the first principle assumed to the final inference. But in the book before us, the author seems to place various truths before us in a manner resembling a dissected map. In the empire of knowledge, he shows us certain provinces of truth in their relative situations, and having brought them together, he shows that there is a wide space which must be vacant, unless occupied by the province of scriptural truth. He then introduces this province into its proper place, and shows how exactly it fits the other truths by which it is surrounded, and to which it is related. Now this is to our taste, and is we believe more convincing in moral subjects, than argumentation arranged in a different form.

Whatever may have been true at the first promulgation of the gospel, when the works of Jesus and his apostles bare witness of them, we must at the present day, for the most part, rely on the internal evidences to prove the truth of revelation; and for the obvious reason, that they are as to the greater part of mankind, the only evidences than can be adequately presented. And even upon men of cultivated minds, they are often more effectual than any other, as we have often had an opportunity of observing. An instance once fell under our notice, which very strikingly illustrated the power of the internal evidences. A gentleman in Virginia, of some talents and extensive reading, was led by the light of false philosophy into the cold and dreary domain of infidelity. He exerted the full force of his powerful and discriminating mind, in the examination of the ablest works on both sides of the question, especially so far as the historical argument was concerned. And so fully was he convinced of the falsehood of christianity, that he said publicly at a dinner table, around which were assembled some of the most respectable gentlemen in the vicinity, " christianity is a fable, and I can prove it to be so from history." But in time affliction came. The death of a beloved wife extinguished the light of joy in his heart. He was sad and solitary, seeking rest and finding none. Among the objects which reminded him of the departed one, was a small bible, which now became interesting to him because it was once dear to her. He opened it at the place where she used to read, and he found that the truths which she loved, were just the truths which he needed as a sufferer and a sinner. He continued to read, until in the adaptation of the bible to the wants, the sins, and the afflictions of man, he saw convincing proof of its divine origin. He became a sincere and humble believer in revelation.

Before closing this article, we ought perhaps to give an analysis of the work and to make some extracts which may furnish an illustration of the remarks which we have been led to make. We have thus far viewed the work as a whole, and have not fixed our attention on particular passages, as the texts upon which we have written, or as eminently striking. The volume is a small one comprised in about two hundred pages, and will well repay the perusal. Prefixed to it is a sensible well written preliminary essay, prepared, we understand, by one of the publishers.

In the first sermon Dr. Thompson lays down this important principle, that ' the disbelief of christianity in particular, leads to the disbelief of religion in general." This he illustrates, first, by an appeal to the past history of deistical writings, the tendency of which has been such, for more than two centuries, as to convince every impartial observer " that to atheism we must come at last, if we acquiesce in their positions, and follow out the course which they have pursued." Secondly, to the character of the prevailing infidelity of the day, whose distinguishing feature is powerfully shown to be " a determined hostility, or a settled contempt, for what is sacred,—not merely for the gospel of Christ,—but for all that relates to the belief and the service of the living God."

In the second sermon, Dr. Thompson goes on to illustrate the principle above stated, by appealing, thirdly, to the *objections* which deists have urged against christianity. These, he shows, when properly estimated, and impartially applied, are found to bear as strongly against *natural* as against *revealed* religion. These objections are, that christianity contains much that we cannot comprehend,—that it has not been extended to our whole race,—that many of its principles are still in controversy among its adherents,—and that it implies what is *miraculous*. As to the last objection, Dr. T. enters into a very ingenious comparison of the grounds of assent to Christ's mission, as supported by miracles, and to the being and attributes of God, as deduced from the phenomena of nature. A miracle like those phenomena, is a mere fact, attested by evidence. The argument is in both cases *inductive*. "Certain ascertained facts are combined with certain acknowledged first principles; and these conduct the understanding to certain conclusions in which it rests as inevitable." As a fourth illustration of his leading principle, Dr. Thompson shows, that the *moral causes* which lead to deism, will naturally, and almost necessarily, bear the mind forward to open atheism. These are inconsideration,—intellectual pride,—and moral depravity.

In the third sermon, deism is shown to be "hostile in every respect to the interests of morality;" and in the fourth, to be "destructive of the comfort and happiness of those who embrace it." These two sermons are characterized by great compass and power of inductive reasoning, and most eloquent appeals to the conscience and the heart.

In the fifth and sixth sermons, Dr. Thompson shows that the term "unbeliever" is not to be confined to the mere deist or atheist. It belongs, 1. To those "who reject one part of revelation, while they admit the rest." 2. To those "whose lives are characterized by impiety and immorality." 3. To those "who exhibit in their practices the decencies, and honesties, and charities of a good life, but do so without any regard to the principles of godliness and the authority of the gospel." 4. To those "who are characterized by worldly-mindedness." 5. To those "who live in the wilful and habitual neglect of religious ordinances." 6. To those "whose conduct manifests indifference to the preservation and success of christianity in the world." These two sermons abound in just and forcible appeals to that large class of practical unbelievers in christian lands, who are reposing in a calm reliance on their speculative belief of christianity.

The seventh sermon exhibits with great power, the sinful nature and awful consequences of unbelief, as to the person to whom it attaches. In the eighth and ninth, the whole subject is applied in distinct address to parents,—to young men,—to persons of the higher classes,—to those of the lower classes, —and to ministers of the gospel. These abound in judicious and weighty considerations.

The following extract may serve as a specimen of the style and manner of these sermons.

The very conduct of infidels in spreading their system with so much eagerness and industry, affords a striking proof that its influence is essentially hostile to human happiness. For what is their conduct ? Why, they allow that religion contributes largely to the comfort of man,—that in this respect, as well as with respect to morality, it would be a great evil were it to lose its hold over their affections,—and that those are no friends to the world who would shake or destroy their belief in it. And yet, in the very face of this acknowledgment, they scruple not to publish their doubts and their unbelief concerning it among their fellow men, and with all the cool deliberation of philosophy, and sometimes with all the keenness and ardor of a zealot, to do the very thing which they profess to deprecate as pernicious to the well-being and comfort of the species. Whether they are sincere in this profession, or whether they are only trifling with the sense and feeling of mankind, still it demonstrates the hardening influence of their principles ; and from principles, which make those who hold them, so reckless of the peace and order and happiness of their brethren, what can be reasonably expected, but everything which is most destructive of human comfort ?

It is true the infidel may be very humane in the intercourse of life ; but, after all, what dependence can be placed upon that humanity of his, which deals out bread to the hungry, and clothing to the naked, and yet would sacrifice to literary vanity, or to something worse, whatever can give support in trial, and consolation at death? He may sympathize with me in my distress, and speak to me of immortality, and at the very moment his constitutional kindness may be triumphing over his cold-blooded and gloomy speculations. But his speculations have shed a misery over my heart, which no language of his can dissipate, and which makes his most affectionate words sound in my ear like the words of mockery and scorn. He has destroyed me, and he cannot save me, and he cannot comfort me. At his bidding I have renounced that Saviour in whom I once trusted, and was happy, and have banished that Comforter, who once dwelt with me, and would have dwelt with me as a comforter forever. And he now pities me, as if his most pitying tones could charm away the anguish of my bosom, and make me forget that it was he himself who planted it there, and planted it so deep, and nourished it so well, that nothing but the power of that heaven, whose power I have denied, is able to pluck it out. Yes, after he has destroyed my belief in the superintending providence of God, —after he has taught me that the prospect of a hereafter is but the baseless fabric of a vision,—after he has bred and nourished in me a contempt for that sacred volume which alone throws light over this benighted world,—after having argued me out of my faith by his sophistries, or laughed me out of it by his ridicule,—after having thus wrung from my very soul every drop of consolation, and dried up my very spirits within me,—yes, after having accomplished this in the season of my health and my prosperity, he would come to me while I mourn, and treat me like a drivelling idiot, whom he may sport with, because he has ruined me, and to whom, in the plenitude of his compassion,—too late, and too unavailing,—he may talk of truths in which he himself does not believe, and which he has long exhorted me, and has at last persuaded me, to cast away as the dreams and the delusions of human folly! From such comforters may heaven preserve me! "My soul come not thou into *their* secrets. Unto their assembly mine honor, be not thou united!" pp. 165–170.

THE CULTIVATION OF THE TASTE.*

Three persons standing on a peak of the mountain range just north of us would receive very different impressions from the scene around them. One of them, looking at the objects before him with a "brute unconscious gaze," might receive only a faint and vague impression attended with no emotion. He might, in his indifference say: "I see the river, the meadows and the mountain, but all these I could have seen without climbing to the top of Holyoke." Another, looking at the same objects, might say: "This is a valuable river—for bringing down lumber. These are valuable meadows—for raising grass or broom corn. These mountains are useful—in furnishing fuel for the inhabitants." His maxim is:

> "The real value of a thing
> Is just the money it will bring."

The third is delighted with every part of the landscape all around him, to the utmost limits of the wide horizon. He loves to gaze at the river moving on in quiet beauty in long and graceful windings, as if it were willing to pause here in its pilgrimage to the ocean. He loves to compare mountain with mountain, Holyoke with Tom, Sugar-loaf with Toby, that he may catch the distinctive features and coloring of each; while those that are far in the hazy distance he strains his vision to behold, invested as they are by the imagination with a mysterious interest. He sees a beauty in everything around him; in the wild wood-lands, made vocal; in the cultivated plains, where men are laboring or cattle grazing;

*An Address delivered at the thirteenth Anniversary of the Mount Holyoke Female Seminary, South Hadley, Mass., Aug. 2, 1850, by William C. Fowler.

in the sloping hills; in the villages with their taper spires; in the shadows as they chase one another along the earth's surface; in the blue sky that bends over him; in the Day-god throned in that sky, sending forth his arrows of light. Drinking the spirit of the whole scene into his soul, he turns back once and again to behold it as he reluctantly descends the mountain.

Do you ask how it happens that the same scene makes such a different impression upon him, from what it makes upon the two others? My answer is, he has a Taste for what is beautiful and they have not.

The term TASTE is borrowed from one of the bodily senses. If an appropriate substance be taken into the mouth, the impression on the palate is that of sweetness, or sourness, or pungency, or bitterness, or saltness. To these impressions the term taste was originally applied. This term is now used in a wider sense as applicable to impressions made upon all the senses, and also upon the imagination and the higher powers. According to Alison, it is "That faculty of the human mind by which we perceive and enjoy whatever is beautiful or sublime in the works of nature or of art." This definition may be accepted as sufficiently correct for my purpose in the following remarks.

The term beauty was originally applied to objects of sight. As the epithet sweet denotes what is pleasing to the palate, and harmonious, what is pleasing to the ear, as what is soft denotes what is pleasing in objects of touch, so the epithet beautiful originally denoted what is pleasing to the eye. It is now used in a wider sense as applicable to objects addressed to the other senses, and likewise to mental and moral objects.

The inquiry here meets us, is it desirable to possess a taste for the beautiful in nature and art?

To this question a distinct answer has often been given in the negative by the lovers of utility, who, in their contempt for the lovers of beauty, charge them with being a brood of triflers, moon-struck bards, drones in the hive, born only to consume the fruits of the earth, and dying only to relieve society of a burden.

In opposition to this opinion, I shall, in the following remarks, endeavor to sustain the affirmative of the question.

That God intended we should have a taste for the beautiful, is evident from many considerations.

The soul of man, the product of his creating skill, is so related to the external world, in which it is to pass its first years, that in accordance with the laws of its nature, it feels emotions of beauty upon the bare presentation of certain material objects. As in certain cases it perceives truth by intuition, and right by intuition, so it perceives beauty by intuition. When the philosopher surveys nature in order to establish the principles of mechanics, his reason is chiefly concerned. When the moralist examines the forms of actions in order to discover what is right, his conscience is brought into requisition. When the poet looks out upon nature in order to discover beauty, his taste is brought into exercise. Truth, right, and beauty, are thus so related to the soul of man, that the reason is conversant with the one, conscience with the second, and taste with the third. There is therefore the same ground for believing that the Creator intended that the taste should be exercised upon what is beautiful, that there is for believing that he intended that the reason should be exercised upon what is true, and the conscience upon what is right. God, the Mighty Parent, gave to all the race these internal powers to be employed on his works. Indeed, the love of beauty is a constituent part of the soul of man, revealed by the infant when he grasps at the lighted taper, by the child when he chases the rainbow, and by older persons in their pursuit of various forms of physical, mental, and moral beauty.

To this constituent principle of the human soul, implanted by the Creator, external nature is adapted by the same designing mind. I speak not merely of the more striking forms of beauty and grandeur which sometimes come over the soul with an overwhelming force. I speak not of the coming glories of the morning light, which clothes the mighty form of nature with its robe of beauty, instead of the pall of darkness. I speak not of the gorgeous coloring of a summer's landscape in which stream and waterfall, hill and valley, the far-off mountain and the far-off ocean, the sky above and the earth beneath, seem to vie with each other for your admiration. I speak rather of the humble forms of nature; of the flower that hardly lifts its head among the grass; of the crystals beneath the earth's surface, which have been styled the "flowers of minerals;" of the forms and colors of animals, whether they are inhabitants of the earth, the air, or the sea. And I ask how it happens that the Creator has thus made everything in nature beautiful on the one hand, and on the other, formed the soul of man so that it can take delight in these objects around it, unless he intended that man should have a taste for the beautiful?

The same thing is evident from the services of the Jewish religion, established by Jehovah. He not only brought the children of Israel into a goodly land, in which was the glory of Lebanon, the excellency of Carmel, and beautiful for situation, Mount Zion, the joy of the whole earth on the side of the north, but in the services of religion, he took especial care that their taste for the beautiful should be consulted and cultivated. In the construction of the tabernacle, not only the most costly materials were used, but as peculiar skill was necessary, he raised up Bezaleel the son of Uri, and Aholiab the son of Ahisamach, filling them with wisdom and understanding in all manner of workmanship, to have the entire charge of the whole business. He did not, however, leave it to these workmen, or even to Moses, to contrive the form of the sacred building in any respect. He himself formed the plan of the building and of the furniture in the most minute particularity, and then solemnly charged Moses, saying "see that thou make them after their pattern which was showed thee in the mount." I cannot stop to describe the gorgeous workmanship of the tabernacle and its furniture. You remember how the sides of it were ornamented with planks of shittim wood, covered with gold, and supported on ninety-six massive sockets of silver, every socket weighing a talent, how the curtains, ten in number, were made of fine twined linen, and blue and purple and scarlet, made with cherubims of cunning work, how each of these curtains were twenty-eight cubits long and four broad, furnished with clasps of gold. I will say nothing of the splendid altar, of the golden candlestick, with its bowls, knobs, and flowers, or of the altar of incense, or of the ark of the covenant, or of the mercy seat, and the cherubs, with their outstretched wings of pure gold, looking towards each other. Between these cherubs, God dwelt in a visible brightness. Besides this there was a temple built according to the command of the same God, at an expense of "a hundred thousand talents of gold and a thousand thousand talents of silver, and of brass and iron without weight by reason of abundance." Seen at a distance, by those who were approaching the city, it appeared, it is said, "like a mountain covered with snow;" for all over, except where broad plates of gold and silver dazzled the eye, it glistened with the whiteness of wrought marble. "He that never saw Jerusalem in her glory," say the ancient Jewish Doctors, "never saw a lovely city; and he that never saw the temple, with its buildings, never saw the most noble palace under the sun." The city was called, "The perfection of beauty, the joy of the whole earth." Here God chose His dwelling place. He loved the beauty which he intended we should love. "A thing of beauty is a joy forever" to God and to man.

In the heavenly Jerusalem, He also appeals to the love of the beautiful. "And He called me," says the Apostle John, "away in the spirit to a great and high mountain, and shewed me that great city the holy Jerusalem, descending out of heaven from God, having the glory of God: and her light was like unto a stone most precious," "And the building of the wall of it was like jasper; and the city was pure gold, like unto clear glass. And the foundations of the wall of the city were garnished with all manner of precious stones. The first foundation was jasper; the second sapphire; the third a chalcedony; the fourth an emerald; the fifth a sardonyx;

the sixth a sardius; the seventh a chrysolite; the eighth, beryl; the ninth a topaz; the tenth a chrysoprasus; the eleventh, a jacinth; the twelvth, an amethyst. And the twelve gates were twelve pearls; every gate was of one pearl. And the streets of the city were pure gold, as it were transparent glass." "And he showed me a pure river of water of life, clear as crystal, proceeding out of the throne of God and the Lamb."

What the utilitarian would say to this course of thought, I know not, but to me it is evident from the constitution of our minds, to which nature around us is adapted, from the services of the Jewish religion, and from the description of heaven, that God the Creator of all, and the Author of true religion, intended that we should have a taste for the beautiful and the sublime in this world and in heaven as he has.

But taste is, however, possessed by men in very different degrees. I would beg leave therefore to offer a few remarks on the origin of this diversity.

There is a difference in the constitutional susceptibility of individuals to the emotions of beauty, upon the perception of the same object; just as there is a difference in the bodily senses or in the faculty of reason. Thus one person has originally a keener relish for music than another, discoverable even when they were infants. The soul of one, in its constitutional susceptibilities, may have been more finely touched to each fine impulse, than the soul of another.

There is also a difference among men arising from the improved perception of beauty which some have acquired beyond others. Two men will agree in admiring "Auld Lang Syne" upon the first hearing, who would differ entirely in their emotions upon hearing for the first time one of Beethoven's Symphonies. The cause of this difference may be found in the circumstance that one of them has cultivated his perceptions so that he can from the very first understand this latter tune, while the other cannot either understand or admire it until he has heard it several times. If two persons should read Milton's Paradise Lost, one of them might perceive much more beauty than the other, from having cultivated his perception of beauty.

Moreover there is a difference among men in this respect, arising from their difference in imagination. In the contemplation of an object, the emotion of beauty may be excited by the imagination, which will often assemble around the object contemplated, other objects connected with it by some law of association, which will throw upon it some of their own beauty. Let a person of a feeble imagination, but slightly acquainted with the history of New England, visit the landing place of the pilgrim fathers. To him, Plymouth rock would be as any other rock, the beach, as any other beach. But if one of the sons of those sires, animated by their spirit, and acquainted with their history, should stand there, his imagination, if an active one, would fill the whole scene with objects of the deepest interest, which would lend their beauty to every visible object around him. He sees that bark tossing in the bay. He sees the weather-beaten mariners on the beach. He hears their praises for deliverance, and their prayers for protection. He then thinks of the fair inheritance which their posterity enjoy in answer to their prayers. Thus his imagination, associating with the scene objects of interest, invests it with a beauty that awakens, even in the gloom of December, the deepest emotions of his soul.

There is also a difference among men, arising from difference of judgment. In the contemplation of an object, the emotion of beauty may be excited by the judgment, which may pronounce it true to nature. If Napoleon, or General Washington should be exhibited in a painting, in the dress of a priest, our judgment would tell us that the painter had made a mistake in not giving a military man a military costume. A palm tree represented in Canadian scenery, would be a deformity, because the judgment would pronounce it not true to nature. When a vessel sails well, the sailors call her a "beauty;" for their judgment decides that she is adapted to the end for which she was designed. A house that is eminently convenient, commends itself to a man in whom judgment predominates, as a beautiful house. "If I had seen a ghost," says Partridge in Tom Jones, on seeing Garrick in Hamlet, "I should have acted exactly as that little man did." His judgment being satisfied that Garrick personated the ghost correctly, excited in his mind the emotion of beauty.

From these causes it happens that some have a delicacy of perception beyond others, which enables them to discover beauty in every combination. "It is with good reason," said Sancho Panza, in Don Quixote, to the Squire with the great nose, "that I pretend to have judgment in wine. This is a quality hereditary in our family. Two of my kinsmen were once called upon to give their opinion of a hogshead of wine, which was supposed to be old, and of a good vintage. One of them tastes it, considers it, and pronounces it to be good, were it not for a small taste of leather which he perceived in it. The other, after having used the same precautions, gave his verdict also in favor of the wine, but with the reserve of a taste of iron, which he could easily distinguish. You cannot imagine how they were both ridiculed for their judgment. But who laughed in the end? On emptying the hogshead, there was found at the bottom an old key with a leather thong tied to it." The close analogy between mental and bodily taste, will lead us to apply this story. A quick and delicate perception of beauty and deformity must be the perfection of our mental taste; nor can a man be satisfied with himself while he suspects that any excellence or blemish in a work of art has passed unobserved.

The question then very naturally suggests itself, is this talent improveable?

Both analogy and facts abundantly prove that it is improved by cultivation, like the judgment or the senses. When an object of beauty is first presented to an uncultivated mind, the taste cannot perceive the excellence of the performance; much less distinguish the particular character of each excellence, and ascertain each quality and degree. But allow one to acquire experience in the class of objects to which it belongs, he not only perceives the beauties and defects of each part, but marks the distinguishing species of each quality, and assigns to it suitable praise or blame. The mist dissipates which once hung over it. In a word, the same dexterity which practice gives to the execution of any work of art, is also acquired by the same means in judging of it.

"It has frequently happened," says Sir Joshua Reynolds, "that many of those whom the keeper of the Vatican had conducted through the edifice, when about to be dismissed, have inquired for the works of Raphael, and would not believe they had already passed through the rooms where they were preserved, so little impression had these works made on them. One of the first painters in France once told me that this circumstance happened to himself. I remember very well my own disappointment when visiting the Vatican, but on confessing my feelings to a brother student, of whose ingenuousness I had a high opinion, he acknowledged that the works of Raphael had the same effect on him, or rather that they did not produce the effect which he expected. This was a great relief to my mind.

"In justice to myself, I ought to say, that though disappointed and mortified at not finding myself enraptured with the works of this great master, I did not for a moment conceive or suppose that the name of Raphael, and those admirable works in particular, owed their reputation to the ignorance and prejudice of mankind. On the contrary, my not relishing them, as I was conscious I ought to have done, was one of the most humiliating circumstances that ever happened to me.

"It was necessary, as was expressed on a very solemn occasion, that I should become a little child. I viewed them again and again; and in a short time new perceptions began to dawn upon me."

This is an exact description of the origin and growth of a taste for the beautiful in nature and in art.

Many a young person has been deeply pained by a sense of his deficiency in a taste for what is beautiful. Neither music nor poetry, sculpture nor painting, architecture nor landscape gardening, which are appropriately called the fine arts, attract his admiration. Nature, too, however bright she may be above, or below, whether with her earthly or her heavenly face, has no charms for him.

You ask what such a one ought to do? Shall he sit down in despair? Shall he learn to despise and ridicule in others what he does not possess himself? I answer, he should do just what Sir Joshua Reynolds did, in order to improve his taste in a particular branch of art. He should diligently study the objects of taste in nature which is always before him, and in the fine arts so far as he has an opportunity. In short, he should do the same substantially that he does in the improvement of his reason or his conscience. If a man wishes to improve his Reason, what course does he take? Why he betakes himself to the investigation of things, that is of real existences, whether they are material substances or the actions or opinions of men; discovers their relations, and then comes to his conclusions. Besides this, he may examine the principles of reasoning as they are developed in the arguments of others or in logic. If he wishes to improve his Conscience, he carefully considers the moral relations of those actions which fall under his notice; or he studies the functions of conscience and the rules for its direction in some work on moral philosophy or in the Bible. He too who wishes to improve his Taste, can go either directly to nature and apply his mind to those objects in which beauty resides; or he can go directly to those works of art which are composed upon correct principles and are in accordance with nature whether in the world of vision, the world of thought, or the world of passion.

But you say, that living as we do in a country where but little attention has been paid to the fine arts, we cannot have access to those models of beauty which might in their contemplation improve the taste. There is truth in this remark. But shall we, because we have not the best possible advantages, neglect those which we do enjoy? We have not before us the best possible specimens of architecture ; we have not before us the Parthenon, still the ornament of Athens, or St. Peter's, the glory of Rome ; yet any one who chooses, can become acquainted with the principles of architectural beauty so far that he can understand what it is that constitutes the difference between an awkward, ill contrived house and one that is graceful and attractive. You may not have before you, in statuary, the Apollo Belvidere and the Dying Gladiator, or in painting, the Last Supper, by De Vinci, and the Last Judgment, by Michael Angelo. But casts in plaster can, in a good degree, supply deficiencies in the one branch of art, and the graver on copper-plate, and the pencil on stone, are furnishing very beautiful illustrations of the other. In both, original productions of native genius are, every year, whether in private collections, in Art-Unions, and Academies, increasing and becoming accessible to all for the improvement of the public taste. You can hardly take up a handsome book, without finding in it beautiful engravings. In landscape gardening, which has been considered as one of the fine arts, great progress has been made in our country within a few years, so that it is not very uncommon to find grounds tastefully laid out. Music and poetry, the two remaining branches of the fine arts, every one has an opportunity to study who chooses, since every one has access to books or recitations for the one, and to the living teacher or performer for the other. I would gladly persuade every one who wishes to improve his taste that he can have such an acquaintance with the fine arts, some of them at least, that they will be of great service to him. By accurate observation, by carefully comparing one specimen of art with another, his perceptions become acute, his judgment correct, and the emotion of beauty a strong one in his soul. Thus genius, which ever has a passionate admiration for the beautiful forms and harmonious colorings of nature, embodies them in works of art, that others may learn to admire, when thus embodied, what in nature would hardly have attracted their notice.

But in order to improve your taste, you must above all, seek for beauty in the visible forms of nature, as it stands in its freshness, commending itself to the common heart of man. You must carefully look for beauty of color, beauty of form, and beauty of sound, and beauty of motion, as it is found in every part of the world around you and above you. And besides this, you should carefully notice whether the beauty which you admire in an object is original and inherent, or whether it is relative and reflected; as some objects shine by their own, and some by borrowed light. Thus you may regard some tree as beautiful, on account of the form of its trunk and branches, the color of its foliage and flowers, or its motion in the breeze. In this case it is the inherent beauty of the tree that excites your admiration. Or you may regard the tree as beautiful because it reminds you of the pleasant hours you have spent in its shade, of the sports of your childhood, of the birds which sang in its branches, of the dear friend with whom you sat in a summer's day, beneath it. In this case, it is the borrowed beauty of the tree that excites your emotions.

I have spoken both of going to nature and to art for the improvement of your taste. I will add that great advantage will often result from comparing the one with the other. Thus if you wish to improve your taste either for external nature or for descriptive poetry, compare a scene in nature with the description of some such scene by a distinguished poet. For example, to follow a hint of Isaac Taylor, visit some water-fall with Southey's celebrated description of the Cataract of Lodore in your hand. Then compare the scene before you with the description, in all the particulars which are indicated by the multitude of epithets so playfully employed. Nature, thus interpreted by art, would fix your attention upon the beauty of the water-fall described, and thus quicken your sensibility to the beauties of all similar scenes. Or you may go through the same process with Cowper's Address to Winter, or with any other well written description of external nature. You can also derive great benefit from trying to produce from your own conceptions or from imitation, something that is beautiful. The very effort, whether successful or unsuccessful, will give you a more distinct idea of the qualities in which beauty is found, and also of the impression which it produces on your own mind. An earnest attempt to make a beautiful drawing of an object, to write a beautiful hand, to compose a beautiful sentence, to cultivate beautiful flowers, or even to make a beautiful garment, can hardly fail to improve your taste, for it makes your conceptions more distinct, and teaches you what is the cause of your success or your failure.

As contributing to the same end, you will find great advantage in the general improvement of your minds from observation and reflection, from reading and conversation. One person will, upon reading a passage in Milton's Paradise Lost, or upon visiting Athens, or upon gazing at some historical painting, feel strongly within him the emotion of sublimity from associations which can be awakened only in a mind highly cultivated. While it is true that a mind can be furnished with stores of knowledge, and yet be deficient in taste, it is also true that a vacant mind cannot enjoy the same associations which a full mind can. If you are deficient in taste for a class of subjects because your mind is vacant of knowledge pertaining to them, the remedy is obvious. Furnish your mind with stores of thoughts and facts connected with these subjects, and innumerable bright forms of beauty will dawn upon your soul. These forms will no longer be to you "as is a landscape to a blind man's eye," but distinct visions "swarming with enchantment," along your daily walks.

> "Earth will breathe in one great presence of the spring;
> Life will turn the meanest of her implements
> Before your eyes to price above all gold."

In these several ways your perceptions and your sensibilities will be brought into harmony with that standard of taste recognized by the common heart of man, and distinctly exhibited in the fine arts.

But you ask me what are the advantages of having a cultivated taste.

One advantage is found in the enjoyment which it affords. Go where you will, you will find the beauties of nature open before you; and whether you have the property, you may have the enjoyment of some of the wonders of art. If you have a cultivated taste, your soul is always in harmony with external nature.

> "For you the Spring
> Distils her dews, and from the silken Gem
> Its lucid leaves unfold. For you the hand
> Of Autumn tinges every fertile branch
> With blooming gold and blushes like the morn.
> Each passing hour sheds tribute from her wings;
> And still new beauties meet your lonely walks,
> And loves unfelt attract you. Not a breeze
> Flies o'er the meadow, not a cloud imbibes
> The setting sun's effulgence, not a strain
> From all the tenants of the warbling shade
> Ascends, but whence your bosom can partake
> Fresh pleasure unreproved."

"On one of the last mornings of our stay in Athens," says our countryman, Dr. Robinson, "I went very early to the Acropolis to see the sun rise over Mount Hymettus. The morning was clear and cold. I was alone upon the Acropolis, in the midst of the solemn grandeur of its desolations. Seating myself within the ruins of the Parthenon, where the eye could command the whole horizon through the columns of the eastern portico, I waited for the rising sun. The whole sky was so resplendent, that for a long time I could not determine the point where the orb of day would appear. The sunlight already lay upon the eastern plain, and on the northern mountains, falling between Hymettus and Pentelicus. Small fleecy clouds came floating on the north wind; and as they hovered over Hymettus and were met by the rays of the sun, were changed to liquid gold. At length, the first beams fell upon the Parthenon and lighted up its marble and its columns with a silvery splendor. It was one of those moments in the life of man that can never be forgotten."

It may not be our lot to visit Attica. But go where we will we can behold architecture raised by the Great Builder of all, this "majestical roof fretted with golden fire," more solemn and grand than the Parthenon. Elsewhere we can behold other mountains ascending as high as the Hymettus, other streams flowing as beautiful as the Illyssus, other woods waving as well as those over "Delphi's steep." Elsewhere the sun, rising as glorious, changes the clouds into "liquid gold." The man of cultivated taste sees and enjoys them all.

> "The meanest flowret of the vale,
> The simplest note that swells the gale,
> The common sun, the air, the skies,
> To him are opening paradise.

As every one should have some regular and stated occupation, so every one should have some seasons of relaxation and leisure, when he can lay down the weapons of his labor. Apollo does not always bend the bow. It is in those seasons of leisure that the man of taste has resources above those who are devoted to mere sensual enjoyments, to the neglect of refined pleasures. "In those rural seasons of the year," says Milton, "when the air is calm and pleasant, it were an injury and sullenness against Nature, not to go out and see her riches and partake in her rejoicing with heaven and earth." It is only the man of cultivated taste that can cordially partake with Nature in her rejoicing.

Another advantage of a cultivated taste is found in the improvement which it communicates to the useful arts. As beauty is associated with truth in all that is theoretical, so it is connected with utility in all that is practical. A man of taste will make a better shoe or a better coat, a better plow or a better wagon, than another, for the plain reason that much of the beauty consists in the adaptation to the end as all of the utility does. And the products of his skill will meet with a ready sale, even to those who profess to be governed only by utility. In certain articles, France and Italy command the market of the world because they show more taste in their manufacture than any other nation; just as individuals command the smaller markets, or bear off the palm at industrial fairs, for the same reason. Many a manufacturer has made his fortune simply by combining in a single article the beautiful with the useful. And in the domestic arrangements of a family taste has also much to do in promoting comfort, inasmuch as it promotes that neatness and orderly arrangement which are essential to health and quiet. Many a city and many a family have suffered from diseases which they would have escaped had they, under the influence of taste, been cleanly in their persons, and habitations, and streets. So too in agriculture, the most beautiful farms are generally the most profitable; the most beautiful meadows are the most productive; the most beautiful fields of grain are those which yield the largest harvest; the most beautiful animals are the most valuable. In houses, in furniture, in dress, in all the necessary arts, beauty is sought for as the concomitant of utility. This is true universally, except in cases where individuals are the most degraded or where nations are lowest in the scale of barbarism.

Another advantage of having a cultivated taste is that it helps to free him who has it from the arbitrary power of Fashion, that fickle goddess that rules the multitude. You well know that great numbers are governed in their opinions as to what is right, as to what is true, as to what is beautiful by Fashion, as if she were the sovereign arbitress over the intellect, the conscience, and the taste. Is that true? Yes, for every body says so. Is that right? Yes, it is the general custom. What a beautiful bonnet that is! Yes, it is of the latest fashion. Indeed "beautiful" and "fashionable" are by many considered as synonymous. Thus it happens that what is beautiful now, was, in their estimation, ugly ten years since, as it will be again ten years hence. To show the absurdity of many of these fashions, it was once proposed by a celebrated wit that a depository should be established for all the various fashions in dress that successively prevail, so that at a glance the follies might be seen into which men run. The evils produced by fashion in matters of taste, if not as great as those produced by matters pertaining to truth and duty, are sufficiently great to attract our notice. Now the reason why dress or furniture, or language or manners appear beautiful when in fashion, and the reverse when not, is that when in fashion, they are beautiful from associations which are destroyed as soon as they cease to be in fashion. Now if the mind by cultivation were fixed on the permanent principles of beauty, instead of being placed on these evanescent associations "these meteors of caprice, these new blown bubbles of the day," it would not be changed from admiration to disgust, and from disgust to admiration, according as the same thing is fashionable at one time and unfashionable at another. It would understand the nature of the illusions to which itself and others have yielded. It would bring every thing regarded as beautiful to a fixed standard, and would cease to be capricious. Do you say that tastes are different, and that there is no standard? You may say this when your own taste is called in question; but you should never say it when you call in question the tastes of others, since by so doing you offend their personality representing yourself as superior to them. The very fact that you call in question the taste of another, implies that there is a standard to which you refer his taste. Opinions are different, but still there is a standard of truth. The moral habits of men are different, but still there is a standard of right. Tastes are different, still there is a standard of beauty. In order to become acquainted with the principles of correct taste, works which treat upon the subject should be carefully studied and their doctrines applied to the various objects of taste which come under your notice. Whether these works differ in some respects from each other or not, is of little consequence, in comparison with the fact that they agree in their influence upon the mind in giving breadth and exactness to its views. Burke may dwell more upon the objective view, presenting us with those qualities in external things which produce the emotions of beauty. Alison may dwell more on the subjective view, presenting to us the emotions themselves in their relations to each other, as they exist in the soul. They may agree, however, in elevating the mind from the tyranny and the caprice of fashion into the appreciation of those principles of beauty and of taste which are founded in nature and which are permanent.

Another advantage of having a cultivated taste is found in the improvement which it communicates to the other faculties of the mind. I need not say to you that whatever has a tendency to take off the attention from low and gross pursuits, and fix it upon what is elevated, refines and improves the mind. The greater the susceptibility one has to a beautiful object, the stronger impression it will make upon his mind, the more lively will be his curiosity, and the more thorough will be his investigation. An object of beauty is related to the judgment as well as to the sensibility. Accordingly the received doctrine is that the grand characteristics of taste are deducible to two, delicacy and correctness. The first of these implies a high degree of sensibility, the second a sound judgment. A man in the cultivation of his taste will often be led to inquire why it is that this object and that excite in his mind the emotion of beauty; and in answering this inquiry, his reasoning faculty will be exercised and strengthened. Thus in aiming at correctness of taste his judgment will be improved. Delicacy of taste implies sensibility even to minute beauties, and sensibility is favorable to the exercise of the imagination. By the cultivation of the taste the imagination is furnished with materials from which it can select groups of beautiful ideas which others will admire. Thus taste is closely connected with genius. Indeed it may with some truth be said that genius is but taste in its extacy; and that taste is but genius in its repose. The great charm of Cowper's poetry consists in the selection of beautiful thoughts on common subjects, which his imagination, improved by the cultivation of his taste, enabled him to make. Thus we may understand how it is that the cultivation of the taste improves the mind in all its faculties, imparting eagerness to the attention, retentiveness to the memory, discrimination to the judgment, and activity to the imagination.

Another advantage of having a cultivated taste is found in the improvement which it communicates to the social affections. Many objects of desire beget selfishness in those who pursue them. Inasmuch as they can fall to the lot of only a few, they produce rivalry in all, disappointment in the losers, and it may be pride in the winners. This is true of the objects of ambition, of avarice, of pleasure. The social feelings of two men who are striving as candidates for the same office, will not be improved by the competition. Go then to the political caucus, to the marts of commerce, to the halls of justice, and you can see causes in operation to keep men apart, and to widen the distance between them. Thus it happens that instead of the law of attraction, which ought to bind men together in sweetest harmony, the law of repulsion reigns.

Now the difference between an object of taste and these other objects is, that two persons, who admire the same object of taste, love each other the more, on account of this common admiration. What delightful friendships have existed between the lovers of nature and of the fine arts; between Raphael and Julio Romano, Gray and West, Southey and Wordsworth! When Dupaty was enjoying the exquisite landscapes at Tivoli, he exclaims, "Why are you not here, my children, who are so dear to me, my Adela, my Adrian, my Eleonora, my Augustus, to pluck these beautiful flowers? How delightful it would be to see them dispersing themselves among the groves, striving to trample down these grass plots, hiding themselves in all these in the shades of evening!"

Go into a family who are bound together by their common love of music, or of landscape-gardening, or of poetry, or even of house-plants, and you will be convinced that this common love for the same objects of beauty has a permanent as well as a delightful influence on the social affections. The celebrated Haydn, loaded with years and with honors, derived the most delightful enjoyments from tuning those simple airs which he sung with his father and mother, when being a child he stood between them, and beat time with two pieces of wood, one of which served him for a violin and the other for a bow. Many a one like him has found that the pleasures of taste, enjoyed in the family, have kept alive his affections for kindred long after they have been sleepers in dust.

Communities likewise in which there is a taste for public and private improvements, in beautifying parks, or the streets, or the gardens, or the burial grounds, or in erecting monuments or statues, show more of genuine friendly feeling in private intercourse and to strangers, than do those communities in which the love of gain or party spirit is the master passion. Napoleon, in the midst of reverses, when all Paris was in a state of extreme agitation, ordered the dome of one of the conspicuous public buildings to be covered with gilding; for he knew that the minds of the Parisians, withdrawn from agitating topics by this beautiful object, would be calmed into quiet. The God of Israel intended that the magnificent temple, the common object of attraction, to the nation, should be the means of union among the tribes; for he knew that those who walked about Zion, and numbered her towers, and marked her bulwarks, and considered her palaces, would be prepared to pray for the peace of Jerusalem.

There is some foundation indeed for the opinion that those religious denominations among Christians show most of the love, and gentleness, and sincerity of the gospel in the intercourse of private life, which are distinguished for the cultivation of taste. The Moravians might be mentioned in the way of illustration. "Their burying ground is a garden, the walks in which are marked out by funeral stones for the living as well as for the dead. By the side of each stone is placed a flowering shrub. On Easter day divine service is performed in the garden, at which the resurrection is announced in the midst of the tombs. All present at this act of worship know the stone that is to be placed over their coffin, and already breathe the perfume of the young tree whose leaves and flowers will fall upon their graves."

Another advantage of having a cultivated taste is found in its moral effects upon the heart. The objects of taste, whether found in the fine arts or in nature, withdraw the attention from temptations which seduce the soul from duty and from God. They calm the temper which is liable to be disturbed by the cares of business and the disappointments of life. Nature around and above is but an image of Him who is the first Good and the first Fair. It is hardly possible therefore to look at the beauties of nature without having the mind raised towards Him whom they thus image forth. As it was out of Zion, the perfection of beauty, that God shone, so from the higher beauties of nature He shines forth still. Whenever the objects of the material world afford delight, they are the signs or expressions of the higher qualities by which our moral sensibilities are called forth. They are the reflections of the image of God. Devotion and the emotions of beauty are naturally associated in the mind. Accordingly in the scriptures the most devout feelings are expressed in the beauty of poetry, and in the services of the temple, music, by divine authority, was made to lend its attractions to duty. "While Canitz, one of the German poets, was upon the bed of death, he requested to be raised on his couch in order to take a last look of the setting sun. Oh, said he, if a small part of the Eternal's creation can be so exquisitely beautiful as this, how much more beautiful must be the Eternal himself!" Thus divine truth beaming into the mind through the medium of a cultivated taste, kindles up the flame of devotion on the altar of the heart. Attracted then by the beauties of nature toward the High and Holy One who made them serve Him in the beauty of holiness on earth, and He will beautify you with His image in Heaven. Having while on earth been led by your admiration of physical beauty in the works of nature and art, to the higher admiration of the moral beauty of which He is the perfect expression, He will cause you to "be what you admire," when He glorifies you in His presence.

Thus have I endeavored distinctly, though briefly, to set

forth some of the advantages of cultivating the taste, that I might persuade all who hear me, and especially the young, to enter upon a course of self-improvement in some such manner as the one I have described. Do you wish to increase the innocent enjoyments of your earthly existence? Do you wish to promote improvements in the useful arts? Do you wish to free yourself from the arbitrary power of fashion? Do you wish to improve the other faculties of your mind, and your social affections, and your moral feelings? Carefully cultivate your taste for what is beautiful in nature, in art, in moral sentiment, and in great and virtuous actions.

In this seminary, we rejoice to believe that the pupils are instructed in the elements of truth as related to the reason, the elements of duty as related to the conscience, the elements of beauty as related to the taste. The principles adopted here, you will carry out with you into practical life. We rejoice to know that many have gone forth from this seminary after having enjoyed the advantages of the prescribed course, with an earnest and devoted attachment to truth and duty in their various forms, and to the beautiful in nature and art, in moral sentiment and conduct. We rejoice to know that in the domestic circle and in the school, they are now in many States in our wide country, teaching as well as acting out the principles which they learned here, and showing, each in her own sphere, something of that love of order, that beauty of arrangement, that decorum, and neatness, and propriety which prevail here. We have seen some of them, each in a circle of confiding pupils, imparting to other minds the principles of learning and religion which they have received in this seminary. We have seen them in woman's world, her home, each in the center of that world, by an attractive influence, binding in accordance sweet every member of the household system to its own orbit of duty, and diffusing light and joy to every part of that system. And we can see some of them now with the eye of faith after sinking in the waters of death, rising in the firmament of the new heavens, "glittering like the morning star, full of life, and splendor, and joy." In their light beaming on you from that clear upper sky, you can still walk.

Before closing this address, I would say in the name of this great assembly, that we rejoice to meet those, who on this day are to close their connection with this seminary, and to go forth into the community to illustrate and diffuse the principles which they have learned here, and to send forth a radiant and gentle influence in their several spheres. Allow me, my young friends, as you are about to part from teachers and friends tenderly loved, to express our best wishes for your welfare. May you carry with you the light of heaven in your hearts to cheer you on your earthly pilgrimage. Do what you have to do in this scene of action, in a beautiful womanly spirit, with modesty. Suffer what you have to suffer in this vale of tears, in a beautiful womanly spirit, with patience. Cultivate in yourselves and in others, the love of the true, the good, the perfect, and the beautiful, so far as you find them on earth.

It may indeed be your lot to be placed in circumstances not favorable to the cultivation of your taste. It may be your lot to pass your life in want, in weariness, in watching, toiling on, suffering on at the calls of duty. While thus in the patience of hope and the labor of love, you prove that you aim to be

> "A creature not too bright and good
> For human nature's daily food,"

still, though embarrassed by the necessities of your condition, so cultivate your taste that your soul

> " Will be a mansion for all lovely forms,
> Your memory a dwelling place
> For all sweet sounds and harmonies."

And if in your external circumstances it should be your fortunate lot to dwell in the midst of scenery more lovely, to form purer friendships, to witness virtues more attractive than you have found here, still in memory you will delight to return to this lovely landscape, to the dear friends whose hearts in graceful sympathy were knit to yours, to the beautiful devotions in which you were accustomed to unite. And when those forms now in the fulness of youthful life, shall be disfigured by time, and those faces now bright with joy shall have faded, and those hearts now beating with strong pulsations shall be hushed in death, may your souls, freed from their clay, ascend on high to behold there in full vision the first true, the first good, the first perfect and the first fair, and to be changed into that divine image from glory to glory.

READING AS A MEANS OF CULTURE.

In the early ages of the world, before the art of writing was invented, men had to depend, for the acquisition of knowledge, chiefly upon oral instruction. In this way, each generation were, in turn, the pupils of the preceding, and the teachers of the following generation in the reception and the transmission of the traditionary lore of the times. And as the family bond was then a strong one, each child was, in a preëminent sense, the pupil of his parent, and each patriarch was, in a preëminent sense, the teacher of his child, when he "sat with him in the house, and when he walked with him by the way, when he lay down, and when he rose up."

After the invention of alphabet-writing, and before that of printing, oral instruction was still the principal means of imparting knowledge. Readers were few; books still fewer, and not accessible; transcription was expensive. So valuable, indeed, were some works, that, in order to obtain the loan of a book, it was necessary to pledge an estate for its safe return. Indeed, in some instances, books were kept chained, so that they could not be removed from the place where they were kept.

But since the art of making paper was invented, and, as related to this, the art of printing, a mighty change has taken place in respect to the number of books and the number of readers. In our own country, especially in this part of our country, where all enjoy the advantages of popular education, all are readers.

All, therefore, must be interested in the subject which I have chosen, namely, READING AS THE MEANS OF SELF-CULTURE.

In treating this subject, I hope, in some degree, to supply a felt want frequently expressed by those who are engaged in self-culture, whether they are at school or at home, whether they are at college, or engaged in some professional employment.

What end shall I aim at in reading?

What time shall I spend in reading?

What mode shall I adopt in reading?

What books shall I read?

These are interrogatories prompted by a desire of self-improvement on the part of the modest and earnest aspirant, whatever be his position; and they demand a careful and a correct answer.

WHAT, THEN, IS THE END TO BE AIMED AT IN READING?

Now, a large class of readers propose to themselves no end at all in their reading. They feel attracted to the page of a book, or to the column of a newspaper, just as they are to a garden of flowers, or to a winding river. They have no purpose in view; they have no object to be accomplished. The act of reading terminates in itself, so far as any end is concerned. It is just a matter of present gratification, of present amusement.

Another class read only to kill time, which otherwise would hang heavily on their hands. Their minds are listless, or they are tormented with sad thoughts, or inward upbraidings, or remorse, or shame, from which they wish to escape; and by killing time in this escape from themselves, so far forth, they commit suicide.

Another class read in order to make a show of learning. They read incessantly, and incessantly boast of what they have read. They are ostentatious; they are vain of their knowledge, and pedantic.

The true end of reading, as the means of self-culture, is evidently, in the very statement of the terms of the proposition, self-culture. Now, self-culture aims at the improvement of all the higher powers of our nature. Just so far, then, as reading contributes to self-culture, it contributes to improve, and elevate, and refine our whole nature. By holding intercourse with the great minds of the world, as they still live in their works, we can become like them. Our memories can be stored with the treasures of knowledge gathered by them. Our imaginations can rove freely among the forms of thought among which they expatiated with delight. Our judgment can decide correctly in view of the facts which they have collected, and the principles which they have evolved, and the reasons they have elaborated. Our wills can be confirmed by the motives they administer. Our hearts can be brought into harmony with their hearts by contemplating what awakened their emotional nature. Our moral feelings can become assimilated to theirs by inhaling their spirit..

In books we have the concentrated wisdom of past ages and of the present, which we can appropriate to ourselves, for our own improvement and that of others. The true end of reading is to make this appropriation. Lord Bacon's rule is the best; "Read, not to contradict and confute, nor to believe and take for granted, nor to find talk and discourse, but to weigh and consider."

The improvement of your intellectual and your moral powers being the true end of reading, I shall proceed to the second question: WHAT TIME SHALL I SPEND IN READING?

The answer to this question must depend upon the circumstances in which you are placed and the duties you have to perform. You are in the district-school, or the academy, or the college, or in the preparation for some professional employment, or in the practice of some profession, or are actively employed in family duties. Now, whenever reading, by consuming time, interferes with your regular studies, or your professional employments, or your family duties, it should be avoided, even though at a sacrifice of inclination.

Moreover, when it creates a distaste for studies or other duties, by withdrawing the attention from them, by impairing the intellectual vigor, by weakening the moral power so as to disqualify you for study or labor, it defeats the main purpose for which you were placed under instruction, or for which you devoted yourselves to labor. For instance, if a student has in his room a book that creates a distaste for the study of arithmetic, a branch which he is pursuing, he had better spend no time in reading that book, for the plain reason that arithmetic, in relation to his duties as a student, is of more importance to him. If a merchant's clerk has a book which creates a distaste for his ledger, he had better spend no time in reading that book, for the plain reason that it disqualifies him for his paramount duties.

And so too, when reading fatigues and exhausts the mind, it should be avoided. Some books are so exciting to the attention, to the imagination, to the passions, that they produce a mental debauch, which, if often repeated, destroys the firm tone of the mind, and renders it fitful and inefficient in its exertion.

Moreover, reading should be avoided when it interferes with necessary repose, as it does when pursued at a late hour of night. It then has a pernicious influence upon the health first, then upon the spirits, then upon the mind itself. The knowledge gained in this way is for the most part of but little value, for it is gained at the expense of mental vigor, and sometimes even of life itself. The celebrated William Pinckney, the great Maryland orator, fell a sacrifice to late reading. To read when you ought to be in bed, especially to read when in bed, is to inflict a great evil on yourself without an equivalent. It is to injure your eyes, your brain, your nervous system, your intellect.

Again, reading ought not to interfere with the due cultivation of the social affections, whether by personal intercourse with friends, or a punctual correspondence. Some are such bookworms that they become insensible to the sweet charities of domestic life, and all the delightful amenities of general society.

Finally, only so much time should be spent in reading as will allow leisure for reflection upon what has been read, in order that it may become our own, for the purposes of mental discipline and strength. Now, it happens that one may have a great appetite and a poor digestion. He may read much and think little. Hence, what he reads, not going through the process of assimilation, instead of invigorating, burdens the mind. Thus addicted to mental gluttony, thus suffering from mental repletion, he is incapacitated for high achievements. He is

'A bookful blockhead ignorantly read,
With loads of learned lumber in his head.'

He is, it may be, a living lexicon, a walking encyclopædia; but he is motionless and dead, so far as practical usefulness is concerned.

With these cautions and exceptions, endeavor to find time, if possible, to read every day of your life. Read, if you can, in the morning, in the sweet hour of prime, if it be only for five minutes. Read, if you can, when resting from your toil at noon. Read especially more or less during the long winter evenings. Read in the season of youth, when the impressions made on the mind are permanent. Read in middle life, when the judgment is strong. Read in the season of old age, when your minds become contemplative, and the body unfitted for active life. Let some book furnish daily food for the mind, as the table does for the body.

We are now prepared to answer the third question: WHAT IS THE BEST MODE OF READING?

The best mode of reading is that which is best adapted to accomplish the ends of reading. And the highest end of reading, as in every part of education, is to furnish and discipline the mind, and thus to prepare it to act in accordance with its high capacity on earth and in heaven. In order to gain these high ends, the mind must be tasked to a high effort.

But, as a matter of fact, there is often careless reading when there ought to be the closest application of the mind. There is often reading, in the common sense of the word, when there ought to be study, because the former is easier than the latter. It has been said, with some appearance of truth: 'Study is labor, and labor is pain, and no one loves pain.' There is, therefore, a temptation to substitute the pleasure of negligent reading for the pain of study. Reading is often identical with study, as when one is said to *read* law. For success in study, the higher powers of the mind must be put in requisition. There must be the full vigor of the attention without any of its wanderings, the full retentiveness of the memory, the full activity of the imagination. In the examination of the subject, the judgment must be ever vigilant; the will, even in the midst of discouragement, must never swerve from its high purpose. The affections must often be summoned from their repose, to give impulse to the intellect. And the body, too, in that much study which is a weariness to the flesh, must be roused from its languor only to writhe and quiver under the chafings of the intellect. In short, for successful study, there must be the highest efforts of the best powers of the mind. But in reading, the mind is often in nearly a passive state, like that of dreaming or reverie, in which images flit before the mind without any act of volition to retain them. In rapid reading, it is nearly in the same state as yours is when you are whirled through a country in a post-coach or a railroad-car. How much do you know of that country in the one case? How much do you know of the book in the other?

A person mentally indolent may be fond of reading. He may love to read in a recumbent posture until he falls asleep, every day or every night of his life. It might be too much to say that his room resembles the famous cave of the god of sleep. But he furnishes proof in his experience, that the leaves of a book are as sure an opiate as the leaves of the poppy, the symbol of that god. Indeed, we have known those who regularly take a book to bed with them every night, as 'a shoe-horn to pull on sleep with.' Indeed, we have seen a whole family, each with a book in hand, to which he seemed to be bowing in devotion, except one bright young girl, who archly sung:

'We are all noddin', nid, nid, noddin';
We are all noddin' at our house at home.'

On the supposition that you propose to yourself the true end of reading, and are ready to adopt the appropriate means to arrive at it, you will take care to understand your author thoroughly. A vague and general impression is not sufficient. You must bestow the whole vigor of your attention on the words, the phrases, the periods, the paragraphs. If, at the first perusal, you do not understand a passage, peruse it a second or a third time. If you then fail in discovering its meaning, mark it for examination after you have read the book through. When you can do it, be careful to furnish yourself with every necessary help in books of reference, such as dictionaries, general, classical, and biographical works on sacred and profane antiquities, geography, and chronology.

If a word occurs whose meaning you do not know, be careful to refer to your dictionary, even though it may for a moment interrupt the course of the narrative or the argument. If you meet with an allusion to a fact with which you are unacquainted, immediately turn to your book of reference for the necessary information. For instance, you meet for the first time with the phrase, *ultima thule*, in a sentence like this: 'In that science, he reached the *ultima thule* of discovery.' Instead of guessing at the import of the phrase, carefully ascertain the meaning, once for all. Again, you meet for the first time with an allusion to the bow of Ulysses, in a sentence like this: 'He cannot bend the bow of Ulysses.' Instead of being satisfied with a conjecture, read the story of the suitors of Penelope, who were put to the test of bending the bow of that hero, her husband, and you will understand the point of the allusion.

But you say that this is a very slow and tedious way of reading. Slow it may be, but not tedious, because your curiosity is constantly awakened and constantly gratified. It is not tedious, any more than it is, in traveling through a country, to take time to examine the most grand and beautiful objects in nature and art. Instead of being tedious, it is the only way of becoming deeply interested in any highly intellectual and finished work. It is the only way in which you can transfer the views of your author to your own mind, and transfuse his spirit to your own soul. And as to slowness, you may, on this subject, adopt the adage: 'The more haste, the worst speed.' You proceed more slowly in the first part of your course, in order that you may make the greater speed in the end. Interruptions will become fewer and fewer as you advance.

But you say that you can understand what you read without all this trouble. Perhaps you can; and perhaps the reason is, that you read those ephemeral productions that require as little labor to read them as it did to write them.

In order thoroughly to understand a work, it is frequently necessary to read it a second or even a third time. One of the first scholars of the age said that he 'read Demosthenes three times before the beauties of that divine author began to appear.' One part of a work throws light upon another part. After you have read the conclusion of a work, you can better understand the commencement.

Lest I should myself fail of being understood, I will adduce one or two more instances. Suppose that you should, in conversation, use the word *water* in the hearing of two persons, the one a child of six years, and the other an accomplished chemist. Ask the child if he understands what is meant by the word, and he will promptly say: 'O! Yes.' And yet how inadequate is the meaning of the word as it stands in his mind, compared with that which stands in the mind of the other, who is acquainted with that substance in its elements and combinations!

Take another instance. Read the lines of Pope, descriptive of creative power, in the hearing of two persons, one of whom has and the other has not reflected on the subject to which it relates:

> 'Builds life on death, on change duration founds,
> And bids the eternal wheels to know their rounds.'

To the one, these lines may be little more than mere words. To the other, they are full of meaning. In them, he sees the earth's face renewed by the breath of the Almighty, and nature for ever changing, yet the same for ever, like the phœnix, springing up into the beauty of the present out of the ashes of the past.

Take another instance:

'So Zembla's rocks, the beauteous work of frost,
Rise white in air and glitter o'er the coast:
Pale suns, unfelt at distance, roll away,
And on the impassive ice the lightnings play,
Eternal snows the growing mass supply,
Till the bright mountains prop the incumbent sky:
As Atlas fixed, each hoary pile appears,
The gathered winter of a thousand years.'

The full beauty of this piece you cannot perceive unless you bring before your mind each brilliant portion of the whole of this winter landscape. And this you cannot do, unless you make yourself acquainted with phenomena of a winter beyond the Arctic circle. And even then you cannot do it unless you dwell long enough upon each image, to give it a distinct local habitation in the range of your conception. You are to gaze upon each part and on the whole as you would upon the picture of it on canvas, or as you would upon the original scene itself, looking, one while, upon the glittering ice-mountain springing from the shore far into the upper sky, piercing the clouds with its hoary head, and supporting, like another Atlas, the heavens; and then looking at the sun fast struggling above the edge of the far-off southern horizon, sending along the intervening ocean his level, ineffectual rays; and then at the lightnings, the 'dread arrows of the clouds,' glancing off from the unscathed brow of the giant mountain.

In the dawn of our intellectual existence, before bad mental habits are formed, we adopt the true mode of gaining knowledge. The child, when a new object is presented, gives up the whole of its little mind to its examination. He gazes at it with intense interest, carefully surveying every part. He applies all his senses, so far as he can, to its examination, when it is within his reach. And so strong is his curiosity, that he will break to pieces what he values, in order to discover its properties. In this way he transfers to his mind a distinct and full image of the admired object, which, in the absence of that object, he can gaze upon in his contemplations, with the same interest that he could upon the object itself, if it were present to the bodily eye. These images, thus carefully formed in early life by the faculty of conception, under the guiding influence of nature, continue distinct and beautiful in the faithful keeping of memory, uninjured by time. In this way, it happens that the young ideas, which, under the teachings of nature, shoot forth from the soul in the spring-time of life, are perennial plants, continuing beautiful in leaf and in flower under the summer's sun of manhood and in the winter of old age.

From the teachings of instinct in early life, reason should learn a lesson to be applied in maturer years. True, the objects that we examine through the medium of words and sentences are often intellectual, not sensible. But in order to become intimately acquainted with them, there must be the same eager and thorough observation, the same deep emotion, the same curiosity, which the child exhibits. Indeed, the distinct perception and full comprehension of abstract ideas, seen through the dispersive and refractive medium of language, require superior concentration of attention, full earnestness of curiosity, and the quickening influence of emotion. If, on the other hand, there is no curiosity felt, no interest excited, and no vigor of attention, it is all in vain that the eye traces the words on the page.

But you say that you get ideas in this superficial way. So you may, but they are ideas of words, not of things. You may get ideas by reading the naked columns of a spelling book, but not connected thought. When I speak of understanding a work, I do not refer merely to the words themselves in their lexical signification, but to their relations in sentences, in paragraphs, in chapters, in the whole, in its general drift and scope.

And when I speak of understanding a work, I do not refer

merely to pure intellect, but to all the faculties that are addressed by the work. Sometimes a subject is presented in the 'dry light' of the intellect; and sometimes, to use another expression of Bacon, it is 'drenched in the affections.' In the one case, the intellect of the reader is put in requisition; in the other, his affections likewise. For instance, Samuel Clarke, whom Voltaire called a 'reasoning machine,' writes a book which can be understood by that reader only who, in the perusal, exerts his reasoning faculty. Jonathan Edwards writes a work under the guidance of his heart, and no one can thoroughly understand it whose heart has not given a lesson to his head. Milton, on the seraph wings of ecstacy, passed the flaming bounds of space and time; and who can follow him, without the aid of imagination, up to the living throne and the sapphire blaze?

While different writers, in this way, exhibit a predominance of different faculties, it likewise is evident that no reader can fully enter into the spirit of a work, who does not, in the perusal of it, exert that faculty which is predominant in the author. Indeed, for fully understanding a writer and thoroughly entering into his spirit, it is necessary for you to give yourself up wholly into his hands, to put yourself in the same state of mind, when you read, that he was when he wrote. You are in this way to go through the letter into the spirit. *Qui haeret in litera, haeret in cortice.*

At the same time, you are to bestow your attention upon the language which an author employs to embody his thoughts, as well for the purpose of learning what those thoughts are, as for being able to embody your own thoughts when you shall address others. As language is the medium of thought, it is as necessary to understand the nature of that medium, as it is to understand the nature of the medium through which you see objects with the bodily eye. In dioptrics, you know that if you view an object through one glass, it will appear magnified; and through another, it will appear diminished; and through another, it will appear distorted; and through a fourth, it will appear colored; and through a fifth, it will appear just as it is, in form and size and color. The same is true of language in modifying thought. Five men will present the same thought in five different ways. One will elevate it; another, degrade it; a third, distort it; a fourth, color it; and a fifth, employ such appropriate language that the reader, at the first view, sees it just as it is. If you will carefully observe how good authors express themselves, you will from them obtain such command of language, that whenever you have a thought to express, words, like 'nimble servitors, will come to their places' at your bidding.

I know that some have affected to underrate the knowledge of language in comparison with the knowledge of things. True, there is a difference between an idea and the expression of it; and in order to express it, you must first have it. But men who are to have intercourse with their fellow-men, and who are to influence them by means of knowledge, must embody their knowledge in language, otherwise they have no instruments by which to work. There are thoughts which, sometimes in happy moments of inspiration, dart through the mind with the brightness of electric fires. In that brightness we behold, as with a prophet's ken, the secrets of the world unknown, revealed to us as through the parting cloud. But as they come, so they go, like lightning. The clouds come together again, and our pathway becomes dark as before. Could we but arrest these flashes of thought and make them permanent in their radiance, they would serve to guide and cheer, and not merely to dazzle. This it is the office of language to do. There are 'men endowed with highest gifts, the vision and the faculty divine,' yet wanting the accomplishment of words, men 'who live out their time, and go to the grave unthought of.'

'To give solidity and permanence to the inspiration of genius, two things are especially necessary. First, that the idea to be communicated should be powerfully apprehended by the speaker or writer; and next, that he should employ words and phrases which convey it in all its truth to another.' A man who entertains such conceptions will fail, unless suitable words wait upon his thoughts. Language has been fitly called a vast labyrinth. The man who has not the clue must wander in its mazes.

In your reading, mark the meaning of the words and phrases employed by your author. Carefully associate language with your thoughts, so that thought and language shall become one in your mind.

Beside understanding the views of an author, and the language in which his views are conveyed, you must understand the subjects upon which he writes. It is one thing to learn what an author thinks of a subject, and another to learn what is true of that subject. Hear what Locke, the great master of reason, says on this subject:

'Reading furnishes the mind only with the materials of knowledge; it is thinking makes what we read ours. We are of the ruminating species, and it is not enough to cram ourselves with a great load of collections; unless we chew them over again, they will not give us strength and nourishment. All that is found in books is not built upon true foundations, nor always rightly deduced from the principles it is pretended to be built on. The mind of the reader is often backward in itself, to be at the pains to trace every argument to its original, to see upon what basis it stands, and how firmly; but yet it is this that gives one man so much advantage over another in reading. The mind should, by severe rules, be tied down to this at first uneasy task; use and exercise will give it facility, so that those who are accustomed to it readily, as it were with one cast of the eye, take a view of the argument, and presently, in most cases, see where it bottoms. Those who have got this faculty, one may say, have got the true key to books, and the clue to lead them through the mizmaze of variety of opinions and authors to truth and certainty. This, young beginners should be entered in and shown the use of, that they might profit by their reading. Those who are strangers to it will be apt to think it too great a clog in the way of men's studies. But I would add, this way of thinking on and profiting by what we read will be a clog and rub only in the beginning. And to those that aim at knowledge I may say, that he who fair and softly goes steadily forward in a course that points right, will sooner be at his journey's end than he that runs after every one he meets, though he gallop all day, full speed.'

In reading, 'truth is the measure of knowledge' and therefore is to be mainly sought. While, in the words of Burns, 'some books are lies fra end to end,' most are composed of a mixture of truth and error in different proportions. Now whether they are the counterfeit presentment of truth, or have in them only so much of the alloy of error as brings them to the common currency, or have in them only pure gold, they should be brought to the touchstone. In some instances, you may perceive almost intuitively that what you are reading is false. This happens when you are acquainted with the subjects upon which they treat. In other instances, by comparing what is said in one part of a book with what is said in another, and thus discovering the inconsistency, you can see where the error lies. It not unfrequently happens that the same author furnishes both the poison and the antidote.

Besides this, you can sometimes examine what you read in the light of your own observation. If you are reading some description of external nature, you can limit, correct, or extend the views presented by others, from your own observation; and this, too, whether those are scientific or political, whether they are found in Paley's 'Theology,' or Thompson's 'Seasons.' When you read. some work on human life and manners, as Addison's 'Spectator,' or Franklin's 'Essays,' you are to cast your eyes around upon the forms of life and manners with which you are acquainted, to discover whether these great moral painters are, in the outlines and coloring of their pictures, true to the original. If you are reading some work on the human mind, you are constantly to watch the working of your own mind, that you may see whether the principles which your author advocates are in accordance with your own consciousness. If you are perusing some historical or political work, inquire whether the writer was a candid man, whether he leaned to a particular theory or party, and in this way learn to make the necessary allowance for his prepossessions and prejudices. To arrive at truths on litigated points, it may be necessary to read both sides.

In order to profit from reading, it is advantageous to converse with those who have read the same books, or are interested in the same topics. Two persons of equal capacity shall read the same book, and yet receive from it very different impressions. By exchanging their views in the commerce of thought, each is a gainer. The difficulties which one meets with are solved by the other, and the truths upon which they agree are more firmly fixed in the minds of each. By thus bringing their minds in contact with each other, in conversation upon the work, their feelings are warmed into more vigorous exercise, and by the collision of their opinions the light of truth is struck out. Moreover, by conversing concerning the books that you read with those that are older and have read more than yourselves, and have had better opportunities for observation, you will be the better able to form a correct estimate of what you read. Their experience will help to guard you against the errors and evil tendencies of the work, or enable you to appreciate its excellences.

If you will adopt the practice, so far as the courtesies of life will allow, of discussing the various subjects which you meet with in your reading, you will always be furnished with interesting and useful topics of conversation, which will render you an acceptable visitor with the select sober few or the gayer circle. In the 'feast of reason and the flow of soul,' you can spend your social interviews, avoiding the error, on the one hand, of sitting in silence because you have nothing to say on the topics that are up, and the greater evil, on the other, of saying an 'infinite deal of nothing.'

Another practice to be attended to, in order to profit by your reading, is, to use your pen as an instrument of thought. When you are reading a work, it is profitable to take notes of what is true and beautiful in thought or expression on the one hand, and likewise of passages that are erroneous or ungraceful, that you may be able to refer to them at pleasure. This will help to form the mental habit of distinguishing between truth and falsehood, beauty and deformity.

In some cases, it may be well to take an abstract or make an analysis of the work. In others, it may be better to write short comments, in the way of refuting what is false, and clearing up what is obscure, and confirming what is true. In expressing the thoughts of your author in your own language, and in connection with your own views, you will receive a benefit like that which you gain in translating from another language, in the distinctness and permanency of your impressions. You will be furnishing yourselves, for the future, with the history of your mental progress. Coleridge was so much in the habit of doing this, that his friends were anxious to lend him books, that he might write notes in the margin. So much was President Edwards in the habit of using his pen as an instrument of thought, that it might be said of him, '*Nil sine calamo.*' Of course I shall be understood as referring to those works only that are worth a careful perusal.

It is useful sometimes to place before you some admired passage of some (English) author, and translate, if I may use the term, the thoughts contained in it into your own language. In this way, by comparing the original and the translation, you can see accurately your own deficiencies and excellences, as well as those of your author.

With respect to the practice of making extracts of passages that you admire, either on account of beauty of expression or correctness of thought, I cannot speak with so much confidence. I see not why those who labor in the mines of literature, may not with advantage arrange the gems of thought, as in a cabinet, as specimens of what is true and beautiful.

It should constantly be remembered that the end of reading is to furnish nourishment to the mind, that it may grow into the full greatness and vigor of which it is susceptible. But the mind grows, like the body, by expansion from within; and not like a crystal, by accretion from without. Now in order to obtain nourishment from what you read, the mind itself must decompose what is received into it, in order that assimilation may take place. While what you read remains a mere undigested mass in the memory, it is of but little worth. Rumination is indispensable.

And here I may with advantage quote the example of a distinguished scholar of our own country.

1. Before I commenced an author, I made myself thoroughly master of the whole scheme of his work, if a table of contents enabled me to do so.

2. I then studied the author in the following manner: After reading the first sentence, I meditated on it, developing the author's thoughts as well as I was able, and reducing the whole, as nearly as possible, to a single distinct concise expression. I then read the second sentence, and did the same. I next compared the two sentences together, meditating on them, and gathering out of them their substance. Thus I went through the paragraph, and reflected on the whole until I had reduced it to a single sentence, containing its essence. I then studied the next paragraph in like manner; and having compared the two, I gathered out of them their substance. The same plan was followed in the comparison of sections with sections, and chapters with chapters, books with books, until the author was finished.

3. A third rule was to pass nothing unexamined, nothing without reflection, whether in poetry or fiction, history or travels, politics, philosophy, or religion. Nor ought I to omit the three rules of Professor Whittaker, of Cambridge, given to John Boyse, one of the eminent translators of the Bible in the time of James the First. 1. To study chiefly standing or walking. 2. Never to study at a window. 3. Not to go to bed, on any account, with cold feet.

Thus much for the manner of reading.

I now proceed to answer the fourth question, namely, WHAT BOOKS SHOULD BE READ?

The time was when this question, if asked by one who intended to be a scholar, might be answered, *All.* Books were few, and every learned man was expected to read every book to which he could gain access. Even some time after the art of printing was invented, an industrious scholar might be expected to read every book that had been put to press. But with the improvements in mechanical arts connected with printing, at the present rate of increase, at no distant period, the world itself, in the language of an authorized hyperbole, cannot contain the books that are printed.

If the youthful student visits some large library in an athenæum or a college, or reads over the catalogues of these libraries, or looks into a fashionable periodical review, he finds a great many standard works, and a great many new works, each lauded to the skies, as the offspring of genius. The press, urged on by the power of steam, is as prolific as Berecynthia, the fabled mother of the gods, and like hers too, if he may credit the voice of flattery at every new birth, all its offspring are immortal. Beside the attractions of splendid binding and typography, the power of the pencil and the graver have been summoned to furnish designs to enliven dulness or grace the creations of genius. At his first introduction to these delights of learning in some favored spot, he may, if his is a poetical temperament, fancy that he has found the home of all the muses, and that each of those bright-eyed daughters of Jove is contending for his favor, as did the three goddesses on Mount Ida for that of Paris.

In this multitude of books, as no one can read all, evidently every judicious person must go on the principle of selection. 'Some books,' says Bacon, 'are to be tasted, others are to be swallowed, and some few to be chewed and digested.' It is only the 'few' that are to be chewed and digested. It is only the standard works that should be anxiously sought and carefully read, though others may be occasionally tasted. While the mind is in the forming state, such books should be read as are adapted to form it to admire virtue, truth, and beauty. When formed, it may gather truth from every part of the fields of literature, as the bee gathers honey even from poisonous flowers. The youthful student should fix his intense regards upon standard works, and bestow only a passing notice on those ephemeral productions which fall from the press upon the current of literature, 'thick as autumnal leaves that strow the brooks of Vallambrosa.'

Their name is legion. They meet you in the book-stores, in steamboats, in railway cars.

> 'The dog-star rages, now 'tis past a doubt,
> All Bedlam or Parnassus is let out.
> Fire in each eye and paper in each hand,
> They rave, recite, and madden round the land.
> By land, by water, they renew the charge;
> They stop the chariot and they board the barge.'

In the fashionable literature, or the 'yellow-covered literature,' as it has been called, a bad spirit reigns, or rather all spirits congregate, 'black spirits and gray.'

In one of these works is found the spirit of infidelity, 'squat like a toad,' undetected unless touched by the spear of Ithuriel, yet doing its work surely. In another, immorality multiform lurks. Every fiend nestles among those books in disguise. There, breathing revenge, is Moloch, 'the strongest and fiercest spirit that fought in heaven.'. There, in his beauty, is Belial, whose 'tongue drops manna, and can make the worse appear the better reason; but to noble deeds timorous and slothful.' There gloating over his gold sits Mammon.

Exposed to such malign influences, it is not strange that many a youthful reader should become the victim of infidelity and vice, as they thus ambush his path.

There is a practice that prevails among youthful readers in colleges and elsewhere, of reading every thing that comes to hand. They make haste to be wise, and think that wisdom consists in having read every thing that comes in their way. They are almost as rapid in their course of reading as a certain coxcomb who boasted that he had read Euclid's 'Elements of Geometry' in one afternoon, only leaving out the *A's* and *B's*, and the crooked lines, which seemed intended merely to retard his progress. Book-worms they might be called, were not book-butterflies the more appropriate term. They skim over the meadows of learning, alighting for a moment on the flowers, but collecting nothing valuable.

But you say that the rule which I have given you of reading standard books, is not sufficiently definite, inasmuch as the number of standard books is so great that one could hardly expect to read them all in a long life, much less in the leisure hours from his studies while in the school, the academy, the college, the workshop, or the counting-house. You ask me what particular books you should read. In reply, I would say: Tell me what are your mental defects, and I will tell you what books will help to remove them.

Are you deficient in taste? Read the best English poets, such as Gray and Goldsmith, Pope and Thomson, Cowper and Coleridge, Scott and Wordsworth.

Are you deficient in imagination? Read Milton, and Akenside, and Burke.

Are you deficient in power of reason? Read Chillingworth, and Bacon, and Locke.

Are you deficient in judgment and good sense in common affairs of life? Read Franklin.

Are you deficient in sensibility? Read Goethe and Mackenzie.

Are you deficient in vigor of style? Read Junius and Fox.

Are you deficient in political knowledge? Read Montesquieu, the 'Federalist,' Webster, and Calhoun.

Are you deficient in patriotism? Read Demosthenes, and the 'Life of Washington.'

Are you deficient in conscience? Read some of President Edwards' works.

Are you deficient in piety? Read the Bible.

This I give you as a sort of specimen list. For a number of these works, others equally good for the purpose can be substituted. Without a reference to the principle which lies at the basis of this rule, reading, besides being a waste of time, may be positively injurious, increasing rather than remedying the mental defects. For instance, if a person has already a morbid sensibility, if he is already infirm of purpose, having hardly force of character enough to get his regular lessons if he is a student, or perform his regular duties on the farm or in the shop if he is called to labor, it is plain that the lighter species of literature will be injurious to him. What he needs is solid thought, to brace his mind up to the regular performance of his duty. Again, if a student is so unfortunate as to have his mind set on fire by party spirit in politics or religion, and if the reading of a paragraph in the newspaper, or a controversial pamphlet, is sufficient to set his feelings all in a blaze, then it is evident that he had better abstain from that kind of reading. What he needs is, the tranquilizing effect of a higher and a purer literature.

Books contain for the faithful seeker a treasure of untold value. They contain the collected wisdom of ages unimpaired. 'The Iliad flourishes as green now as on the day when Pisistratus stamped upon it its present order.' Plato still speaks in the language of the immortals the lessons of philosophy. The Æneid is just as tender and as touching to the human heart as when the mother of Marcellus swooned under the power of its pathos. Milton 'still rides sublime on the seraph wings of ecstacy, passing the flaming bounds of space and time.' Bacon is still the prophet of the sciences. Still

> 'Shakespeare, fancy's sweetest child,
> Warbles his native wood-notes wild,'

captivating us as he captivated the heart of the Virgin Queen. And above all, God himself, breaking the silence of nature, still utters forth his own truth in the same tones as when he spake to holy men of old.

In good books, we hold converse with the great minds which composed them. We contract an undying friendship for those great minds that have ministered to our happiness and our improvement. As we advance in years, other friends fall off, or prove treacherous, or die; but those minds continue the same, and we turn to them, from a frowning or a smiling world, with increasing confidence and delight, as to old friends and tried friends that will ever be dear to us.

EDUCATIONAL INFLUENCE OF LIBRARIES.

DURHAM CENTER, CONNECTICUT, April, 1868.

To the Secretary of the Board of Education :

Dear Sir.—In reply to your favor, in which you request me to furnish some information "concerning the Town and Village Libraries, which, in various parts of the State, were the educators of our fathers," I have to say, that the shortness of the time, and my previous engagements, have not allowed me to bestow that attention on the subject which its intrinsic interest demands. These libraries are now numbered with the things that were; but for fifty or a hundred years they were a living power in the Commonwealth, as we may still learn in the fast fading light of tradition.

Books were for a long time scarce in Connecticut, as elsewhere in New England, except in the libraries of some of the eminent clergymen; and so much valued were they, that when a certain distinguished clergyman in Massachusetts died, who was in possession of a valuable library, a clergyman in Stratford, Connecticut, offered to bring up and educate his orphan son, then only five years of age, on condition that he might have the use of that library until that son should want it. And so good a use did he make of that library, that he was offered the Presidency of Yale College, which he declined.

BOOKS were the foundation of Yale College. The foundation was laid on this wise: Ten of the principal clergymen of the Colony, having formed themselves into a society, met at Branford. "Each member brought a number of books, and presenting them to the body, said these words; "*I give these books, for the founding of a college in this colony.*" Then the trustees took possession of them and confided them to the care of the Reverend Mr. Russell, the Librarian. The number of the books was forty folio volumes.

The opinion of these founders was, that a college is a *mental and spiritual structure*, built on the foundation of the prophets and apostles of learning, Jesus Christ being the chief corner stone. These books were, at once, the symbols and the sources of learning, the exponents of those donors who founded Yale College, and the fountains from which the students could thereafter slake their thirst for knowledge.

As showing the high appreciation of books, in 1717, when the college library was removed from Saybrook to New Haven, a large number of men resisted the removal, and "in the struggle that ensued, about *two hundred and fifty volumes of valuable books* were conveyed away by unknown persons, and were never recovered." Whether any of those books formed the basis of the valuable library not long after established by individuals in the three towns of Saybrook, Lyme, and Guilford, I am not able positively to say. Some circumstances point that way.

The year 1733 was signalized by the noble donation of one thousand volumes to Yale College, by a distinguished divine of the church of England, Dean BERKLEY, afterwards Bishop of Cloyne. This caused great rejoicing among the friends of the college in the Colony, and inspired high hopes of its success.

It is remarkable that in a few months after this event, in the same year, namely, October 30th, the first "BOOK COMPANY" in Connecticut, or what is supposed to be the first, was formed. From that time to about 1800, and perhaps later, libraries were established in the different towns. The ministers and intelligent men reasoned in this way: If large libraries are useful in large cities in Europe and elsewhere, small libraries may be useful in the small towns in Connecticut, where all enjoy the advantages of common school education, which prepares them to derive pleasure and profit from books. And many of the people reasoned in this way: I have learned to read, why shall I not make a profitable use of what I have learned, and extend my knowledge by reading books? They thought much like STONE, the celebrated self-made mathematician, who, when asked how he had been able to acquire such a great amount of knowledge, replied, "Why, I first learned the *twenty-four letters of the alphabet*, and then I found that, by means of these, I could learn any thing else that I wished to learn."

Moreover, members of the Colonial Legislature, which met twice in the year, often had conversations with each other about the establishment of libraries as the means of elevating the tastes and intelligence of the people in the several towns. And after they had been established in some towns, the members from those towns were consulted by those from other towns, as to the results, and as to the mode of proceeding in forming and conducting them, and as to the choice and character of the books to be purchased. And afterwards, when "book companies" had become common in the colony, the members frequently, in their social intercourse, conversed with one another about the books which belonged to the libraries in their respective towns. This statement I had from those who received it from one who was as influential as any other in the establishment of such libraries, and who was a member of the legislature, at least seventy-four sessions.

These *book companies* were voluntary associations of persons in the several towns who were desirous of establishing a library. A number of the intelligent men of the town would meet together, appoint a committee of four or five persons, and a clerk, who was often the library-keeper. These officers were afterwards appointed annually. Each member contributed a certain sum, say twenty shillings, as an entrance fee, and an annual tax, say one shilling. The books were drawn out by the members, or by some of their families, to be returned in a fortnight, or at some longer time, perhaps, in some places. A record of the books drawn was kept by the clerk, a fine being charged for want of punctuality in returning them. Sometimes, through neglect, the taxes and fines would amount to so much that the committee would declare the rights forfeited. The moneys collected were applied by the committee to the purchase of books from time to time. The question what books should be purchased was considered to be a very important one, and was often discussed by the committee. In one case the clerk and library-keeper held his place forty-nine years.

It was, I believe, not uncommon that the clergyman was the clerk. At least I was acquainted with one who acted as such something like thirty years, meeting the members of the book company statedly for drawing the books; when he would describe to them their character, with remarks adapted to lead them to their perusal, he himself having carefully read them. He wished to imbue the minds of the readers in his parish with scholarly tastes, to make them understand that though the bodies of the great ones in mind's empire lie in the " caves of death," their minds still live and breathe in their works as if immortal; lifting, as with an angel's wing, the souls of their readers above earth's vanities. He wished to take off their attention from the petty questions and the party disputes of the day, which divide or weaken congregations, and to fix it upon the great truths and great duties in which all could agree to unite. And he was successful. He left what continues to be, at the distance of forty-four years, one of the largest and best congregations in the country towns in the state. We know men from the friends whom they choose; he knew many of his people from the books which they read, those silent friends who teach without offending, and admonish without wounding, and who form the character.

The annual meetings for the choice of officers, and for hearing the report on the condition of the library, was a sort of literary festival, when there was " the feast of reason and the flow of soul," when the members eulogized their favorite authors, quoting them as if they were old friends, and ready to say with Bacon, " libraries are the shrines where all the relics of saints, full of true virtue, and without imposture, are preserved and reposed."

The following preamble to the by-laws adopted in one town, is given as a specimen, which may help one to form a correct idea of a " Book Company " in those times.

" Forasmuch as the subscribers hereof, being desirous to improve our leisure hours in enriching our minds in useful and profitable knowledge by reading, do find ourselves unable to do so, for the want of suitable and *proper books:* Therefore, that we may be the better able to furnish ourselves with a suitable and proper collection of books, for the above said end, we do, each of us, unite together, and agree to be copartners in company together by the name of the BOOK COMPANY of Durham, united to buy books ; and we do agree and covenant with each other, and it is hereby covenanted and agreed upon, by each of us, the subscribers hereof, that we ourselves and successors will be in future a society or company of copartners united for that end, viz : to buy books ; and we will each of us, so often as we shall agree by our major vote, bear our equal part in advancing any sum or sums of money at any time as a common stock to be laid out for such books as shall be agreed upon by the major vote of the company, to enlarge our library ; and in pursuance of said design, we have each of us put into one stock the sum of twenty shillings, which is already laid out according to our direction, in purchasing books, which books shall be kept as a common stock library for the use of said company, by some honest person, whom we will choose, each member having an equal right in said library, and the use of the same, under such regulations as we shall agree upon."

In addition to this, there were sixty by-laws carefully and judiciously drawn up.

In my early years I was conversant with several of those libraries, frequented as they were by the members of the company, who drew books and read them and talked about them. The binding was generally in strong sheep or calf, sometimes in double bindings after the first was injured by use. That they were used, the volumes themselves bore witness, as well as the records.

It should be remembered, that during the era which we are considering, the people of the commonwealth were agricultural, living on farms cultivated by themselves as owners, and in homes often separated by broad acres ; that in those homes the several families spent the long winters mostly together, and the rainy days and their evenings, and thus had leisure for reading. It should also be remembered, that with them often dwelt the four cardinal virtues, prudence, temperance, justice, and fortitude, and also the sweet household charities; and what is more, daily prayers were offered in those homes even by many who had never taken the sacramental oath in the sanctuary, and thus they were in a mood of mind to enjoy solid reading. Their public amusements were few ; there were training days with the wrestling matches; there were election days with their raised cake; there were thanksgiving days with their table luxuries and family loves; there were occasional balls conducted with all the formality and decorum of the olden time. Still, as a whole, there was very little outside to draw them from their homes.

In such homes and from such hearts books met a ready welcome as supplying a felt want, whether adapted to the memory, the imagination, or the reason. "*The Universal History*," Josephus' "*History of the Jews*," Watts' works, some of the poetical works of Milton, Pope, Thomson, Goldsmith, the sermons of some of the ablest English Divines, some of the works of President Edwards, "*The Spectator*," some of Locke's works, Montesquieu's "*Spirit of Laws*," "*The Vicar of Wakefield*," and many others, became familiarly known to more or less readers in many towns. And when thus read and appreciated, they of course produced a beneficial effect. This was especially true of the "*Spectator*," composed by Addison and the wits of Queen Anne's time. If it be true that it contributed to elevate and refine the conversation and conduct of the people of England in their social intercourse, it did the same for the people of Connecticut, inasmuch as, in proportion to the population, it was more read.

In the excellent Constitution of Massachusetts, under the head of encouraging literature, it is made the duty of Legislators and Magistrates to countenance "*sincerity, good humor, and all social affections, and generous sentiments among the people.*" What was aimed at by this provision, was, to a large extent, accomplished by the extensive perusal of books like these; while they planted a root of bitterness nowhere, whether in churches or towns. It is true there were many books in these libraries of not so high a character. I have seen "*Arabian Nights Entertainment,*" and the "*Fool of Quality,*" and the "*Pilgrim's Progress,*" and the "*Holy War,*" in one library, and it is very likely that "*Sir Charles Grandison,*" and "*Pamela,*" and "*Robinson Crusoe,*" were found in others. At any rate, there was enough in them to extend the opening mind of the young boy beyond the horizon of his native town to other forms of social life, thus nourishing manly thought; and to expand the budding affections of the young girl into the consummate blossom of maiden loveliness.

A studious youth in a secluded house, would, on some winter's evening, sit down, with his tallow candle, to peruse a book of travels from one of these libraries, perhaps reading portions of it to the listening family. In imagination he would range through various climes, and among various nations, until, in his delight, he could enjoy them as if his own. In the language of Goldsmith he could say,

> "Ye glitt'ring towns with wealth and splendor crowned,
> Ye fields, whose summer spreads profusion round,
> Ye lakes, whose vessels catch the busy gale,
> Ye bending swains that dress the flow'ry vale,
> For me your tributary stores combine;
> Creation's heir, the world, the world is mine."

He could enjoy all the delights of the traveler without his fatigues, exposures, and temptations.

History was favorite reading with those who were older, especially English history. The people were but a few generations removed from their English ancestors, in whom tradition, government and trade kept them interested. They themselves were British subjects until 1776. To understand their rights as such, they must read English history which informed them how these rights were obtained. The rulers of the people, and those who expected to be rulers, were readers of history. Some of the published debates in the Connecticut Legislature show a familiarity with historical facts. It is remarkable that in the Connecticut Convention which adopted the present Federal Constitution, the great argument of Oliver Ellsworth in its favor was largely historical, implying that the members were so much acquainted with history, that they could appreciate its force. Ministers of the Gospel in those days not unfrequently, in their sermons, stated facts of history, as the teaching of Divine Providence. The famous sermon of President Stiles before the Connecticut Legislature in 1783 is largely historical. Many other facts might be adduced to show what were the prevailing tastes and sentiments in the Commonwealth, growing out more or less from the perusal of books furnished by these book companies.

The good influence of these libraries upon every class of the population, from the highest to the lowest, cannot be measured, any more than can the influence of "the all-pervading spirit of literature" generally, any more than can the influence of the light in the firmament, glancing as it does from the highest hill-top down into the lowest vale.

These "book companies" lived, some of them more than a hundred years, accomplishing great good to the several communities; others had a shorter term of life. They all, from various general causes in operation, lost their hold on the hearts of the people, and were neglected. Some of the libraries were sold at auction, and the proceeds distributed among the members. Some were distributed to them, each member receiving his share of books. Some were scattered and lost. And the remains of one, at least, are boxed up in a large chest.

The causes that produced this change began to operate about the commencement of the present century, though they did not produce their full effect until something like thirty years afterwards. To state what these causes were, would exceed my limits.

If this letter, my dear Sir, shall furnish you with any aid in your laudable attempt to obtain materials for an Educational History of the State, I shall have accomplished my purpose in complying with your request.

Very respectfully, your obedient servant,

WILLIAM C. FOWLER.

To Mr. Northrop,
Secretary of the Board of Education of Connecticut.

ELOQUENCE.

Every one understands the difference between theory and practice, when these terms are used in the popular sense. Thus, when you hear the words used in reference to government, or religion, or education, you regard the one, namely, theory, as embracing the general principles of that subject, and the other, that is, practice, as embracing the application of those principles to particular cases.

In the history of human knowledge, it appears that practice comes first, and theory afterwards. Thus, men baked bread, hollowed out canoes, and erected cabins, before they formed theories in chemistry, ship-building and architecture. Art collected the facts ; science developed them into a system. But in the process of time the tables are turned ; the order is inverted. Theory or science moves first in the exhibition of grand principles ; practice follows, in the application of those principles to particular cases. Science becomes the herald of art, as art was primarily the forerunner of science.

It has often happened that those who have been profoundly acquainted with general principles, as they are comprehended in theoretical science, have failed utterly in their attempts to apply those principles in the arts to particular cases. Thus the famous Mr. Locke was profoundly acquainted with the science of government, but was entirely unsuccessful in the application of his doctrines in the constitution which he framed for South Carolina. Like many other ingenious schemes, this did not work well, for it was not the result of practice as well as theory. Sir Isaac Newton was thoroughly versed in those astronomical and mathematical doctrines which are applied to navigation, yet, from want of practice in their application, he would probably have been but a poor navigator in his first voyage, if he had chosen to make one. On the other hand, Captain Hull, of the American navy, possessed great practical skill in navigation, though but little versed in science. And Dr. Franklin, though an able practical statesman, could not be compared with Locke in his knowledge of the doctrinal principles of political philosophy. Both the gallant commodore and the sagacious statesman owed their success to their practical skill.

Having spoken of the general relation of practice and theory, I now propose to present for consideration some thoughts on the particular relation between the practice of eloquence and its theoretical principles.

One advantage, let me premise, which is to be derived from the practice of eloquence, is that it will enable one better to understand the theoretical principles of eloquence. These principles are presented in form in our text-books, and though often studied thoroughly and recited with discriminating exactness, are, after all, not very adequately understood compared with their importance. And when their importance is insisted on either by the author or the teacher, there is often some incredulity in the mind of the pupil, which shows itself in something like good-natured derision. Or, if they be received as true, they still have not much depth or strength of meaning in his mind. For instance, when he reads the famous saying of Demosthenes—who, when asked what was the first, second and third excellence in eloquence, answered to each, " action,"—he attaches but little meaning to this repeated answer in comparison with that in the mind of him who uttered it. Indeed, the great orator himself learned the full meaning of the term, and the value of the thing, from repeated failures and final success in practice.

The same is the fact in a thousand cases. Take that of articulation : you might tell one who had never pronounced the letters L and R, that in the first he must interrupt the voice by placing the tip of the tongue against the upper gums, and in the latter, by placing the middle of the tongue against the roof of the mouth. Now, this is a true rule, and an indispensable rule, and one easily understood; still it could not be adequately understood without practice.

I know it was said, in classic times, that a philosopher is a shoemaker, even though he has never made shoes, since he is theoretically acquainted with the mode in which they are made. But put him to the proof, in the actual manufacture of a pair of shoes, and he would hardly satisfy one of those well-dressed-men who promenade Broadway and Chestnut street.

Even in religion the importance of practice, in order to the full understanding of principles, is distinctly set forth. "He that doeth His will shall know of the doctrines whether they are of God."

It need not seem strange, then, or peculiar, that the practice of eloquence is necessary in order to the full understanding of its theoretical principles.

Another advantage which one will derive from the practice of eloquence is the correction of any false principles which one may have adopted on the subject. Along with what is true, your accidental reading or observation, or deductions, may have led you to adopt much that is false, either in regard to the true end of eloquence, or the means by which that end is accomplished. The finest orators that the world has seen, have been able, by practice, to correct certain false notions which they once entertained as to what eloquence is. Cicero, in the first public cause which he pleaded, in defence of Roscius of Armeria, uses the following language, which he afterwards condemned, when practice had corrected his theoretical views. Having occasion, in the course of his plea, to mention that remarkable punishment which Latin legislators had contrived for the murder of a parent, of sewing the criminal in a sack, and throwing him into a river, he says: "The meaning of it was, to strike him at once out of the system of nature, by taking him from the air, the sun, the water, and the earth; that he who had destroyed the author of his being should lose the benefit of those elements whence all things derive their being. They would not throw him to the beasts, lest the contagion of such wickedness should make the beasts themselves more ferocious; they would not commit him naked to the stream, lest he should pollute the very sea, which is the purifier of all other pollutions. They left him no share of anything natural, howsoever vile or common; for what is so common as breath to the living, earth to the dead, the sea to those who float, the shore to those who are cast up? Yet these wretches live, (as long as they can,) so as not to draw breath from the air; die, so as not to touch the ground; are so tossed by the wavês as not to be washed by them; so cast out upon the shore as to find no rest even on the rocks." This piece of extravagance, Cicero's better taste, taught by practice, condemned. Many a young orator has found by experience that those decorations which he once admired as true eloquence, are of no more use in the strife of debate, than are the nodding plumes on a warrior's crest amid the fury of the onset. Our great western orator, Henry Clay, by a course of experience, corrected his early errors of style, so that, instead of rant, in which he formerly indulged, he presented subsequently and uniformly what was effective, judicious, and tasteful.

Another advantage which you may derive from the practice of eloquence is, that it will make you familiar with the application of the true principles of eloquence. Two men shall understand the principles of eloquence equally well, and one of them will be an eloquent man because he is familiar with the application of those principles, while the other is utterly destitute of eloquence. The latter may be very fully acquainted with the subject at issue in debate, and likewise with the true principles of logic and rhetoric, and yet fail in his contest with one inferior to him in everything but a practical familiarity with the principles of eloquence. This has been finely hit off by Scott, in the interview between Advocate Pleydel and Domine Sampson. "When the man of law began to get into his attitudes, and his wit, naturally shrewd and dry, became more lively and poignant, the Domine looked upon him with that sort of surprise with which we can conceive a tame bear might regard the monkey upon their being just introduced to each other. It was Mr. Pleydel's delight to state, in grave and serious argument, some position which he knew the Domine would be inclined to dispute. He then beheld with exquisite pleasure the internal labor with which the honest man arranged his ideas in reply, and tasked his inert and sluggish powers to bring up all the heavy artillery of his learning for demolishing the schismatic or heretical opinions which had been stated; when, behold, before the ordnance could be discharged, the foe had quitted the post, and appeared in a new position of annoyance on the Domine's flank and rear. Often did he exclaim 'prodigious!' when marching up to the enemy in full confidence of victory, he found the field evacuated, and it may be supposed that it cost him no little labor to attempt a new formation." In allusion to this contest Colonel Mannering remarks: "Even our friend, the Dominie, is returned thrice the man he was, having sharpened his wits in controversy with the geniuses of the Northern Metropolis."

"'Of a surety,' said the Dominie, with great complacency, 'I did wrestle and was not overcome, though my adversary was cunning in his art.'"

"'I can bear witness,' said the Colonel, 'that I never saw an affair better contested. The enemy was like the Mahratta cavalry; he assailed on all sides and presented no fair mark for artillery; but Mr. Sampson stood to his guns, notwithstanding, and fired away now upon the enemy and now upon the dust he had raised.'"

This describes, it may be somewhat in caricature, the condition of many a man who has not learned by practice to apply the principles of eloquence; who has gathered stores of knowledge which, as an orator, he cannot readily use; who has not a shilling at command, though he could draw for thousands.

Another advantage which you may derive from the practice of eloquence, is found in the readiness of mind that it produces. The study of theoretical principles, while it disposes to largeness of views and logical accuracy of statement, is not very favorable to promptitude either of thought or expression. In order to success, the mind must arrest each idea in succession, until it is viewed in its various associations, and the whole arranged in the order of premise and conclusion, with philosophical exactness. In dwelling on the abstractions of philosophy habitually, the mind becomes cool, comprehensive, far-reaching, discriminating, but slow, considerate, hesitating. When this gets to be a fixed habit of the mind, the man cannot in the highest sense be eloquent. Now the practice of eloquence tends to prevent the formation of this mental habit, by establishing habits of an opposite character; by making the mind prompt in its decisions, discussions, inventions; thus forming the advocate instead of the judge; the actor instead of the philosopher. One thus trained is inspired by the occasion, so that he has his resources at command, and can say more things to the purpose and better things than he expected to say on the particular point at issue; while one who is acquainted with general principles, but has had no practice, will lose himself and his hearers in naked generalities, will omit what ought to be said, and will say what ought to be omitted, and on the review of the effort which he has made, will discover that his, like an Englishman's wit, according to the proverb, always comes afterward.

Another advantage which you will derive from the practice of eloquence, is that it will give you self-possession. For want of this, men of the finest talents and the largest attainments, and the most fluent in common conversations, have utterly failed in public speaking. This, I presume, was the reason that Byron failed so signally in the House of Lords; not being accustomed to speak in public, he lost all command of his faculties. This, too, was the reason why Bulwer failed in the House of Commons. Their minds were full of thoughts, fertile in combination, and deeply interested in the subject, but from want of practice they were not at home in the halls of debate.

In contrast to this, take Mirabeau's first triumph at the as sembly of the *tires-etat*. Duroverai, a distinguished foreigner, was invited in the assembly with some deputies of his acquaintance. He had occasion to pass to Mirabeau a note written with a pencil. One of the most formidable declaimers in the assembly saw this, and asked the member next him, who that stranger was, who was passing notes and interfering with the proceedings. On being informed who he was, he rose and in a voice of thunder, stated that a " foreigner banished from his native country, and residing in England, from whose government he received a pension, was seated among them assisting at their debates and transmitting notes and observations to the deputies of their assembly." The agitation on every side of the hall, which succeeded this denunciation, would not have appeared less terrible had it been the forerunner of an earthquake. Confused cries were heard, " Who is he? where is he? Let him be pointed out." Fifty members spoke at once; but Mirabeau's powerful voice soon obtained silence. He declared he would point out the foreigner to the assembly. " This exile," said he, " in the pay of England, is M. Duroverai, of Geneva, and know that this respectable man, whom you have so wantonly insulted, is a martyr to liberty; that, as attorney-general of the Republic of Geneva, he offended our visirs, by his zealous defence of his fellow-citizens; that a *lettre de cachet*, issued by M. de Vergenne, deprived him of the office he had but too honorably filled; and when his native city was brought under the yoke of the aristocracy, he obtained the honors of exile. Behold, then, the stranger, the exile, the refugee, who has been denounced to you. Formerly the persecuted man sought refuge at the altar, where he found an inviolable asylum and escaped from the rage of the wicked. The hall in which we are now assembled is the temple which, in the name of Frenchmen, you are raising to liberty; and will you suffer it to be polluted by an outrage committed upon a martyr to liberty?" The effect produced by this speech was electrical. It was succeeded by a universal burst of applause. Duroverai was immediately surrounded by deputies, who by their kind attentions endeavored to atone for the insult they had offered him.

Mirabeau was a practised debater, and being, therefore, able to retain his self-possession on this very trying occasion, won the assembly over to his views by this sudden burst of eloquence.

Another advantage which you may gain by the practice of eloquence, is that it will bring your feelings, your thoughts, your words, your gestures, your countenance into harmony. I shall spend no time in showing the importance of this harmony, since without it there can be nothing that deserves the name of eloquence. Now practice, by the law of association, has a tendency to bring the feelings into harmony with the thoughts; the words into harmony with the feelings; the countenance and the whole person into harmony with the words, so that all the powers of the man are concentrated on the single act of persuading the hearers to come into the views and feelings of the speaker.

Besides this analytical view of the subject, the position I have taken is sustained by a multitude of general facts.

And first, men who have been the most distinguished for their knowledge of the true principles of the theory of eloquence, have, from the want of practice, been unable to produce much impression as public speakers. Isocrates, the father of Grecian eloquence, as his school was its cradle, never made but one attempt at public speaking, when he gave up in despair. Aristotle, the ablest critic of antiquity, was far from being an eloquent man. Neither Campbell nor Whately have been considered as remarkable for eloquence in their public speaking, though distinguished for their acquaintance with the true principles of eloquence. And generally teachers of eloquence have not been distinguished among great orators; just as the best teachers of the principles of the military art have not been the greatest warriors. Their devotedness to the study of those principles, without the benefit of practice, tends to produce habits of mind that are unfavorable to public speaking, while their standard of excellence is so high that they despair of reaching it.

Another grand fact, which I would mention, is that many

distinguished orators have found, that they have made improvement in oratory just in proportion to their amount of practice. It was said of Robespierre, by Reybas, on hearing one of his first speeches in the Chamber of Deputies: "This young man has not yet practised; he is too wordy and does not know when to stop, but he has a store of eloquence which will not leave him in the crowd." He afterwards practised with so much success, that he was able by his voice to govern the chamber, then Paris, then revolutionary France. Many a distinguished orator might be named whose maiden speech was a failure. But instead of yielding to discouragement, they went steadily in the way of practice until success crowned their efforts.

Men have attended to pursuits which have led them away from the practice of eloquence, until they seem to be destitute of the power of speaking well, but on resuming the practice have gained the power. When John Quincy Adams was candidate for the presidency a second time a comparison was drawn between him and Andrew Jackson and Henry Clay, in the way of showing that General Jackson was great in action; Mr. Clay great in eloquence; Mr. Adams great only in writing. Now, if greatness either in action or in eloquence is superior to greatness in writing, it was inferred that, on the ground of merit, either General Jackson or Mr. Clay was to be preferred to Mr. Adams. No one at that time pretended that this statement, made by Mr. McDuffie, did any injustice to Mr. Adams, for no one regarded him as an eloquent man. For years, when abroad as minister, and then during twelve years that he was Secretary of State or President, he had been out of the practice of eloquence. He did, indeed, once, on the invitation of the city authorities of Washington, deliver an oration on the Fourth of July, which was regarded by some of his friends, taking the delivery and all into view, as an inferior performance. Indeed, when he was appointed to a seat in Congress, very little was expected of him as a speaker. But he then went into the practice of eloquence, as he was before well acquainted with its theoretical principles, every session improving, until he speedily came to be regarded as another Webster—as the "old man eloquent." Such was the influence of practice that it transformed the retired scholastic statesman, who might be said to live with a pen in his hand, into a ready and terrible antagonist in debate. This it did for him, after he was sixty years of age, when the habits of mind are supposed to be rigid, and new associations are not easily formed.

There is another general fact, which in this connection deserves notice. Men who were distinguished for their eloquence while in the practice of eloquence, lose their power as public speakers, in consequence of laying aside the practice of speaking. Thus men who were eloquent advocates while they were at the bar, when they have been raised to the bench, in a few years lose to some degree the power which they once had. Eloquent preachers, after being, as teachers, for a few years withdrawn from the practice of preaching, cease to be eloquent. Their minds are occupied and their feelings absorbed in other pursuits, until their mental habits are changed. Mr. Webster was an eloquent man in Congress in 1814, and when in 1824 he was sent from Boston, great expectations were entertained that he would exert there a commanding influence on the councils of the nation. But not having recently been in the practice of congressional eloquence, he somewhat disappointed the expectations of his friends. His effort for the Greeks, in the words of an elaborate and practised debater, "was awkwardly made." He failed in carrying the two leading measures which he endeavored to sustain that session. He was evidently inferior in debate to John Randolph, who opposed him on one of those measures, as he was to Henry Clay, who opposed him on the other. But after a few years of practice, he became, if not decidedly superior to all, *primus inter pares*.

After he had been acquiring skill and power by practice some years, Mr. Calhoun, who as Secretary of War and Vice President of the United States, had for twelve years not been accustomed to take part in public debates, came into the Senate with the virtues and talents of an accomplished statesman. The subject of nullification came before the Senate. This brought out these two distinguished men in opposition to each other. Though well matched in other respects, Mr. Calhoun was deficient, from the want of recent practice, in that perfect self-possession which the other had gained by practice; and hence, as was generally supposed, by Whigs, his inferiority on that occasion, in comparison with the orator from New England; an inferiority which he did not manifest in debates after he had been a longer term in the Senate.

The reasonings and facts, then, which I have adduced, abundantly show the importance of practice to the attainment of eloquence.

There are, indeed, exceptions to every general rule. Hamilton, in the British Parliament, without any previous practice there, delivered a single able speech, and ever after kept silence there. This was deemed so remarkable that he has to this day gone by the name "Single Speech Hamilton."

While I would thus urge upon you the importance of practice, I would not have you suppose that I intend to underrate other means, or those qualities of the soul which show themselves in the great orator. I speak not to undervalue solitary study, or theoretical principles, or the treasured stores of learning, as means of improving in eloquence. I would not undervalue the burning passions and the unconquerable will of Chatham, revealed in words of fire, as from a seraph's lips; or the winged imaginations of Burke, which circled over all the creations of nature and art to gather contributions to aid the intellect; or the strong good sense, and the ready memory of Fox, speaking to the common heart of man; or the brilliant wit of Sheridan; or the logical accuracy and sound judgment of Pitt, or the playful fancy of Canning. Nature in her bounty imparted some of these rare gifts, and study furnished them with others; but this would all have been comparatively valueless without practice. Any man of them would have told you so.

"To be a great orator does not require," it has been justly

said, "the highest faculties of the human mind, but it requires the highest exertion of the common faculties of our nature. He has no occasion to dive into the depths of science, or to soar aloft on angel's wings. He keeps upon the surface, he stands firm upon the ground; but his form is majestic, and his eye sees far and near; he moves among his fellows, but he moves among them as a giant among common men. He has no need to reach the heavens, to unfold the system of the universe, or to create new worlds, for the delighted fancy to roam in; it is enough if he sees things as they are; that he knows, and feels, and remembers the common circumstances and daily transactions that are passing in the world around him."

There is nothing, perhaps, in the range of human acquisition that is so earnestly coveted by the student in some part of his collegiate course, as to be an orator. To rise in an assembly with ease and self-possession, to state his opinions with gracefulness and energy of language and manner, to control the will of others, to act with irresistible effect on the passions, to awaken the minds of others to their real interests, to hold a multitude hanging upon his lips, as if they were spell-bound, while he transfuses his mind into their mind, until there is but one beating heart as but one voice, one soul, one resolving will—what student has not aspired to do this? And what student has not at times been inclined to sit down in despair of being able to do this?

In the way of encouragement, then, I would say that, until you have been through a course of practice in eloquence, you cannot tell how much it will do for you. I would say this before you sit down in despair.

In college both teachers and pupils are necessarily employed for the most part in the inculcation and reception of theoretical principles, while the practical application of those principles comes afterwards, if at all. What if any one should say in despair, I never can become a chemist, for though I have studied chemistry, I am not able to analyze a piece of iron ore, or even the common soil beneath my feet? What if one should say, I never can become a navigator, for though I have studied navigation, I could not now even conduct a ship to England? What if one should say, I never can become an orator, for though I have studied rhetoric, I could not speak five consecutive sentences before an audience without embarrassment?

If any one should talk in this way, should we not say that his conclusion was broader than his premises? Should we not say that he was entirely ignorant of the nature and end of a liberal education? Here you are to learn the great principles of the sciences. In professional life you are to learn, if you choose, their practical applications. Having learned the theoretical principles of chemistry, and of astronomy, and of eloquence here; then if you wish to become an analytical chemist, or a practical navigator, or an eloquent man, enter into the school of practice, not fearing but that you will be successful.

I am aware that in college societies, and to a small extent in the regular course, there are some opportunities for practice in eloquence. All the remarks which I have made are intended to apply in their full force to these exercises, as important means of improvement. I know that they are sometimes undervalued in comparison with corresponding exercises in real life. But consider that they will be of use in helping to prepare for those exercises. It was at the Games that the Grecian youths prepared themselves for the strife of war. It was in the Palæstra that the young Romans prepared themselves to be the conquerors of the world. The adventurous boy launching his skiff upon the bosom of the peaceful harbor, acquires by practice a quick eye, a ready hand, a collected mind, and a strong heart, to encounter, on the high seas, the storm when it is up in its frenzy. Use all the opportunities which you enjoy for the practice of eloquence. Reasoning from general principles or from facts, you have enough to encourage you. In a college debating society, Canning prepared himself for parliamentary practice. In a debating club, Brougham laid the foundation of his eloquence. And if need be, we could summon multitudes from the pulpit, the bar, and the Senate chamber, who would bear testimony, from their own experience, in favor of the practice of eloquence in college, in addition to the study of its theoretical principles.

The union of theory and practice is necessary for the highest results. "*Orator fit*" is the maxim upon which every great orator has acted. The poet is born a poet. By inspiration he has the ken of genius, "the vision and the faculty divine." But the orator, on the other hand, is the architect of himself.

It may be profitable, here, to illustrate this statement, by referring to the practice of one who exhibited the greatest devotion to eloquence, both in its spirit and its external forms, and who by practice, took his place among the world's eloquent men, second only to Demosthenes.

In the whole history of Cicero's life, it appears that he endeavored, with the greatest assiduity, first to form an idea of a perfect orator, and then to approximate as nearly as possible to this image in his mind. In his works we have the portraiture of the ideal of excellence, the result of his observation and reflection. In his life we have the history of his efforts to realize in his own person, his ideal of excellence. He was born at Arpinum, now a part of the kingdom of Naples, about 107 before Christ. We are informed that his father made it his chief employment from the first, to give his sons the best education which Rome could afford. They were bred up with their cousins, the young Aculeos, in a method approved by Lucius Crassus, a man of the first eloquence, by those very masters who had taught Crassus himself. After Cicero had thus gone through a most careful course of training at home, he was placed at Rome, under an eminent Greek master. Here, it is said, he gave the first proof of those shining talents, which afterwards made him illustrious. About this time a celebrated rhetorician, Plotius, first set up a Latin school of eloquence at Rome, which was attended by a great number of pupils. Cicero was very desirous of becoming his scholar, "but was over-ruled by the advice of the learned, who thought the Greek masters more useful in forming to the bar."

Afterwards, having for a time been placed under the care of the poet Archias, and having published a poem called *Glaucus Pontius*, he was in the 17th year of his age, placed under the care of Lucius Scaevola, the principal lawyer of that age, and he carefully treasured up his sayings as so many lessons of wisdom for his future conduct. During this period he constantly took notes of what he heard, and made comments on what he read. He likewise habitually applied himself to the task of translating the select speeches of the best Greek orators. He likewise translated Aratus on the phænomenon of the Heavens, and also published an original poem in honor of Caius Marius.

At the age of 21 he is supposed to have drawn up those rhetorical pieces on the subject of invention, that still remain. About this time, Philo, a philosopher of the highest name in the Academy, fled from the fury of Mithridates, who had made himself Master of Athens. Cicero, having become his pupil, was exceedingly interested in his philosophy, which he studied with the greatest assiduity. Not long after this, Molo, the Rhodian, the most celebrated teacher of eloquence, happening to be at Rome, Cicero, immediately under him, resumed his rhetorical studies. After this, he kept in the house with him Diodatus, the Stoic, as his preceptor in various branches of learning, but more particularly in logic, which Zeno, as he tells us, calls a close and contracted eloquence, as he called eloquence an enlarged or dilated logic, comparing the one to the fist or hand doubled, and the other to the palm opened. But while he was thus studying logic, he never suffered a day to pass without some exercise in oratory, chiefly that of declaiming, which he generally performed with M. Piso and Quintus Pompey, two young noblemen for whom he had contracted a friendship. About this time Molo, the Rhodian, came again to Rome, when Cicero a second time put himself under his instruction.

Cicero had now gone through the course of discipline, which he lays down as necessary to form a complete orator. He had learned the rudiments of grammar and languages from the ablest teachers, gone through the studies of humanity, and the polite letters with the poet Archias, been instructed in philosophy by Phædrus the Epicurean, Philo the Academician, Diodatus the Stoic, and acquired a thorough knowledge of the law from the greatest lawyers in Rome, the two Scævolas. At the age of 27, the same age at which Demosthenes commenced his career, he undertook the defence of Roscius of Almeria.

Having been successful in this and some other causes, he traveled abroad for the improvement of his health, injured by study, but more especially for improving his style of speaking, which at that time was monotonous. During his travels he spent six months at Athens, where he took up his quarters with Antiochus, the principal philosopher of the old Academy, under whom he renewed, he says, the studies of his youth. But while engaged in the study of philosophy, he was careful not to neglect his rhetorical exercises, which he performed still every day with Demetrius, the Syrian, an experienced master of the art of speaking. He next, after visiting Asia, went to Rhodes, and applied again to Molo for instruction. The greatest trouble which his master experienced, says Cicero, was to restrain the exuberance of a juvenile imagination always ready to overflow its banks, within its due channel. Having finished the circuit of his travels, he came back again to Italy after an absence of two years, very much improved. The vehemence of his voice and action was moderated, the redundancy of his style and fancy corrected, his lungs strengthened, and his whole constitution improved.

Soon after his return, in his thirty-first year, he was appointed Quæstor for the island of Sicily. While there, in his hours of leisure from provincial affairs, he diligently employed himself, as he did at Rome, in his rhetorical studies, agreeably to the rule which he constantly inculcates, never to let one day pass without some exercise of this kind. The country itself, famous of old for its school of oratory, might afford a particular invitation for the revival of those studies. On his return from Sicily, his oratorical powers, according to his own judgment, were in their full maturity.

I will say nothing of his devotion to those studies which have a more remote bearing upon eloquence. He devoted himself to the whole circle of human knowledge, that he might concentrate the whole to the perfecting of his eloquence. The numerous and valuable fruits of his learning in every branch of science and the polite arts; in oratory, poetry, philosophy, law, history, criticism, politics, ethics, prove his almost incredible industry; while his own declarations, as well as the history of his life, prove that he accumulated those treasures of knowledge for the single purpose of preparing himself to be a finished orator. The spirit of eloquence was the governing principle of his life, animating him to effort through the whole course of it. In his soul was emotion, continued emotion, springing from the subject upon which he spoke, and regulated by reason. Moreover, he was governed by a love of truth, by a strong sense of right, by a vigorous imagination, high sympathies with his fellow-men, and a strong will.

The spirit of eloquence attended him during the whole of his life in its various changes, like the presiding genius of Socrates. It attended him in his childhood as he wandered musing amid the paternal groves on the banks of the cool Filænus, filling his young soul with the love of excellence. From the solitude of this domestic scene it attended him to the metropolis, where he entered the public school to struggle for the palm with the youth of Rome. It attended him when, under the poet Archias, he saw "forms such as glitter in the muses' eye with orient hues," and when successively under the two Scævolas he cultivated an acquaintance with the less attractive forms of law. Whether he traveled into Greece in the pursuit of wisdom, or at home stood up as the advocate of the innocent and the injured; whether in the height of his popularity he was hailed as the father of his country, or driven by a faction into exile; whether in a military campaign, or enjoying *otium cum dignitate* during the ascendancy of Cæsar; whether composing a philosophical treatise, or thundering forth his philippics against Anthony, the spirit of eloquence was the ruling spirit in his soul.

CLERGY AND COMMON SCHOOLS.

Durham, Conn., December, 1867.

Henry Barnard, LL. D.:

Dear Sir:—A few weeks since I had the pleasure of receiving from you a letter, in which you ask me to communicate some facts connected with the common schools in Connecticut "as they were." While I was endeavoring to collect these facts, I met some gentlemen in Hartford who are active in promoting the educational interests of the Commonwealth; one of whom encouraged me to prepare for the press, some remarks which I made on a topic which came up in that interview. This I consented to do, with the purpose of uniting the two topics in one communication.

But to whom shall this communication be addressed? My mind readily turned to you as a distinguished friend and advocate of popular education who has labored long and successfully in this State and elsewhere, first as a pioneer, and then as a victorious soldier, in this good cause. I feel, too, assured that you will welcome every well-meant effort for promoting the same cause, however inadequate it may be.

The topic, last mentioned, is, The Province of the Clergy of Connecticut in the Promotion of Popular Education in this Commonwealth.

These remarks and statements, will, I trust, be well received by them, inasmuch as they are in harmony with the views of the clergy of Connecticut from 1635 to the present time.

The proposition which I shall endeavor to sustain, by the following plain arguments, is this, *Ministers of the Gospel in Connecticut ought to take an active part in promoting popular education.*

My first argument in support of this proposition, is derived from *the nature of Christianity.*

It is a religion which addresses accountable beings through their intellect. Just in proportion, therefore, as you improve their intellect by culture, will you enlarge their capacity of being influenced, in their moral instincts, by the objects of divine truth in that religion. Now as Christianity is a general provision for the spiritual wants of all mankind, we may be sure that all classes of the community ought to experience so much of intellectual culture as will enable them to appreciate and appropriate the full benefit of that provision.

Other religious systems were designed, at least in some of their parts, for certain privileged orders, who should enjoy high mental culture; while the many, the *oi polloi*, were excluded from a full participation. Those systems had their esoteric or secret doctrines, which were communicated to the favored few, the initiated; and their exoteric or superficial doctrines, which were communicated to the common people, who were supposed to be incapable of comprehending those deeper doctrines.

But among Christians it is not so. To the poor the Gospel is preached. To them it is given to know the mysteries of the Kingdom. Now in order that this preaching be effectual, in order that these mysteries be adequately comprehended, some degree of mental cultivation is necessary. Evidently, then, it is the duty of the Christian minister to promote the intellectual improvement of those whom he wishes to influence by his preaching; for in so doing he is preparing them to understand and appreciate the truths and duties of the Christian religion, and to yield their conscience and their heart to Christ the author of that religion. No Christian minister, therefore, is justified in standing aloof from the great cause of popular education; for, without it, the light of the Gospel will shine in darkness, and the darkness will comprehend it not.

In the early period of the Christian dispensation, the Clergy, the great lights of the Catholic church, acted successfully on this principle; though they did not, in the existing social condition, extend it in its application, so far as we can do. They carefully guarded and preserved the learning of the times in which they lived, and, by the establishment of institutions of learning and religion, helped to keep both, in their intimate association, alive on the earth. They carefully preserved the Greek and Roman classics, the Pandects of Justinian, the Hebrew copies of the Old Testament, and the Greek of the New Testament. Thus it happened, through them, that classical learning could revive, and that "the public reason of the Romans" could be silently and studiously transfused into the public institutions of Europe, and the study of the Bible could become general. In many an Abbey and University, the lamp of learning, trimmed by their hands, burned brightly, illuminating a wider or a narrower circle, and sending down its cheering light to our times. Honor to whom honor is due. Let all honor be paid to the Catholic church, as the conservator and promoter of learning and religion. When darkness covered the earth like a flood during the mediæval centuries, that church was the ark which saved for us the learning and religion of the old world. All thanks to the bright example of her heroic missionaries; for the recorded lives of those eminent saints, who, through the long centuries, bore the mingled fruits of learning and holiness,—for such as "Pascal who was all reason," and for such as "Fenelon who was all love."

My second argument is derived from *the nature of Protestantism.*

The right of private judgment, in opposition to human claims to a dictatorial authority, in matters of faith, is an essential article in the Protestant faith. Now this single fact, that we are to call no man master, is assumed on the ground that the followers of Christ are capable of forming, from the Bible, an opinion for themselves; and in order to form this opinion for themselves, from the study of the Bible, they ought at least to be able to read the Bible. For how can a man, in the exercise of the right of private judgment, form a correct judgment except on a correct basis, and how can he have a satisfactory basis in the Bible, unless he understands that Bible?

Besides the acknowledged advantages which they enjoyed in the Catholic church, some of the first reformers desired to enjoy this right of private judgment. They wished to escape from the heavy hand of authority by which they felt themselves humiliated. They were opposed to what was called *carbonaria fides*, "the collier's faith," or implicit faith. A collier being asked what he believed on a certain point, replied, "I believe as the church believes." And being asked what the church believes, he replied, "The church believes as I believe." And being asked again what he and the church believe, he replied, "The church and I believe the same thing."

Leading Protestants, in opposition to this *carbonaria fides*, undertook to have a faith of their own, and to be able to state the grounds of their faith. In the language of Chillingworth, "the Bible, the Bible is the religion of Protestants." In adopting this for their motto they virtually declared that the common people ought to be elevated to such a level in the scale of mental cultivation, that in the exercise of the right of private judgment in the formation of their opinions from the Bible, they would not "wrest it to their own destruction."

The contest on the subject at issue, between Luther and his allies on the one hand, and the Pope and his Cardinals on the other, was like the battle between the gods, as described by Homer, or the battle between angels, as described by Milton. There was great intellectual power and great learning on both sides; and it required intellectual cultivation to judge of the merits of that controversy. Luther translated the Bible; but of what use would that be, unless the people could read that translation? Luther, Melancthon, and Carlostadius, all men of great learning, delivered lectures in the University of Wittemburg, which helped to enlighten the people and give currency to his doctrines. The revival of classical learning near that time contributed largely to the same effect.

In like manner the Protestant religion of England was permeated with learning, which the Episcopal church there have zealously promoted ever since they took possession of the Catholic schools and universities. Indeed, the leading Protestants throughout Europe had been highly educated in the Roman Catholic schools, and were thus disposed to imitate and surpass them in the establishment of such institutions.

Accordingly, in Protestant regions, schools of learning soon shone forth on the earth, thick-set as the stars in the sky above. Voetius, a learned Protestant, boasted that while in the ten Catholic provinces of Belgium there were only two universities, in the ten Protestant provinces there were seven.

It is true that what is now understood by popular education was not then thought of as practicable. The Reformers seem not to have supposed it possible that the delights and advantages of learning could be brought down to the lowest stratum of the population. But they adopted principles and measures that are now operating in Germany in the education of the masses, and which justify the clergy here in promoting popular education by direct and efficient means.

My third argument is derived from *the nature of Puritanism*. Besides the general principles of Christianity and of Protestantism, the Puritans adopted the opinion that the people are capable of *self-government*, both in their civil and in their ecclesiastical polity. This opinion implied that the people should be qualified, by education, to perform the duties involved in self-government. Accordingly, as soon as their circumstances would allow, like the Catholics, like the Protestants, they adopted measures, both in England and in this country, to establish schools and colleges, under the direction of their learned divines. These had generally been educated in the universities of Oxford and Cambridge. In eleven years after the settlement of Massachusetts, they laid the foundation of Harvard College, to the support of which Connecticut annually contributed. In seventeen years, they established a system of common schools. The clergy, as is well known, were active in establishing and sustaining these institutions in Massachusetts. As advisors, as patrons, as teachers and visitors, they exerted a controlling and salutary influence.

Without going into an induction of particulars, it is sufficient for my purpose here to say, that the whole history of the Puritans shows abundantly, that they have been staunch believers in the value of local law. They have believed that a church can govern itself better than any outside person or body can govern it; that a town can govern itself better than a colony or a state can govern it; that the colony can govern itself better than parliament can govern it; that a state can govern itself better than congress can govern it. But in order to this successful self-government, in these several circles of power, they have also believed that the people must be educated in the school of Christ, and at least, in common schools. On this same belief the clergy have acted earnestly and efficiently.

Listen to the prayer made by Eliot, the Apostle John, in a synod of ministers in Boston: "Lord, for schools everywhere among us! That our schools may flourish! That every member of this assembly may go home and procure a good school to be encouraged in the town where he lives! That before we die we may be so happy as to see a good school encouraged in every plantation of the country!" This was the spirit of the early ministers, and their conduct was in accordance with their spirit.

My fourth argument is derived from *the nature of the profession* into which ministers have entered.

The object of that profession is to raise the souls of men from their earthly condition into union with the divine nature, that they may thus become the intelligent, and holy, and happy inhabitants of earth and of heaven; to raise them from the power of appetite and passion into the dominion of reason and conscience. This the minister endeavors to accomplish by commending to them the truths of God's holy word illustrated by the teachings of His providence.

In like manner it is the object of popular education so to raise men in the scale of knowledge, virtue, and happiness, that they become good citizens; to elevate the tastes of the young from sensuality, from the bar and the brandy saloon, from the haunts of loafers and gamblers, into the love and the pursuit of the true, the good, and the beautiful. Thus the minister and the educator are largely aiming at the same thing; though the motives employed by the former are always supposed to be chiefly drawn from a higher world, and the motives employed by the latter may be chiefly drawn from this. The Christian minister has, then, every encouragement to act strenuously for the promotion of popular education, with the full belief that while he is promoting that, he is at the same time promoting the object of his own profession.

The minister and the school-master are fellow laborers in the same field. The field is the world. When "the school-master is abroad," let the minister go forth to meet him and join himself to him as a fellow laborer. Let them encourage each other and bear each other's burdens, both looking forward to "the harvest home," when they shall bring their sheaves with them.

My fifth argument is derived from *the position occupied by the Clergy of Connecticut during more than two hundred years.*

From the early legislation of the Colonies it appears, that a reason given why schools should be supported, was, namely: that the young could in them be so taught that they would be able to "read the Bible" and the "capital laws," and thus be "fitted for service in the church and commonwealth." In the order to establish a free school in 1641, in New Haven, "Our pastor, Mr. *Davenport*," is mentioned with the magistrates, as committee "to consider what yearly allowance is meet to be given out of the common stock of the town," for the support of the school; and also, "what rules and orders are meet to be observed in and about the same." And, in 1644, the General Court ordered that a grammar school be set up and appointed, and that the "Magistrates and the Teaching Elders" be a committee to attend to that, for the same purposes as in the case of the first mentioned or common school. It appears that Governor Eaton and Mr. *Dav-*

enport were the active men in thus establishing a system of free schools in the Colony.

And after the Colonies were united, the General Court, in 1690, ordered as follows: "This Court considering the necessary and great advantage of good literature, do *order and appoint*, that there shall be two good free schools kept in this Colony, for the schooling of all such children as shall come there after they can distinctly read the psalter, to be taught reading, writing, arithmetic, the Latin and the English languages, the one at Hartford, the other at New Haven, the masters whereof shall be chosen by the magistrates and the *ministers* of the said counties, and shall be inspected and displaced by them, if they see cause." These were grammar schools, after the model of the *free*, or endowed grammar schools of England, in which the Latin and the English languages were to be taught grammatically.

While I thus notice the prominence that was given to the clergy in the establishment of free schools, it should be mentioned that by the original Constitution of Connecticut the "supreme power of the Commonwealth" was lodged in the General Court, which for a long time afterwards gave prominence to the clergy in all matters connected with education.

It should be added that the School-Masters were treated with great consideration from the first. They were among the few at the first, who received the title of "Mr.," and not that of "brother," or "good man." The school-master stood next to the minister in the minds of the people; just as he does in Goldsmith's inimitable description in "The Deserted Village:"

> "And still they gazed, and still the wonder grew,
> That one small head could carry all he knew."

He was on familiar terms with the minister, and often derived important aid from him in the government and instruction of his school, and kept him informed as to the proficiency of individual pupils. It is a tradition, that a school-master in Guilford from time to time informed the minister, the Rev. Joseph Elliott, that his son, afterwards the celebrated

Jared Elliott, was not making much proficiency in his studies. On one occasion, when carrying his book to school, Jared let it fall into the water, and when standing by the fire to dry it, he let it fall into the fire. Upon being reprimanded by the master, he replied, "I believe my book is a lunatic, it is oft in the fire and oft in the water." The school-master, as soon as the school was dismissed, hastened to the minister to say to him, "Jared will make a man after all."

Many of the school-masters in the principal towns, one at least in each town, made teaching their principal employment through the year, namely, such as Cheever, and Tisdale, and Jones. Other intelligent men taught school in winter, and managed their farms in the summer; one of these, who was born in 1727, told me that, in this way, he taught school thirty years. Others, chiefly young men, often the flower of the town, well-educated for the times, and from good families, taught school for a few winters, until they were married. Females, called school-mistresses, and school-dames, taught the small schools in the summer. Clergymen often taught select schools in the winter, for the older youth in their congregations.

Among these teachers there were indeed those who were but poorly qualified for their employment. Some such are described by John Trumbull, in his "*Progress of Dullness:*"

> "He tries, with ease and unconcern,
> To teach what ne'er himself could learn;
> Gives law and punishment alone,
> Judge, jury, bailiff, all in one;
> Holds all good learning must depend
> Upon the rod's extremest end,
> Whose great electric touch is such,
> Each genius brightens at the touch.
> With threats and blows, excitements pressing,
> Drives on his lads to learn each lesson;
> Thinks flogging cures all moral ills,
> And breaks their heads to break their wills."

But there were other school-masters who led their pupils gently up the hillside of learning, bearing their burdens, sympathizing with their difficulties, and by kind looks, kind tones, and winning ways, gaining their hearts. They did for them what Aristotle did for Alexander the Great, who, in return, said, he loved him better than he did his father Philip, for the "latter was only the father of his body, but his teacher was the father of his mind." They did for them what Mr. Elmer, her teacher, did for Lady Jane Grey, who, she said, "taught me so gently, so pleasantly, with such fair allurements to learning, that I think all the time nothing, while I am with him, and when I am called from him, I fall on weeping, because, whatever I do else, but learning, is full of grief, trouble, fear, and whole misliking unto me." I could mention the name of a Connecticut school-master, who in 1782 taught a select school. About fifty years afterwards, a pupil in that school made a journey of many miles to see him, and thank him for his counsels and instruction, bestowed upon him when he was only eight or ten years of age.

What a beautiful letter Daniel Webster wrote to his old school-master, July 20th, 1852, the last year of his life! "MASTER TAPPAN, I hear, with much pleasure, through the public press, that you continue to enjoy life, with mental faculties bright and vivid, although you have arrived at a very advanced age, and are somewhat infirm. I came to-day, from the very spot in which you taught me; and to me a most delightful spot it is. The river and the hills are as beautiful as ever. But the graves of my father and mother, and brothers and sisters, and early friends, give it to me something of the appearance of a city of the dead. But let us not repine. You have lived long, and my life is already not short; and we have both much to be thankful for. Two or three persons are still living, who, like myself, were brought up, *sub tua ferula*. They remember 'Master Tappan.'

"And now, my good old master, receive a renewed tribute of affectionate regard from your grateful pupil; with his wishes and prayers for your happiness, in all that remains to you of this life, and more especially, for your rich participation, hereafter, in the more durable riches of righteousness.—Daniel Webster." Mr. Webster was born January 18, 1782.

This letter is a beautiful picture of the feelings entertained by ingenuous children, for good school-masters in the last century.

For a long period the only two BOOKS in common use in district schools, were, first, the "*New England Primer*," which was an equivalent, among the Puritans here, for a small prayer book, called the "Primer" among the Roman Catholics. This, with its frontispiece of John Rogers in the flames, and his wife and nine children looking on, excited in the mind of the young child while learning its first lesson, the deepest sensibility. There was in it the beautiful cradle hymn of Watts, appealing, as it does, to the highest sentiments of our nature; and the shorter catechism, to be committed to memory and repeated every Saturday.

The other book was the "*Psalter*," namely, the book of Psalms printed separately. This also was an equivalent for a certain Roman Catholic book so called.

Arithmetic was taught in these common schools, the teacher only having a book, and writing the sums for the pupil, and showing him how to do them. Sewing was taught by school-dames.

Writing was also taught, the teacher writing the copy and handing it to the pupil with the question, "Can you read your copy?"

At a later period, "*Dilworth's Spelling Book, or New Guide*," published 1740, was introduced. He was an Englishman, and died in England, 1781. His book was for a time in common use. Trumbull alludes to it thus, in 1772:

"Our master says, (I'm sure he is right,)
There's not a lad in town so bright,
He'll cypher bravely, write and read,
And say his catechism and creed,
And scorn to hesitate or falter,
In Primer, *Spelling-Book*, or Psalter."

His "*School Master's Assistant*," an arithmetic, was published, after his Spelling Book had been well received, in 1743, and was dedicated to "*The Reverend and Worthy School*

Masters in Great Britain and Ireland." School-masters in Connecticut used this book in their schools. The sums given out were often cyphered at home in the evening. Classes were also taught by the master in the evening, for which a small stipend was given.

In 1784, *Webster's Spelling Book* began to replace Dilworth's, though with some opposition. "*Dilworth's Ghost*" was written to deter the people of the State from the change. Webster's book was entitled, "*The First Part of the Grammatical Institute of the English Language.*" This book, I have heard him say, was introduced into the schools of Connecticut through the influence of the clergymen of Connecticut; though it was highly recommended by others. After this, the "*Second Part*" in the series, was introduced, which was published in 1790. This was a *grammar*. After this, the "*Third Part*" in the series, was introduced. It was a reading book, and was published in 1792. "*Dwight's Geography*" began to be used in the schools of Connticut, in 1795. It was prepared by Nathaniel Dwight, a brother of Timothy Dwight. Morse's Geography was also used, more or less, soon after its publication.

The first clergymen of Connecticut were educated, many of them, at the Universities in England, and had enjoyed intercourse with the learned and polished clergymen of the Episcopal Church there. As we see them now on the canvas, in their wigs, and bands, and gowns, we are impressed with the belief that they were gentlemen. Their manners were grave, dignified and courteous, and they were regarded by the school-masters, and gentlemen, and all of the people, as the models of *good manners*. Thus it long continued the case with their successors in office. In the schools in the Colony of Connecticut, it was expected that not only learning, and religion, and morality should be cultivated, but also GOOD MANNERS, in opposition to clownishness on the one hand, and rowdyism on the other. The pupils were expected to bow or courtesy, or, in other words, to make their *manners* when they entered the school, and when they left it; and when they began the recitation, and when they retired. They were taught to address the teacher with the title of "Master." They were taught to show respect to age, and station, and moral worth: to take off their hats when they met respectable persons, as the ministers and principal men were accustomed to do. This regard for *minor morals*, carried out in many particulars, prevailed in Connecticut for something like two hundred years. By thus cultivating the sentiment of politeness in the young, their hearts became better, socially, and good manners became common law.

In some of the acts of the General Court, the "GOVERNMENT" of schools is spoken of as if it were as important as instruction. In those days children were expected to be *governed*, not coaxed. This government, in those times, is described as being unreasonably severe. So it was, judged of by our own standard. But in those times there was, in many places, a high type of discipline in the church, in the family, and in the town. They or their fathers had left England in order that they might have a purer church, and how could they have a purer church without discipline? Parents, in those days, had large families; Dr. Johnson malignantly said of them that "they multiplied with the fecundity of their own rattlesnakes." Besides, the Pilgrims had left Holland that their children might not be corrupted. Large families require stricter discipline than small ones. In the town, the whipping-post was a standing proof of the importance attached to discipline. The same doctrine prevailed in the schools, as it also did in the English schools. Ministers, too, were full believers in the doctrine, that "the rod and reproof bring wisdom." Accordingly the rod was used, and the ferule, and the block of disgrace, a sort of "stool of repentance," on which the culprit sat, until he was willing to submit to the rules of the school.

But the clergy of Connecticut exerted a MORE DIRECT INFLUENCE in favor of popular or universal education in the State. Having themselves, most of them, been trained, when young, in common schools, a large number of them became teachers in them or in select schools, during their college course or afterwards. Numbers of them, when settled, kept school in their own houses, for the young people of their congregations. Clergymen founded Yale College, and for more than one hundred and fifty years have controlled it, and presided over it. For one hundred and thirty years a large part of the students of the State, educated in it, were fitted for college by clergymen. When I concluded to go to college I applied to Dr. John Elliot to fit me for Yale. He told me that he " felt under the same obligation to lend his aid in fitting young men for college that he did to preach the Gospel."

Clergymen were on the committee for the examination of school-masters, and the inspection of schools. They visited the schools, at least at the commencement of the season, and at the close. In this way they became acquainted with the comparative merits of the several schools, and of the several teachers, and of the several pupils. They made the condition and importance of the schools one of their common topics in conversation, alluded to schools often in their sermons, and in their public prayers on the Sabbath, they would say, in respect to them and the college, " cast the salt of Divine Grace into these fountains, that the streams, that annually flow from them, may make glad the city and the church of our God." For a long time the town was the parish, and the town schools were the parish schools, which the minister felt, officially, bound to foster. And in doing this they were often rewarded, even while living, with the gratitude, the love, and the confidence of three generations. And when such a one died, great lamentation was made over him. And when carried to his grave, he was mourned by the fathers, and the children, and the children's children, as one who had taught them how to think as men, how to act as Christians, and how to behave as gentlemen; as a light-bearer, who had held for them the torch of knowledge, in the meeting-house, in the school-house, and in the dwelling-house; a torch which some of them were ready to seize and hold up in turn in the church, in the school, and in the family. To these ministers, we sons of Connecticut owe something more than gratitude ; we owe them undying affection as our spiritual and educational forefathers.

In the minds of the early clergymen of Connecticut, the church and the school—the *meeting-house* for the one, and the *school-house* for the other--were closely associated. In the early settlement of a town, as soon as the meeting-house was erected, if not sooner, the school-house was built, *near* the meeting-house, the one a symbol of learning, the other of religion. When the minister was settled, the school-master was sure to follow to establish his little seminary, from which the church was to be supplied with intelligent members, and the town with intelligent inhabitants.

With the type of the old Connecticut school-house, which replaced the one constructed of logs, and its slender appointments, many are acquainted, as some such are still standing. There was the large chimney, often on the north end, with its large fire-place, before which the children could warm themselves when they came in, or after shivering on the outer circle of benches. On one side of the chimney was a small entry, and on the other, was a small apartment for the hats, or buff caps, and bonnets, and which served the purpose of a prison, in which were confined disobedient and refractory children. Long benches, without backs, on which the children sat, and thus learned to sustain themselves.

Having been confined in the school from nine o'clock until about eleven, and from one until about three, they, at the notice of the master, hastened to the play-ground fresh from the "constraint that sweetens liberty." Here they contended with each other in feats of agility and strength. They were encouraged to wrestle and to run well, because they might have to wrestle with the Indians in battle, or to run with them, for escape or for capture. Accordingly some of them emulated the strength of Jacob, who wrestled with the Angel, and some, the fleetness of Asahel, who " was as light of foot as a wild roe."

And when, perchance, some well-known person was passing,

the word would come out from some of them, that parson—or squire—or doctor—or deacon—was coming. Immediately they would leave their play for a moment, take off their hats, or caps, and then resume their play. This ready act of civility, they would pay with a conscious sense of politeness,—with a " proud submission," which raised them in their own estimation. They had been taught in the church, in the family, and the school, to respect what is respectable, and to " do their duties to superiors, inferiors, and equals."

It should be added that in the settlement of the country towns, before the districts were weakened by being divided, the schools were often large. " The boys came to school in the winter, the only season in which schools were usually open, from distances of several miles, wading through the snow, or running upon the crust, with their curly heads of hair often whitened with frost from their own breath."

Visitation day, in the spring, when the inspectors visited the schools, was a great day in the district. The minister and some of the principal men were present. The schoolmaster was in his glory, now that others had come to magnify his office. Many of the parents were present. The inspectors were interested to behold the "*spem gregis*," the hope of the church and the town. The psalter was read by the older children, and the primer by the younger ones. The writing books and the arithmetic books were handed round. In later times, lessons in spelling from the spelling book were put out. The catechism was recited. The inspectors made their remarks, particularly the minister, upon the proficiency of the school, the manners, the morals, the religion. A prayer was then made by the clergyman, in which these several topics were alluded to.

It should be added that a prayer was made by the schoolmaster in a portion of the schools, at nine o'clock, when the school came together in the morning, and at four. In other schools, a prayer was made only at four, when the school was dismissed.

On this subject, listen to the language of President Timothy Dwight: "Of learning and the general diffusion of useful knowledge, the clergy as individuals, have, beyond any other class of men, been the promoters. To this, their own knowledge, the general nature of their office, and their comparative leisure from the busy occupations of life, almost necessarily lead. In the foundation and the regulation of no small number of our schools, they are directly concerned as principals. To our college they gave birth, continuance, a considerable proportion of its property, and the whole system of its government and instruction. They have supported and educated more scholars of charity, than the whole community besides; nor is there at this time, unless I am deceived, a single school of consideration in the State, in which they have not a principal agency."

Thus the meeting-house was the center of illumination for the town, and the school-house was the center of illumination for the district. The lights in both were steady, irradiating the whole surface of the State, like the lights which on some evenings illumine all the northern sky. This was before the cunning artificers of the press sent up their fireworks to dazzle by their glare and mislead. It was the influence of these steady lights that made Connecticut THE LAND OF STEADY HABITS; a model commonwealth, where, from the cultivation of the arts and sciences, from the general diffusion of knowledge, the people have in the exercise of the rights of private judgment, pursued a wise policy in their public acts, and in the administration of their own private and local affairs.

It would exceed my limits to show forth the great results of the educational efforts of the clergy of Connecticut. These would have to be sought not only in the territorial limits of the State, but throughout our broad country, wherever the emigrating sons and daughters of Connecticut have fixed their habitation.

Thus, my dear Sir, have I endeavored, briefly to show, that the ministers of the Gospel ought to take a prominent part in popular education; from the nature of the Christian religion; from the nature of Protestantism; from the nature of Puritanism; from the nature of their own profession; from the position long occupied by clergymen. In doing this, they ought to be encouraged by the towns, as they were formerly.

How they should do this, I do not presume to say. Each of them has his own gift; each his own circumstances. They have that wisdom in the selection of means, which is profitable to direct.

Very respectfully, your obedient servant,

WILLIAM C. FOWLER.

P. S.—Your very valuable Report of 1853, when you were Superintendent of Common Schools in Connecticut, renders it unnecessary that I should enlarge my statements on certain topics of interest.

www.ingramcontent.com/pod-product-compliance
Lightning Source LLC
LaVergne TN
LVHW020242110826
845151LV00003B/1005

9781425530402